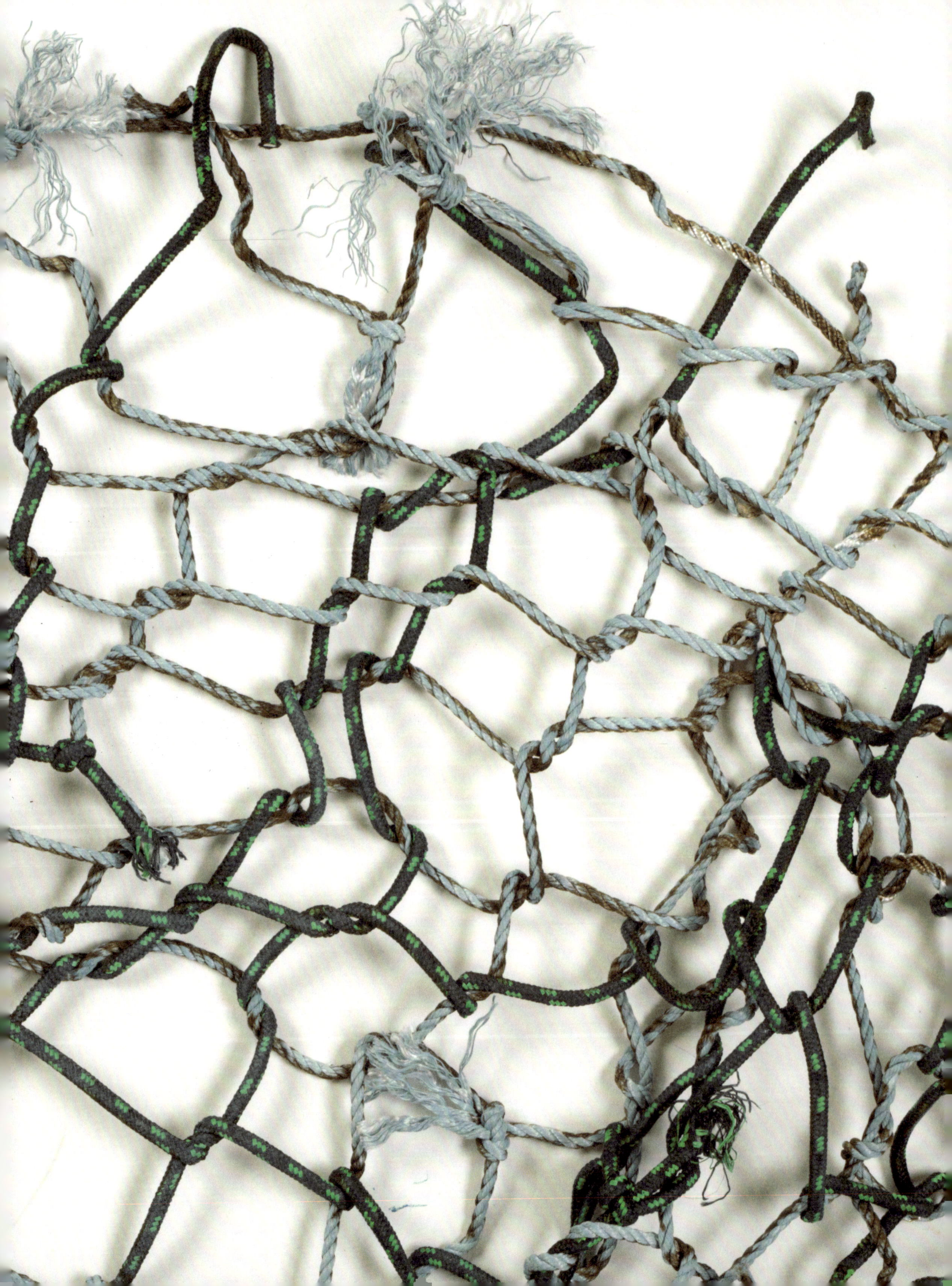

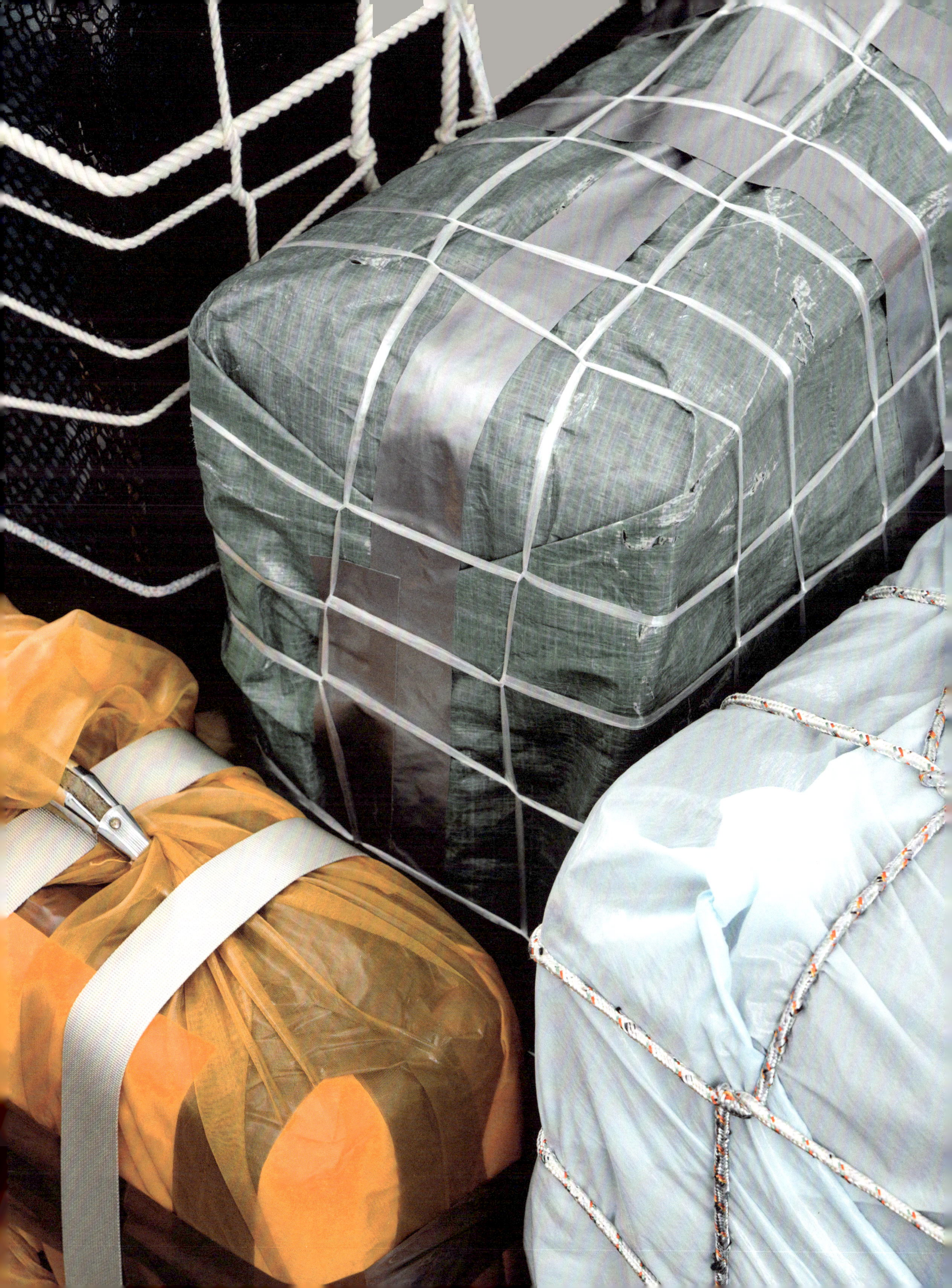

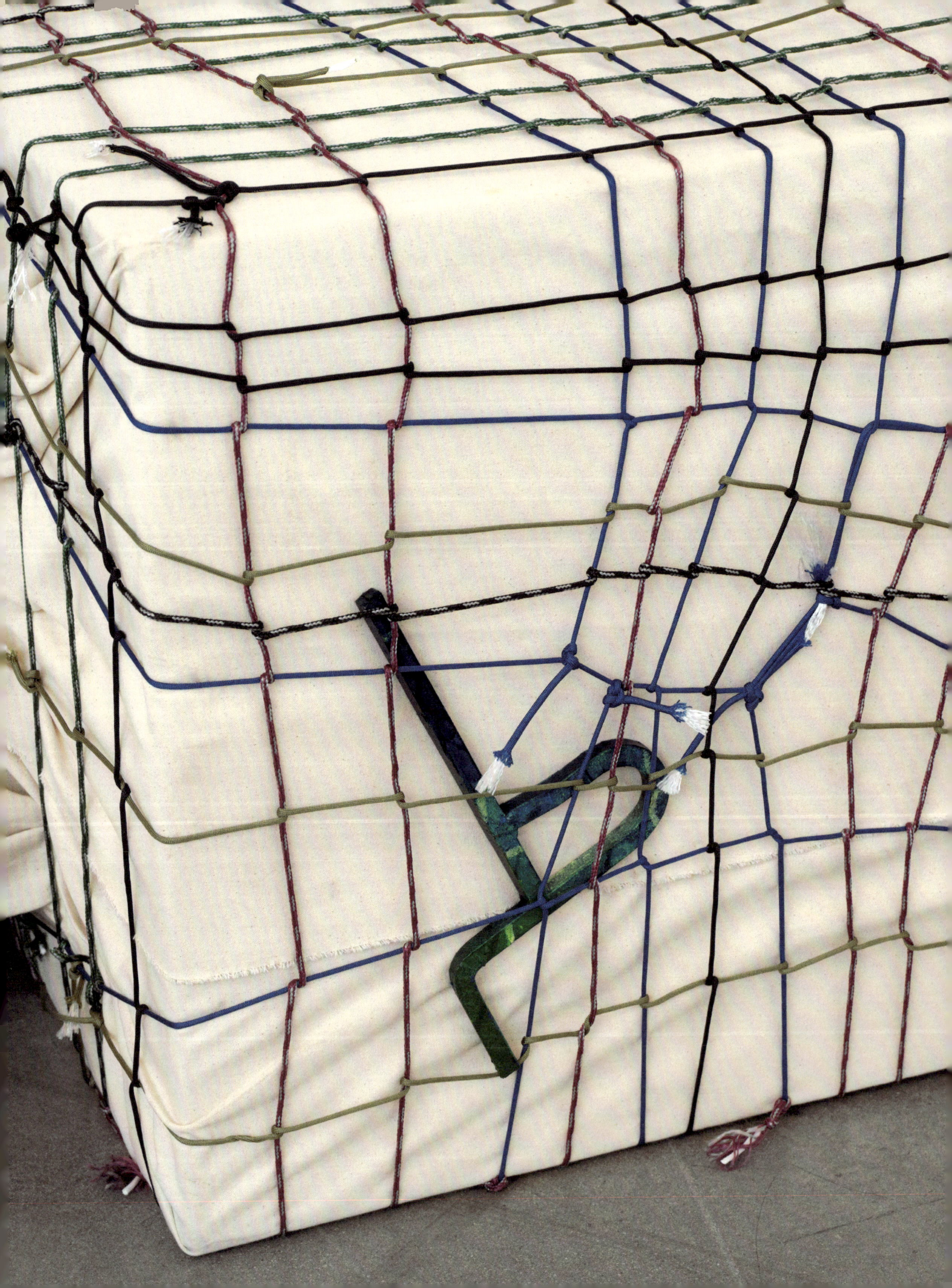

MAIA RUTH LEE

BONDAGE BAGGAGE

RADIUS BOOKS

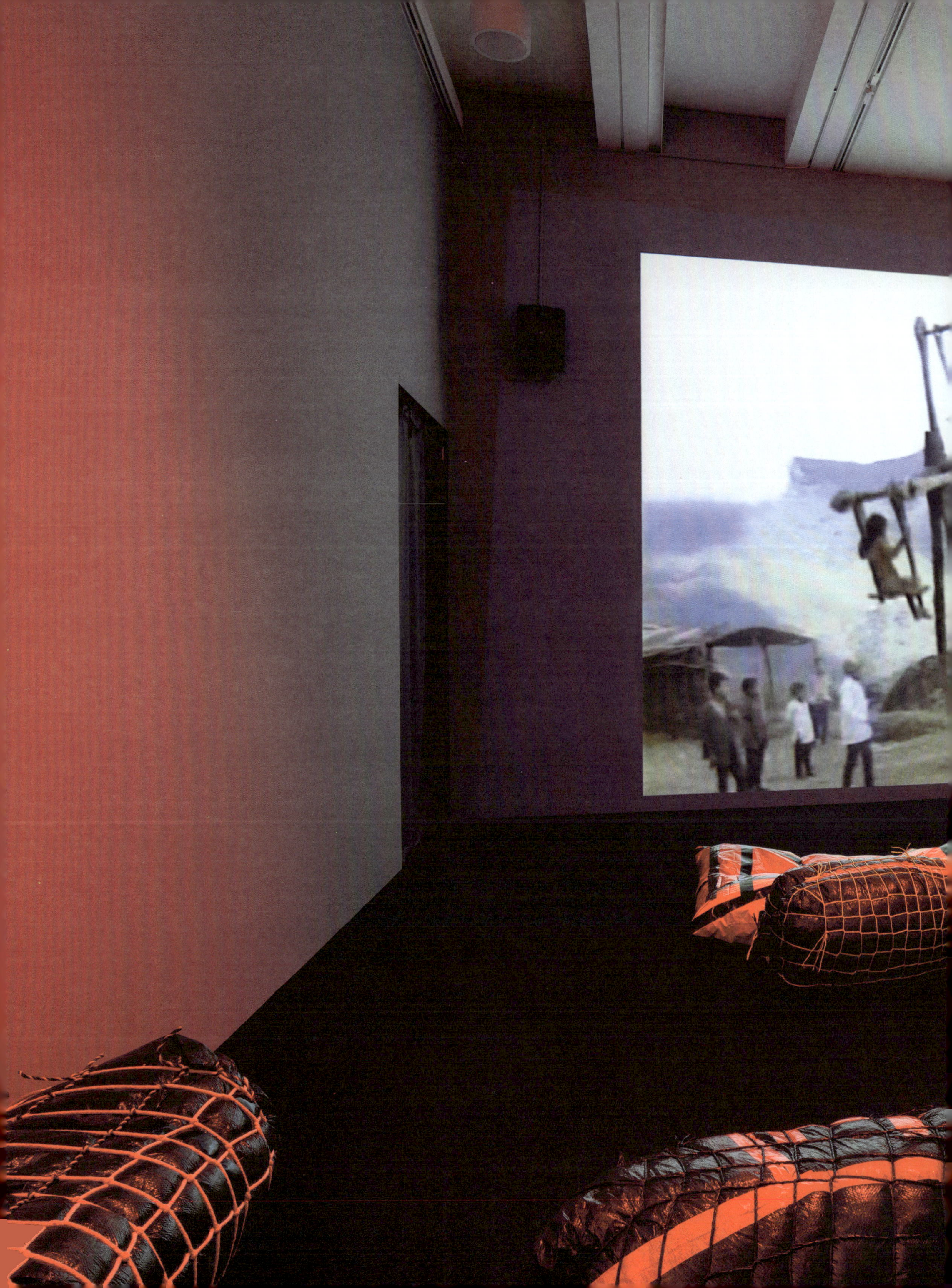

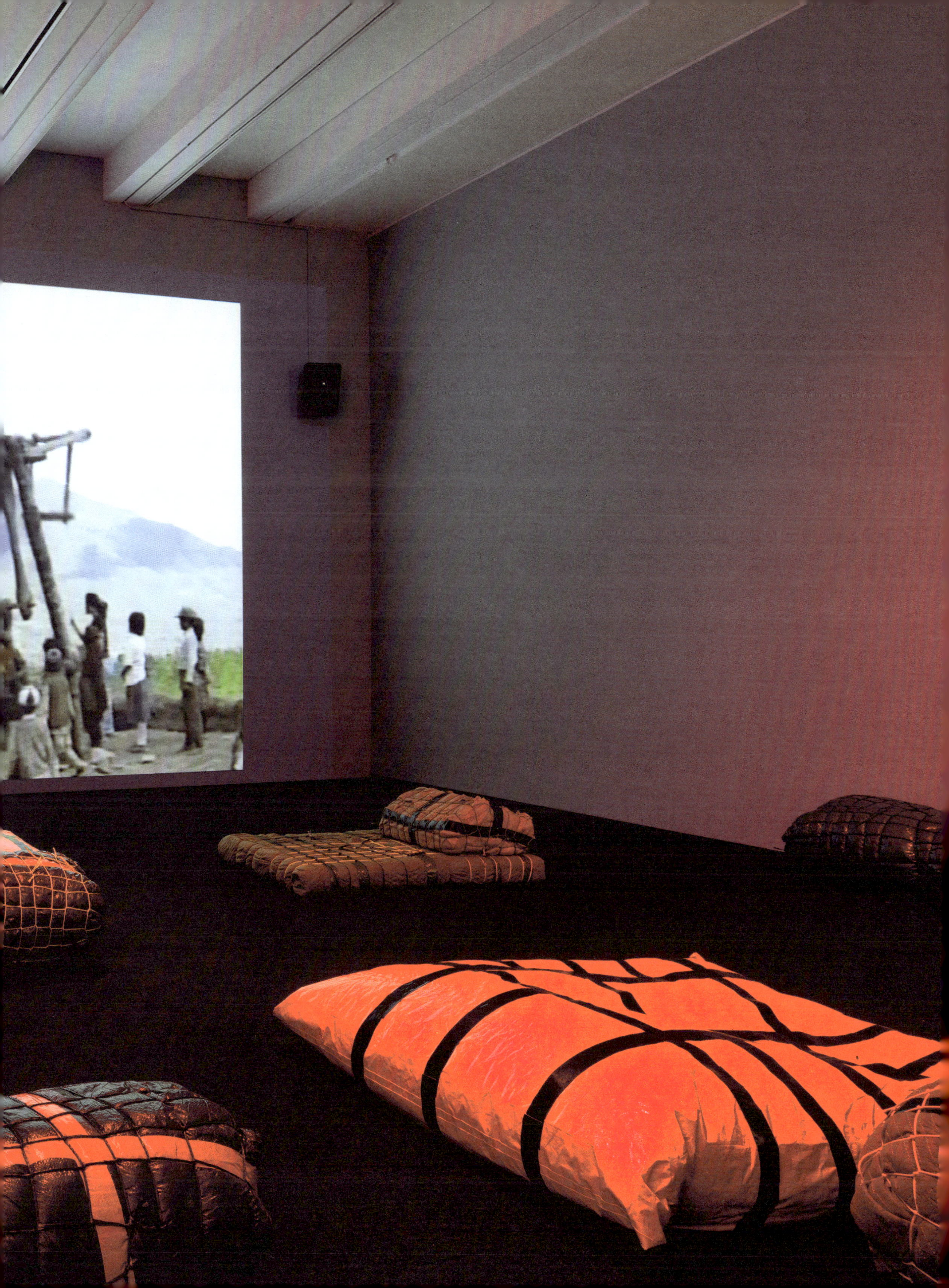

Can there be another / alternate state to the Bondage Baggage?
Can it ultimately change its shape and course?

*Can the bondage break? Can the baggage reduce in size?

If the answer is YES, then HOW?
The structure can become loose - Out of its shape...
Sprawled on a flat surface? Untangled and unraveled?
INSIDE OUT? The exterior wrapper can be a protectant, but equally restri
Can it break away from its current aesthetics?

Alternate self in alternate realities. Can the bondage break??

Shapes can change, but bondage will still be intact..
Exterior wrapper can be omitted, the substance revealed. Contents in vie
Does this change the meaning of baggage? Perhaps.
When content revealed; the hidden flaws and intimate secrets are no long
This frees the subject from its state of intangibility.
Clarity can untangle the neurotic conflicts; hence no more intellectual
baggage. The burdens and impediments can be worked on.

Bondage baggage in TRANSIT - in MOVEMENT. Even more interesting.
BB as a constant state of transformation. Baggage claim.
BONDAGE BAGGAGE CLAIM

Constant flux: The human state/

Bondage baggage as a form of present/gift. A sense of surprise
Maybe unwanted?

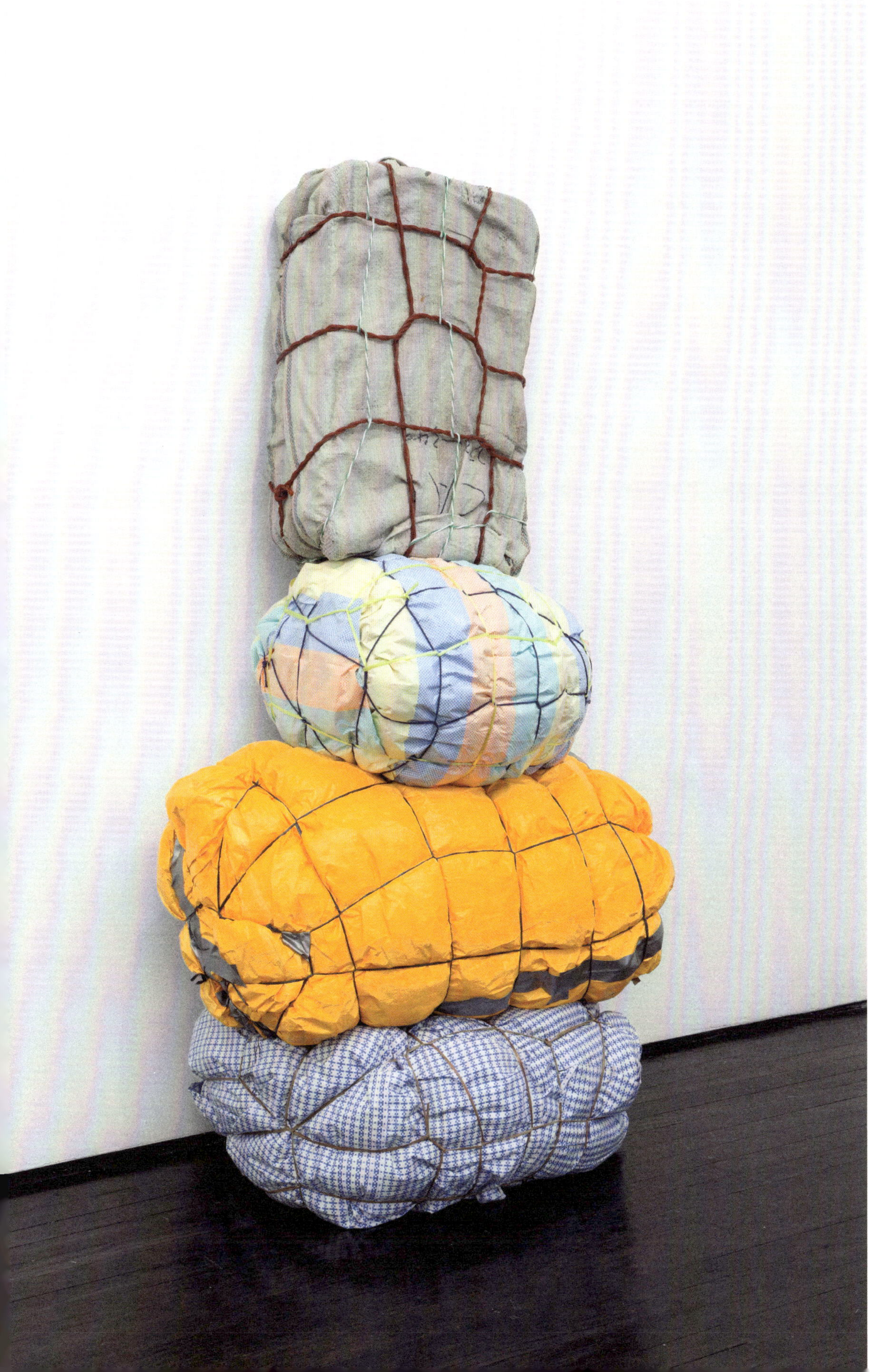

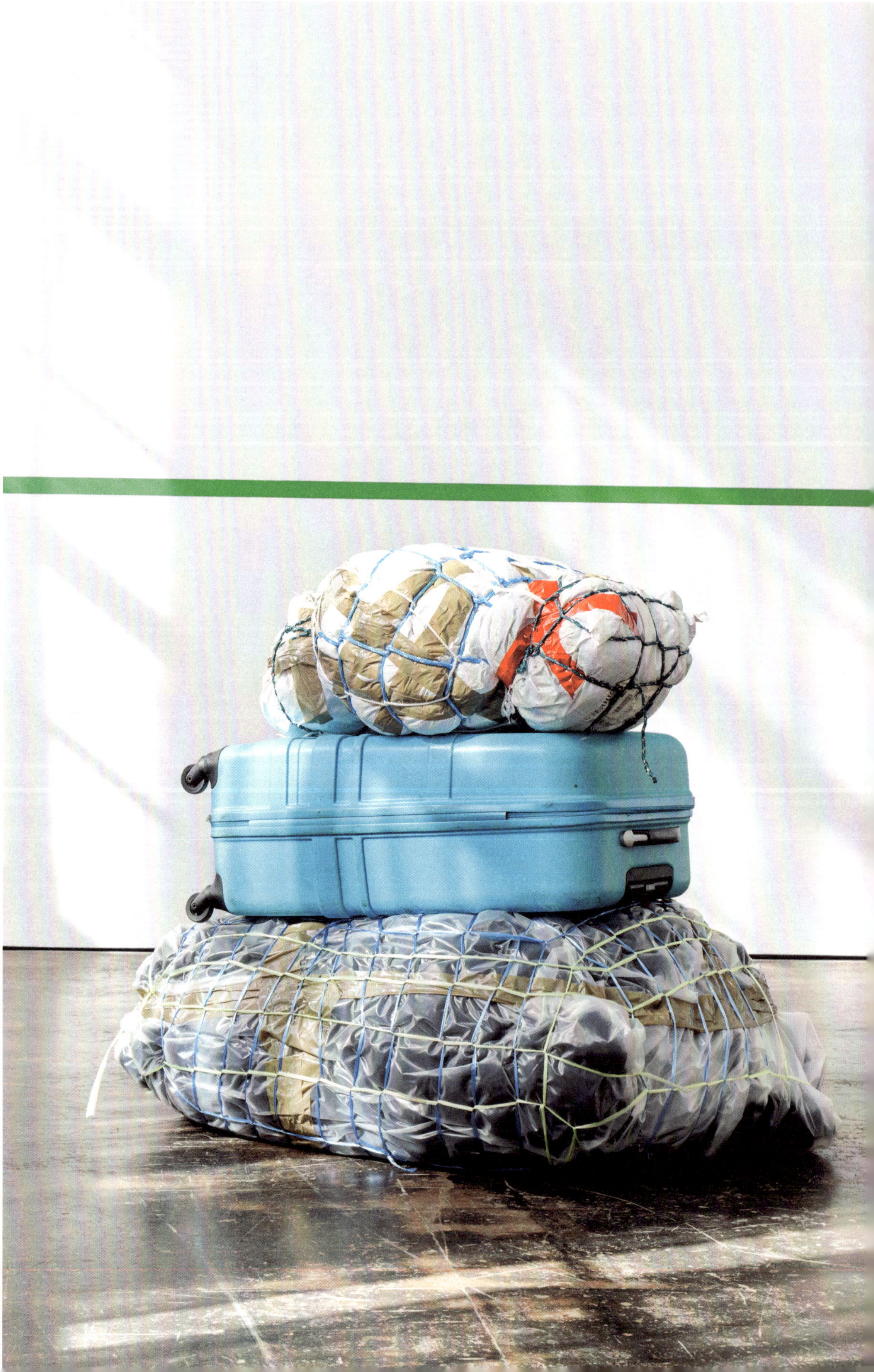

THE END OF THE LINE

Jade Foster

As I look across the horizon line where the sandy earth of Saltburn meets the sky, I think about lines two-fold. The horizon line that haunts the borderlands—the never quite there, never quite here line separating one state from another—and the spine or throughline of an exhibition, an artist's practice, or text. But now, with my eyes drifting out of focus, I return to the page in front of me and trace my fingers along the line *Oigo el llorido del mar, el respiro del aire* (I hear the cry of the sea, the breath of the air).[1] I once again feel orientated within Chicana feminist and theorist Gloria Anzaldúa's 1987 book *Borderlands/La Frontera: The New Mestiza*. Anzaldúa intimately names the geographical borderlines and the intangible psychological, sexual, and spiritual borderlands that affect our internal wayfinder. The horizon line, which is the line between the crying sea and the breath of air that the writer describes, is key to the practice of Colorado-based artist Maia Ruth Lee (Busan; b. 1983), whose own borderlands deeply imbue in her *Bondage Baggage* (2018–ongoing) and *Bondage Banner* (2024–ongoing) series. I am thankful to Anzaldúa, as she makes way for my framing of "line" not just as a visual component in artmaking, but an essential formal element, philosophy, and approach to storytelling within the curatorial.

During the spring equinox, I find myself staring into space inside a gallery housed in a porous, grade II-listed, former-Victorian school building, now an arts organization called Primary in Nottingham, UK. Rather than skies, I see a green strip enticing me into believing that safe passage exists for the "alien," the 외국인 (*oegugin*), the migrant known and unknown. This green horizon line, the thickness of duct tape, encircles the gallery. This line acts as a spine. At eye level, the curatorial mark cuts through the sterility of the studio.[2] Here at Primary, the mark alludes to the worldly and spiritual divide between the bounding of material baggage, ungainly luggage, and heftiness on the downstairs floor and its spiritual and directional release upstairs.

Lee's profound yet tricky task as an artist is to visually—and discreetly—encapsulate a sliver of life's precarity, hope, and impermanence, deciding what to leave unexcavated and concealed from the eye of coloniality, like the luggage she saw arriving at Kathmandu Airport in Nepal back in 2018. The latter philosophical concept, impermanence, is essential Buddhist Dharma for the Nepalese monasteries the artist draws from; it also happens to be that my spirituality aligns with the Buddhist path. Remaining curious while on the beach in Saltburn, I think further, reminding myself of *śūnyatā*, which means "without form," the absence of a fixed or stable self due to dependent origination (*pratītya-samutpāda*)—in other words, the idea that everything relies on one another. The "wheel of life" and its "borderlands" or "middle state" also come to mind, a state where beings may find themselves before being reborn in a higher or lower realm.

Multiple realms are imagined in *Human Life in Motion*, Lee's first solo exhibition in the UK (Primary, March 21–May 31, 2025). The veil of separation is thin between the white cube-esque space of Gallery 1 (animal, worldly, and human; downstairs), featuring the last five commissioned *Bondage Baggage* sculptures compacted with offerings from Primary's community, and Gallery 2 (spiritual and higher; upstairs) with its elongated height and an exposed beam structure that *Bondage Baggage Banner* effortlessly drapes on with gravity being the only hanging mechanism, revealing the structural interdependence. The separation is also thin between what constitutes painting and sculpture. The sixth green banner that "completes the set" (not knowing it was her last) is made from tightly packed canvas bags pinned together on its edges, indented by a gridlocked pattern of tensed knotted rope. The sculptures are then painted with green acrylic and further imprinted through the seeping of black ink around the rope's exterior, appearing as crevices once dried and unraveled flat. The work is no longer with its body. American artist Donald Judd's 1964 text "Specific Objects" is interesting to bring into the fold at this point, as both the exhibition and the *Bondage Baggage Banner* series put into contention what Judd wrote in *Arts Yearbook*: "Almost all paintings are spatial in one way or another."[3] Six individually cascading objects in a line lost their body and took form again once suspended over a beam, becoming spatial paintings or sculpture-paintings. The phenomenological experience of the banners and the physical actuality of their presence in real space is essential to the installation's formality. Painted in green, black, white, yellow, blue, and red—corresponding to the five hues that constitute *obangsaek*, the five cardinal directions and elements in Korean traditional culture—they flow, in sync, in the same direction, toward the entrance.

Every panel is made from one sculpture by a participant in the "Bondage Baggage process," which took place at Primary's Studio A4 on Sunday, March 16, 2025 and included Maia Ruth Lee, Olivia Oyamada, Sofia Yala, Jade Foster, Marwa Soliman, Hanan Shaikh, Maha Hadid, Shahlaa Al-Battawi, and Azza Elkareh from Heya Nottingham. In part, their disorientating stories, which collectively slalom across Iraq, Libya, Egypt, Nepal, Korea, USA, Japan, Britain, and Portugal, are weaved together through the collective human hand. When I heard their narratives, my mind traveled to the Egyptian Revolution, The Tahrir uprising in 2011 (in which mass protests had forced the long-time, dictatorial President Zine al-Abidine Ben Ali to flee his country), the Gulf War, and the War in Iraq. Not dissimilar to Anzaldúa, the British-Australian feminist writer Sara Ahmed is interested in phenomenology, a deep concern about how the world seems to the individual experiencing it and the intersubjectivity about how the world looks—its "borderlands," the "life-world," and the distorted understanding that sometimes comes with it. Ahmed beautifully shares in *Queer Phenomenology: Orientations, Objects, Others* (2006), "Hands... emerge as crucial sites in stories of disorientation.... Hands hold things. They touch things. They let things go."[4] It is the letting things go, *the unhanding*, that recognizes impermanence. Just like the state of life, Lee's objects are fragile. When sculptures turn into paintings, the lines are broken like skin and splinter into a new scatter pattern. That pattern is changed with every hand, individual and collective. These remarkable hands and their stories are forever part of the canvas, will continue to infuse in the work as it moves to another gallery, museum, or home beyond the horizon line.

ENDNOTES

1. Gloria Anzaldúa, *Borderlands: The New Mestiza* (San Francisco: Aunt Lute Books, 1987) 2.
2. At Primary—comprised, in part, of an artist-led studio complex—the public gallery is a studio for the curator.
3. Donald Judd, *Specific Objects*, 1964, https://juddfoundation.org/wp-content/uploads/2016/04/Specific_Objects_1964.pdf.
4. Sara Ahmed, *Queer Phenomenology: Orientations, Objects, Others* (Durham, NC: Duke University Press, 2006), 165, https://doi.org/10.1215/9780822388074.

PAGE 3:

HELMUT LANG COLLABORATION [DETAIL], 2021
courtesy of Helmut Lang; photo: Sean Davidson

PAGE 4:

B.B.TIME_UNTIL LIBERATION 1 [DETAIL], 2024
cardboard, canvas, foam, rope, and steel
26 × 107 × 28¼ inches (66 × 272 × 72 cm)
courtesy of the artist and François Ghebaly, Los Angeles and New York
photo: Paul Salveson

PAGES 6–7:

INSTALLATION VIEW OF **THE STRANGER**, 2018
duration: 23:45; color, sound; in *Mountain/Time*,
curated by Chrisse Iles, Simone Krug, and Anisa Jackson
Aspen Art Museum, Aspen, CO, 2022

PAGE 9:

BONDAGE BAGGAGE PROTOTYPE 4, 2018
tarp, rope, tape, luggage, used clothing, bedding
67 × 35 × 21 inches (170 × 89 × 53 cm)
courtesy of artist and Jack Hanley Gallery

PAGE 10:

INSTALLATION VIEW OF **HUMAN LIFE IN MOTION**
curated by Jade Foster, Primary, Nottingham, UK, 2025
courtesy of the artist and Primary, Nottingham, UK; photo: Reece Straw

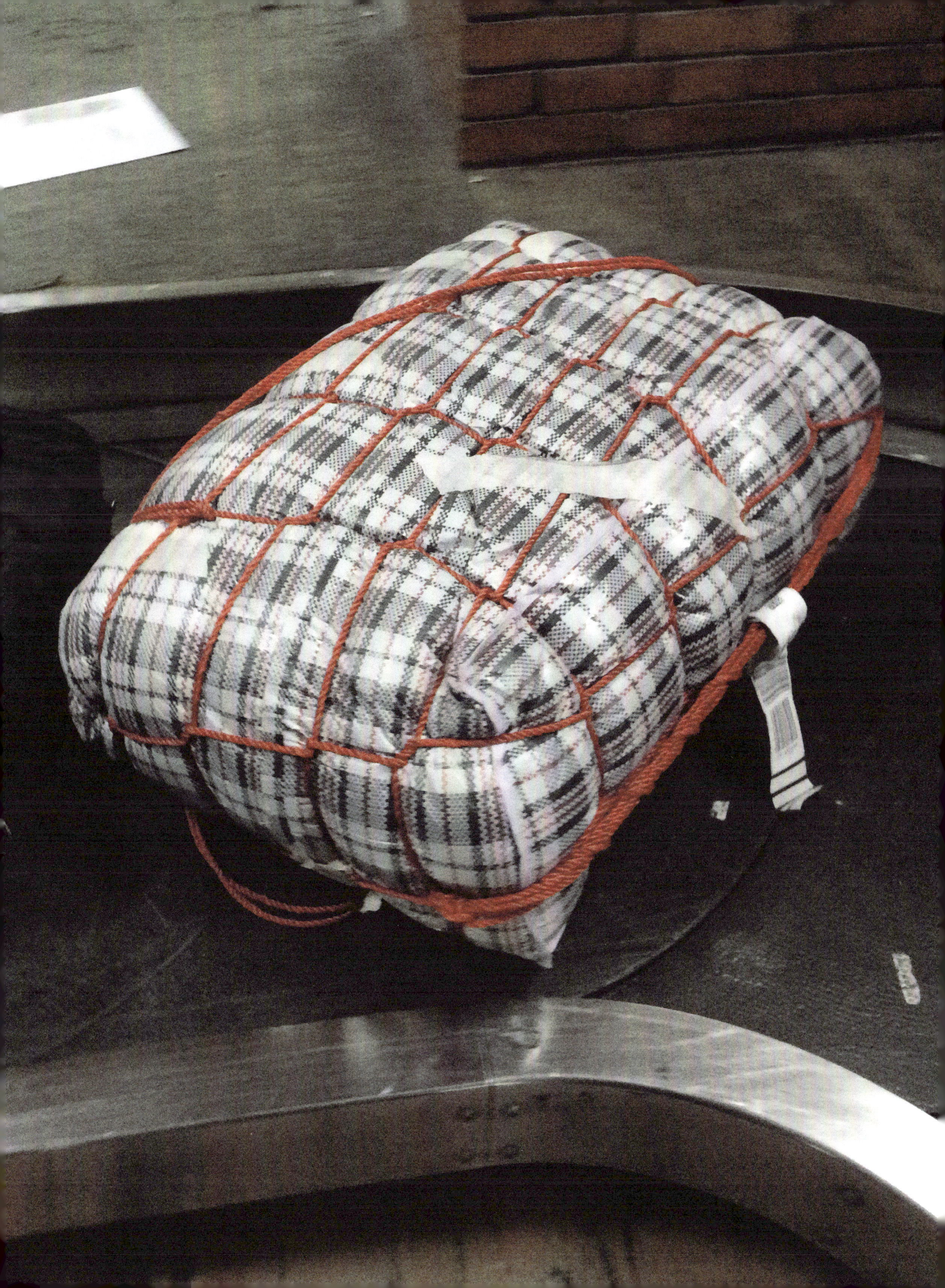

Map → guide → forward → destination

↓

past

↕ memory (geographic / location)

- pattern sensitivity
- nuances of language rhythms
- creative tension
- sense of wholeness

" attitude to wonder "

choose a time (9am -10am) everyday

agony of eros (byung chul han)
to be dead to love is to be dead to thought

erotic experience presumes the asymmetry and exteriority of others
** narcissism is not the same as self love
--- depression is a narcissictic malady --
it derives from overwrought, pathologically distorted self reference// eros puls the subject out of itself toward the Other / depression in contrast plunges the subject into itself

(if something cracks, it's revealing - not destroying)

(handling of the object)
← reflect on this.

home <-----------> host culture

a. integration (maintain both cultural identities, and have positive relations with the hose society)
b. assimilation (only positive relations with host society are important)
c. separation (only maintaining culturel heritage is important)
d. magginalisation (neither outcome is important)

*** six psychological functioning to acculturation (Berry 1997)
1. language 2 cognitive styles 3. personality
4. identity 5. attitudes 6. acculturative stress

(flexibility allows creativity
compromises limit ".)

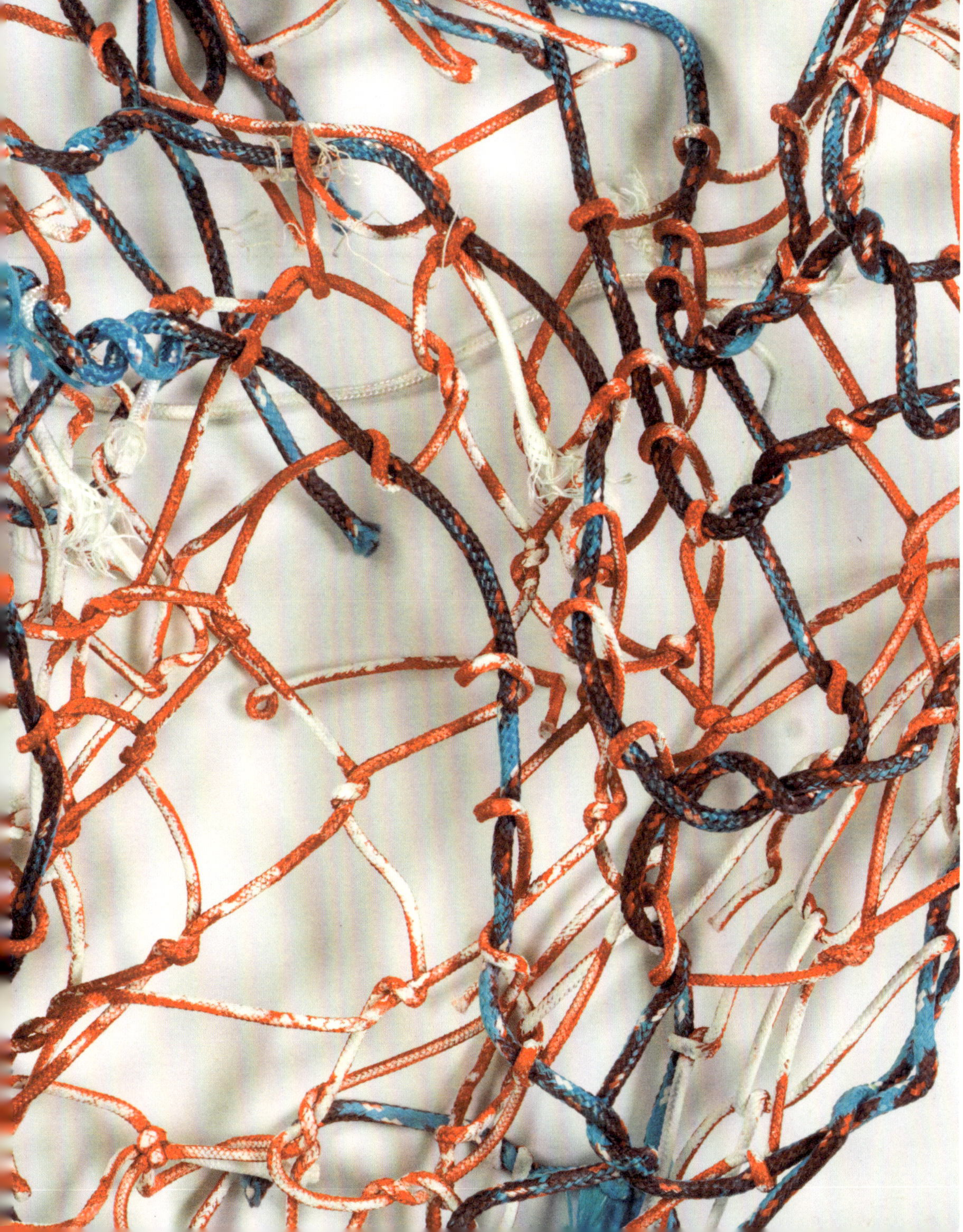

Dear Maia,

I've hesitated to write you a letter. Probably because I find letter writing to be so extremely personal that it's difficult to do out in the open. There's no mask of history and no myth to hide behind. My handwriting here is absent. In essence, the letter is a simple exchange from one to another. But simple is not to be mistaken for impersonal or lacking any depth of emotion. Actually, it is perhaps one of our most personal exchanges. Were I to write just one word to express such passion, what else could it be, but distance? And so, this letter-writing business is not something I often do unless I feel a deep connection to a person. You wrote to me a while back, during a time when I was feeling pretty lonely in my friendships. I worried that your letter might've created a false screen or a false sense of intimacy because the reality of our relationship and the experiences we've had together are very few. So, I hesitated even more to know what to write to you, given that the threads that bind us are so few and fine. But fragility shouldn't be mistaken for any weakness, I decided. My hesitation, I would admit, comes from a stubborn insistence on honesty and a fear of projecting any sense of a false intimacy. I initially connected with you on the subject of pregnancy and having children. A family of my own is something that I dream about, yet, at least up to the day I'm writing this, I have not been able to have one. It will have been a year and a couple of weeks now since my first miscarriage—an experience I find difficult to articulate here. I've lived most of my life very dedicated to solitude. In part, it's in my nature. I've never connected fully with a group of people, and I have the habit of pushing people away. It's a quality I've spent years hating about myself, but I'm working on acceptance. But also, it is how I've managed to dedicate so much time to making art.

I don't want to make art into something that's worth suffering over. I want to say that I try to live a beautiful life. One that is kind to the people in my immediate vicinity and that doesn't pretend to be wider or bigger than is humanly possible. Even though I am childless, I think my biggest dream is to inspire the younger generation to continue to believe in beauty. Fantasy is a powerful refuge for healing and becoming. I don't believe art can save the world, but I'm glad to be an artist who puts thought and care into objects for future generations. Every time we are destructive, we create a hole. And this hole we are able to fill. Without the imagination, we would be a world of holes, with each hole edging into the other until life becomes only a void. A hole is an opportunity. I do not always see us filling these holes with good. In moments of despondency, I feel surrounded by unnecessary inventions. Then, at my most destructive, I bore into the ground, with all my anger and my grief, an opening into which I slowly gather stories. I had this thought that I was claiming my own corner of the world. My desires were stories as pungent and fresh as the scent of damp soil caught in my nostrils, but I didn't understand their roots or even the depth of my own story. The pictures grew with me as the words grew, taking form, making punctuation, finding sentences and paragraphs of tales unknown to me, until I learned they were already recorded in a ledger as common knowledge and by somebody else. All those things I thought I needed were but a figment of someone else's imagination. But whose imagination?

But distance is not a hole. This is an expanse—a widening feeling of space—we create to make room for those instances in which we may need to, for a moment, tear into something.

My dear friend, to beauty and creation, sending all my love,

— Brook

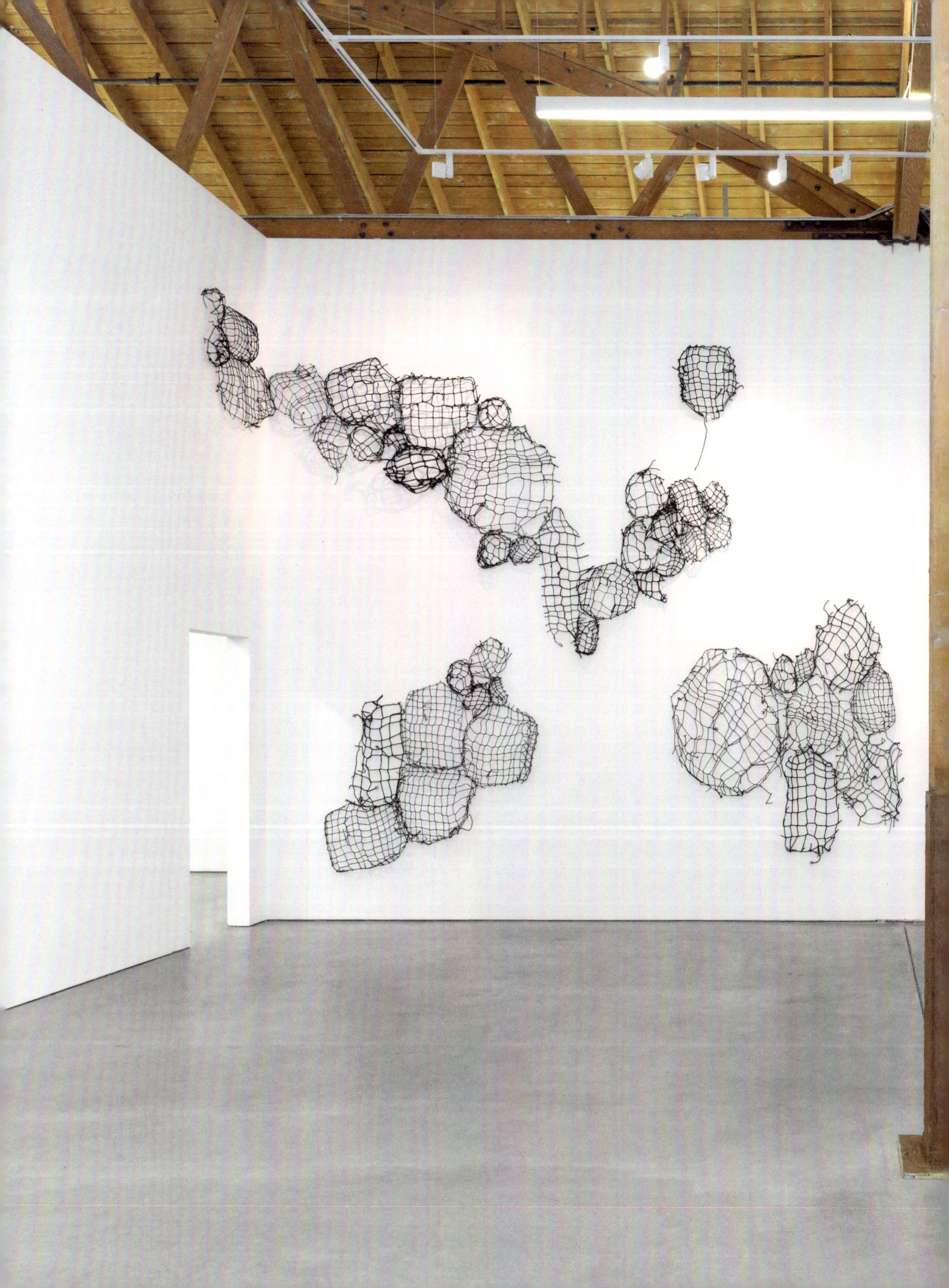

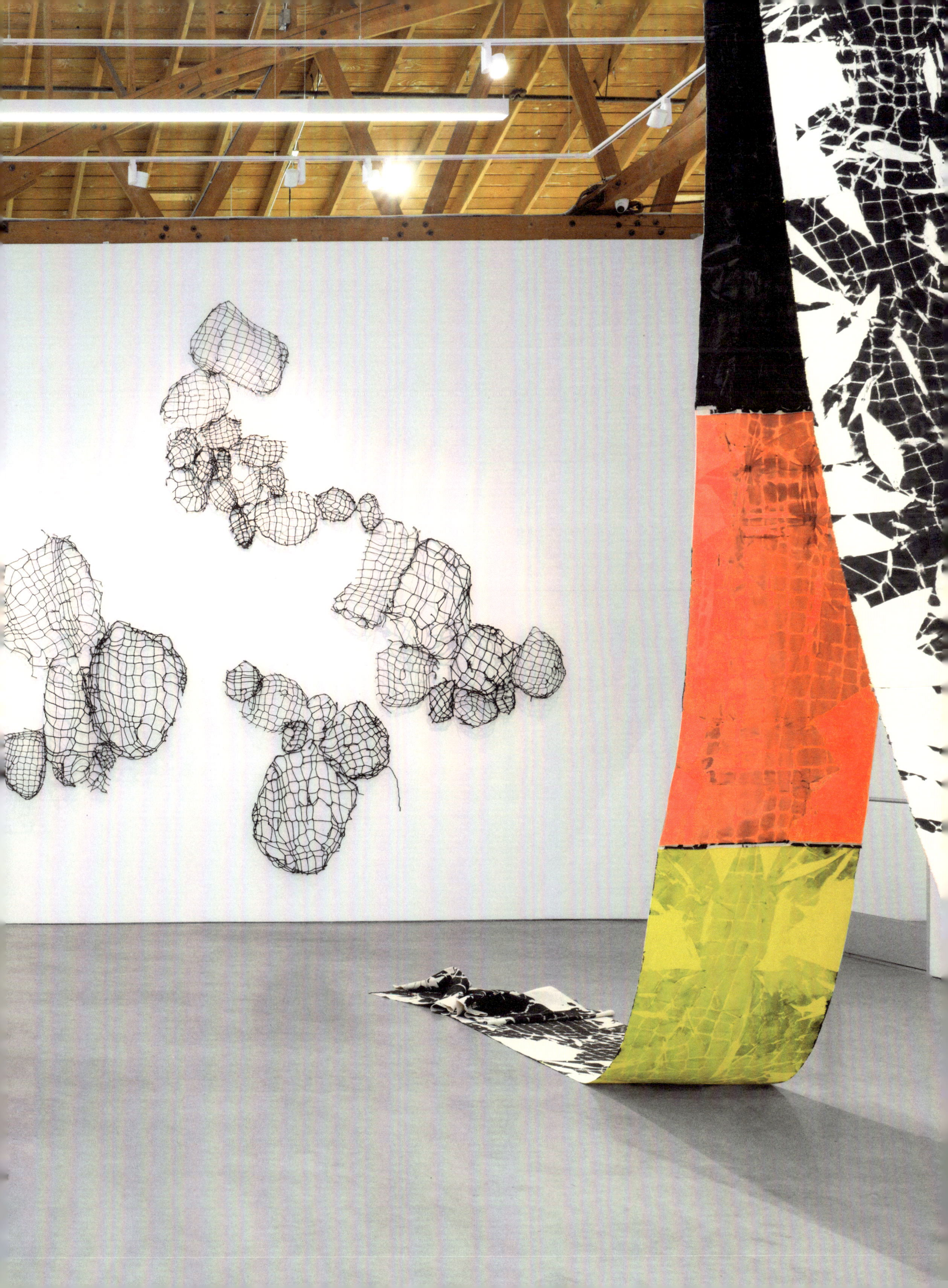

PAGES 26–27:

INSTALLATION VIEW OF **MAIA RUTH LEE: MIGRANT READER**
François Ghebaly, Los Angeles, 2022
courtesy of the artist and François Ghebaly, Los Angeles and New York
photo: Paul Salveson

PAGES 30, 31:

BONDAGE BAGGAGE READER I, 2022
India ink on canvas
80¼ × 78 inches (204 × 198 cm)
courtesy of the artist and François Ghebaly, Los Angeles and New York
photo: Paul Salveson

dear morgan,
i can't seem to write handwritten notes anymore, my wrist bucklesu up, like it forgot to hold a pen. i'm in my new studio set up, dow -nstairs in the basement garage, the door is swugg open to the driveway and the street. and beyond that in the backdrop lies Pike -s Peakright in my view, and since i've been here the white mounta -ins turned into a dark blue gray. this house is also a block away from these beautiful red rocks called garden of the gods, and like its name it s arelly beautiful place to be right now. i'm not mada at it at all, and despite the bouts of despair, anxiety of the pre -sent moemnt and near future, i do feel happy. happy to be with pe -eter, and nim a in this home where peter sepnt most of his life. you know the strange thing is that in this very garage was where peter's mom found peter's father who passed away suddenly from a heart attack, and that might sound morbid, but on the contrary i love this garage, i can feel his spirit in here in some ofhis old things, and it's weird to say, but in some way i've felt a beautif -ul connection with him throughout my relationship with peter. everyday is different, isn't it? yesterday peter had to talk me 'off the ledge', as i was miserable and clearly depressed, and tod -ay i woke up with less anxiety feeling calmer than usual. the ups and downs are hard to keep track of, but now ithink that is just normal.
i remember having that conversation with you about how this year some things will have to change, how that the past years of exerting our energy was not sustainable andwe were feeling deplete --d. that a new chapter needed to be opened. i hope this time away from the city and being home has beena valuable time for you to reassess that. i remember the first time we met, at my studio for my interview, you were so thoughtful, and i remember thinking you were so extraordinary and special. in the years that followed you proved me right and even more than that, i learned so much from yo -u, the way you listen, the way you treat others, your gentleness that brings others ease, your patience shows me your capacity to b

-e truly generous. you've been one of the biggest parts of my lif -e in ny, which i will miss the most. i know you've mentioned in the past that one of your struggles in life is dealing with sadnes -s, but i do think that is because you care, caring is exhausting and requrest s o much from anyone, and i sometihme s think that what if ther's a smart solution for caring? liek caring less witho -ut baring less you know? i hope you take care of the reservoir of love you hold for others morgan, and when you make good use of it, the reservoir will certainlytransform into waves of oceans that is not bound to anyone or anywhere, i hope you can be free from your own boundaries and can let go a little. i love you so much, and i look forward to the day we can see each other and eat sushi at takahachi :)

always
maia, colorado springs
may 2020

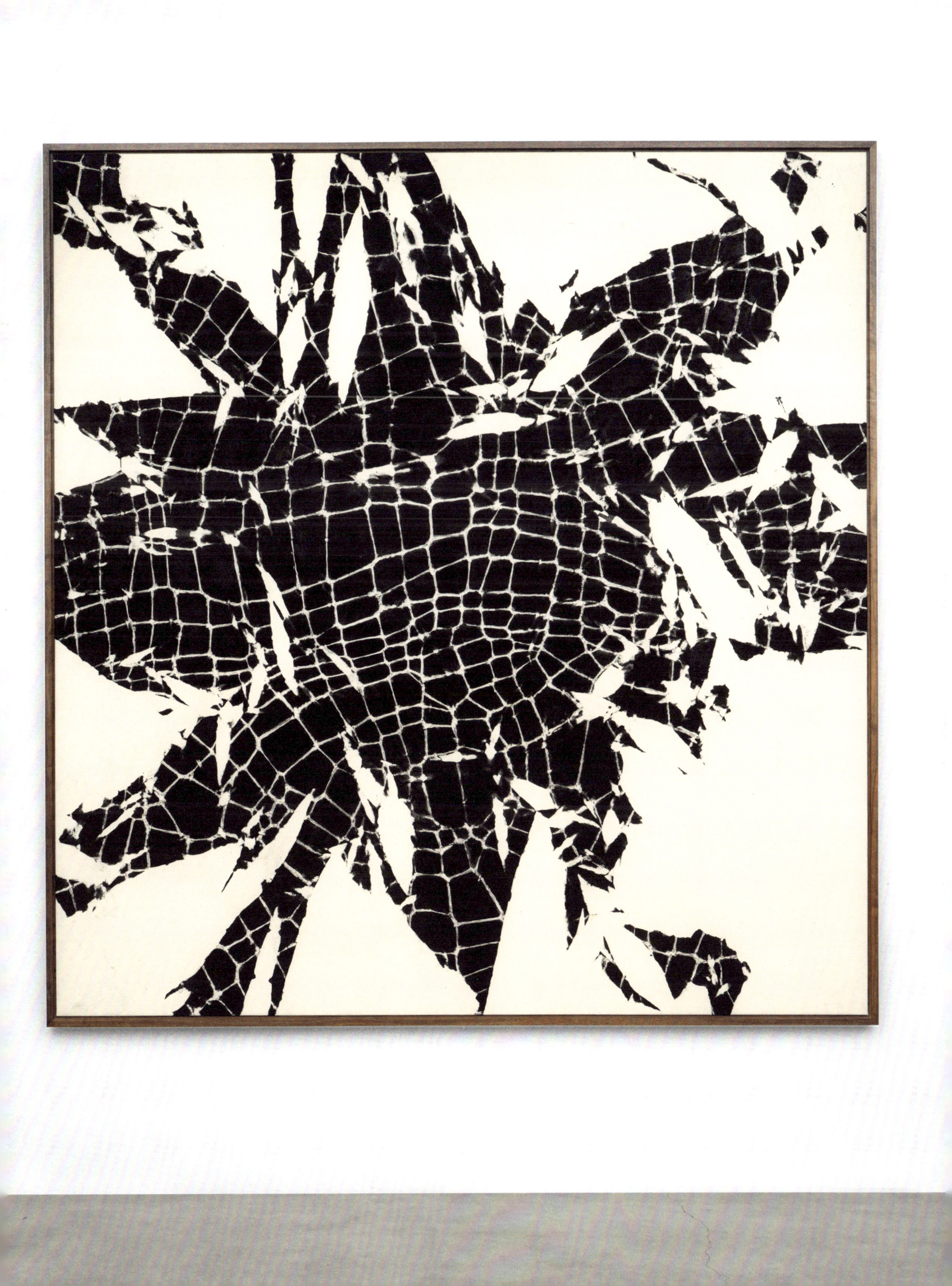

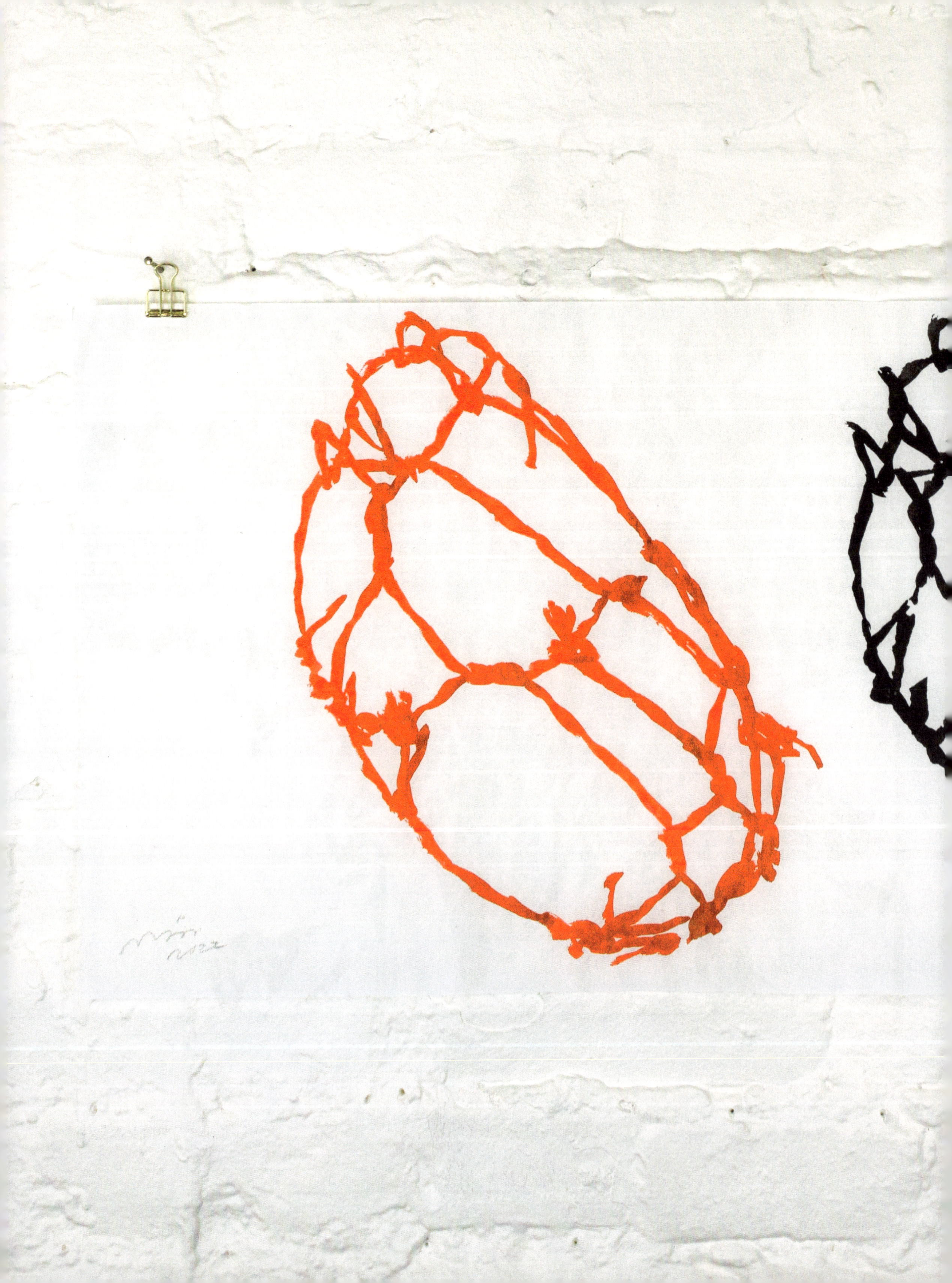

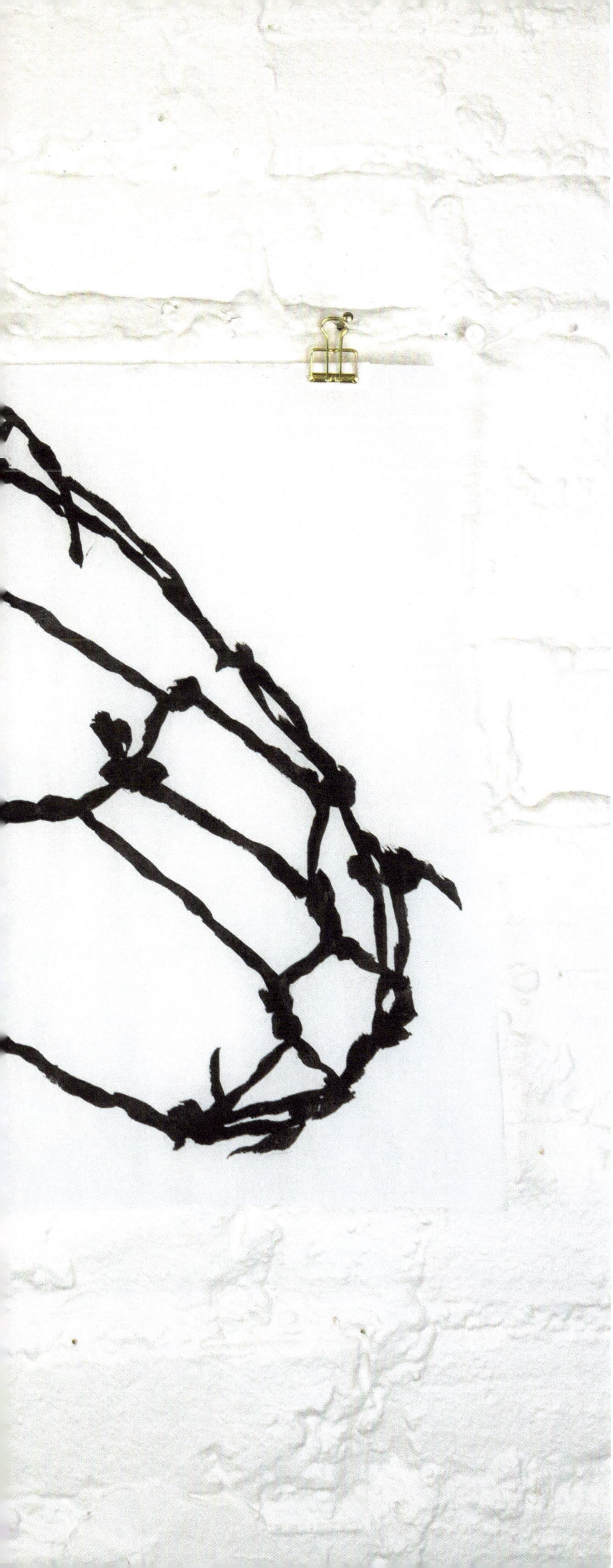

OPPOSITE:

BONDAGE BAGGAGE UMBRA I, 2022
ink on paper
17½ × 31 inches (44.5 × 78.7 cm)
courtesy of the artist and Picture Room

PAGES 34–35:

A TO B, 2022
steel
28 × 136 × 1½ inches (71.1 × 345.4 × 3.8 cm)
courtesy of artist and Jack Hanley Gallery

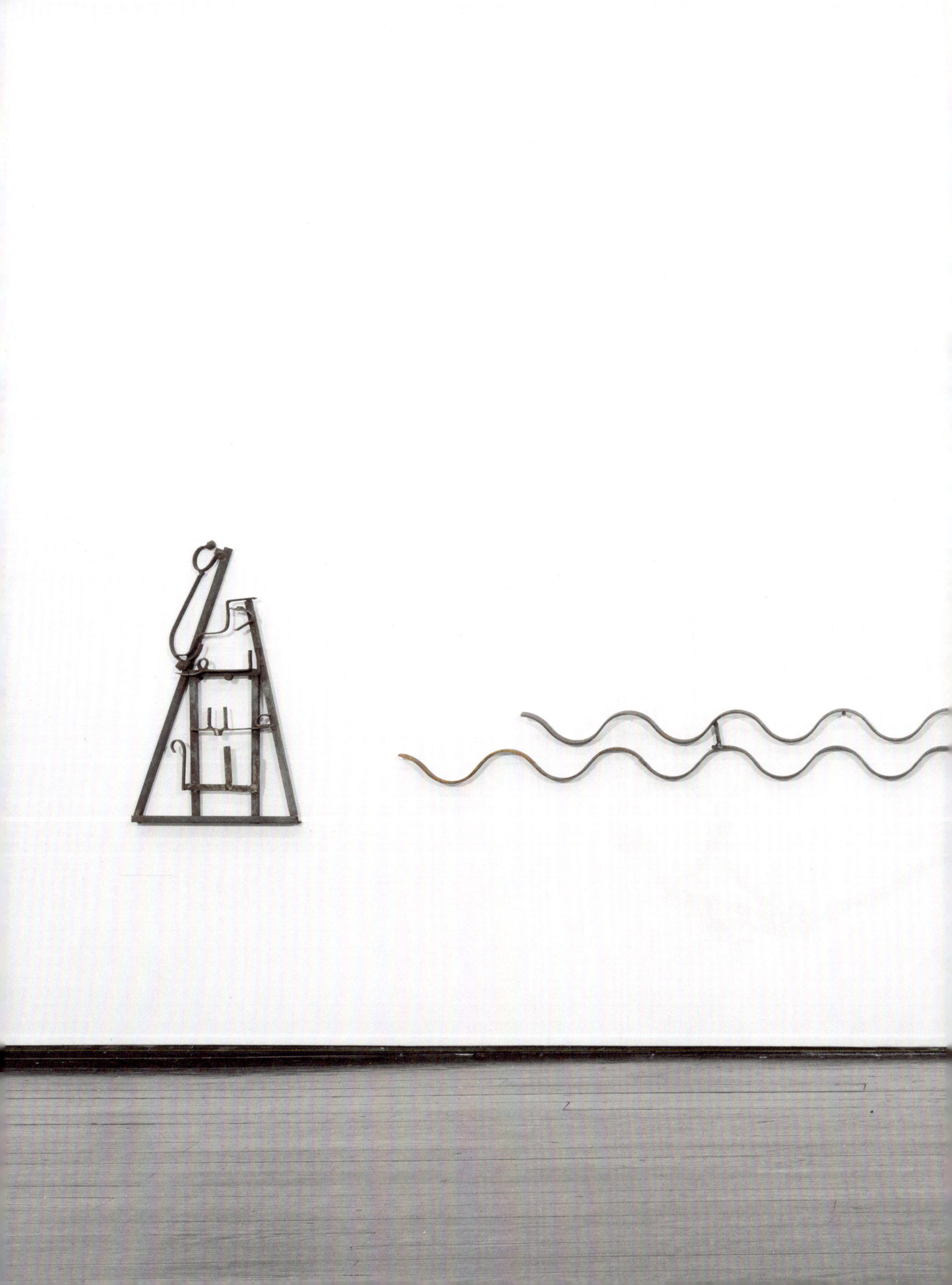

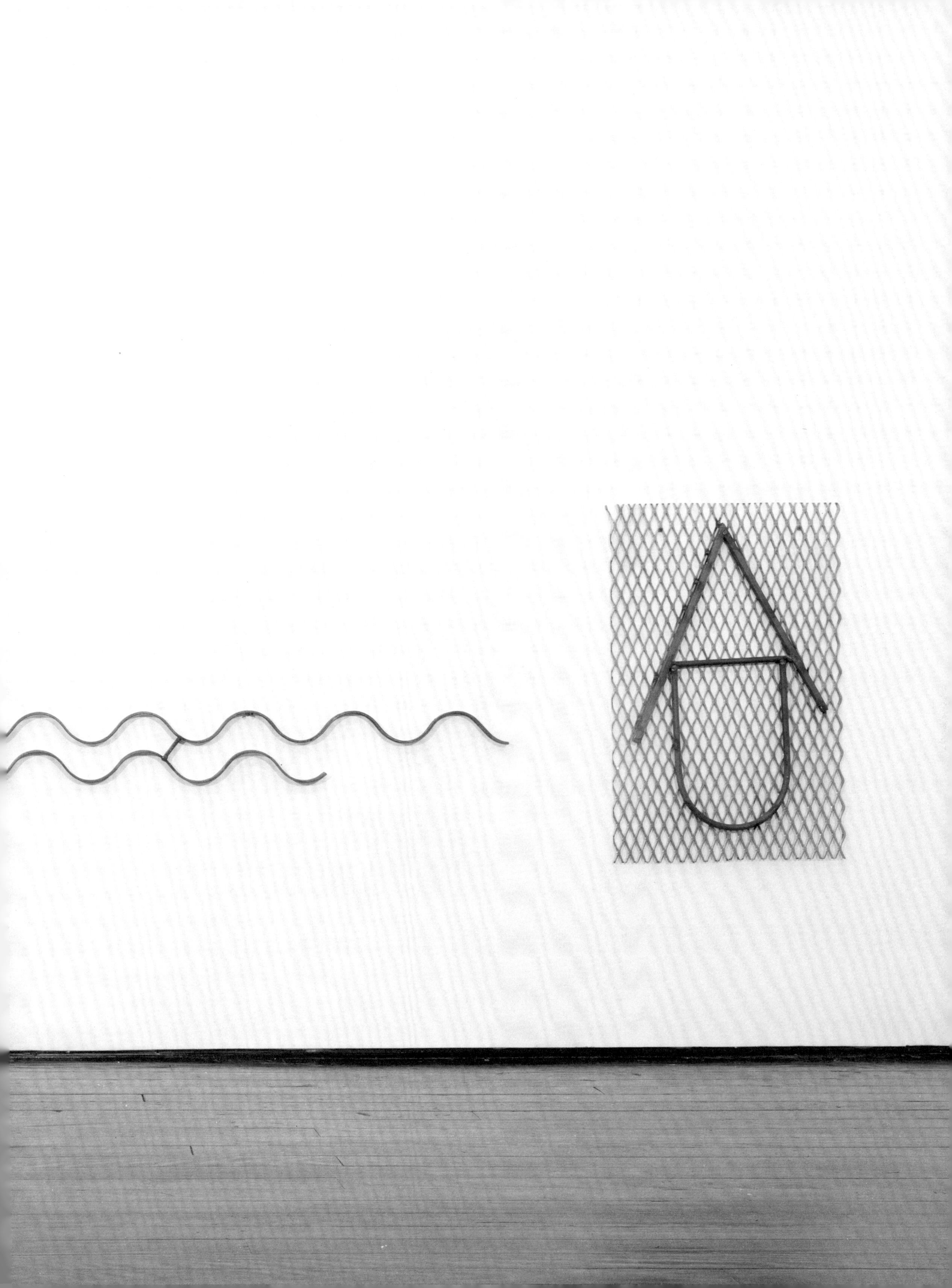

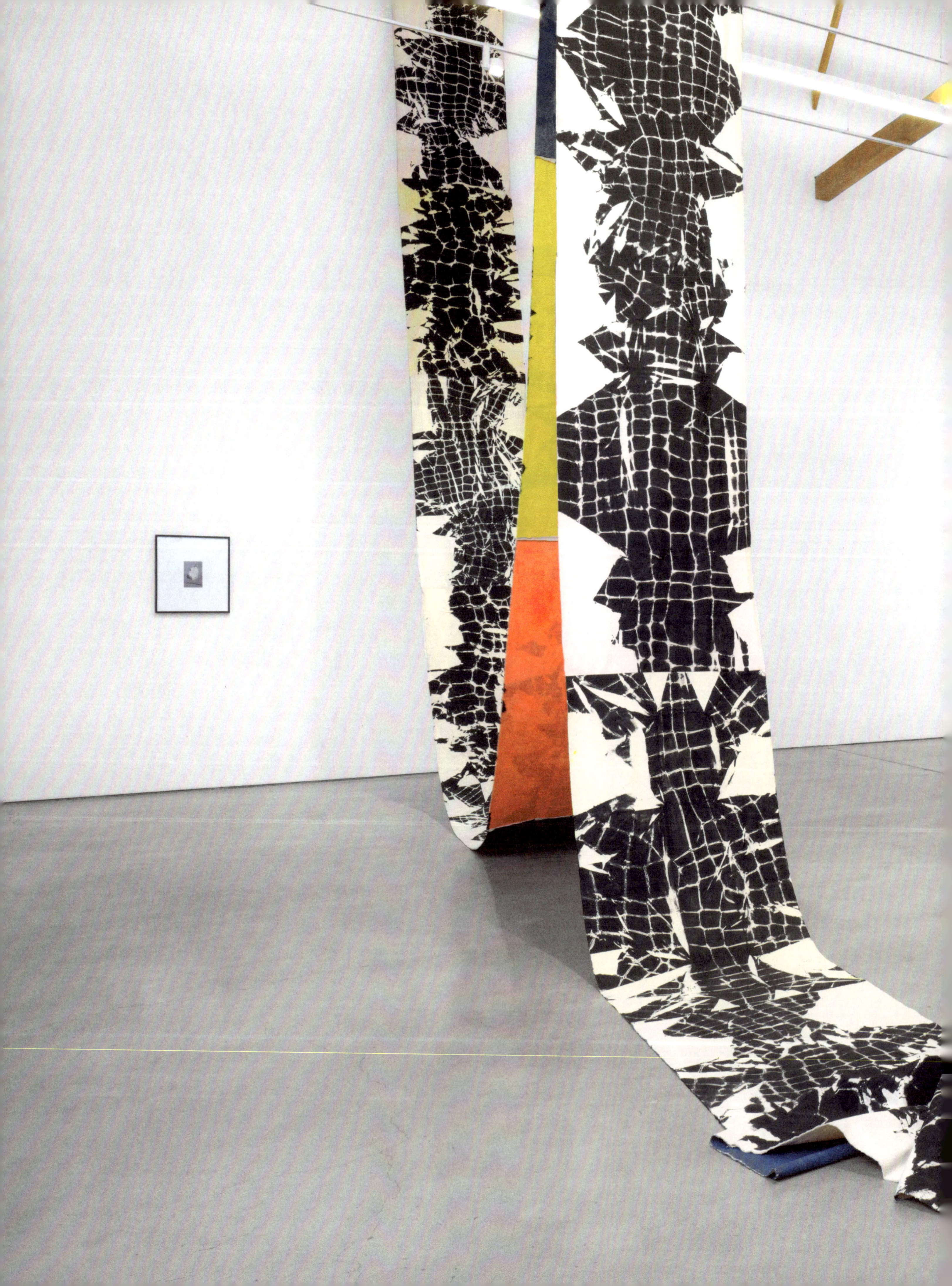

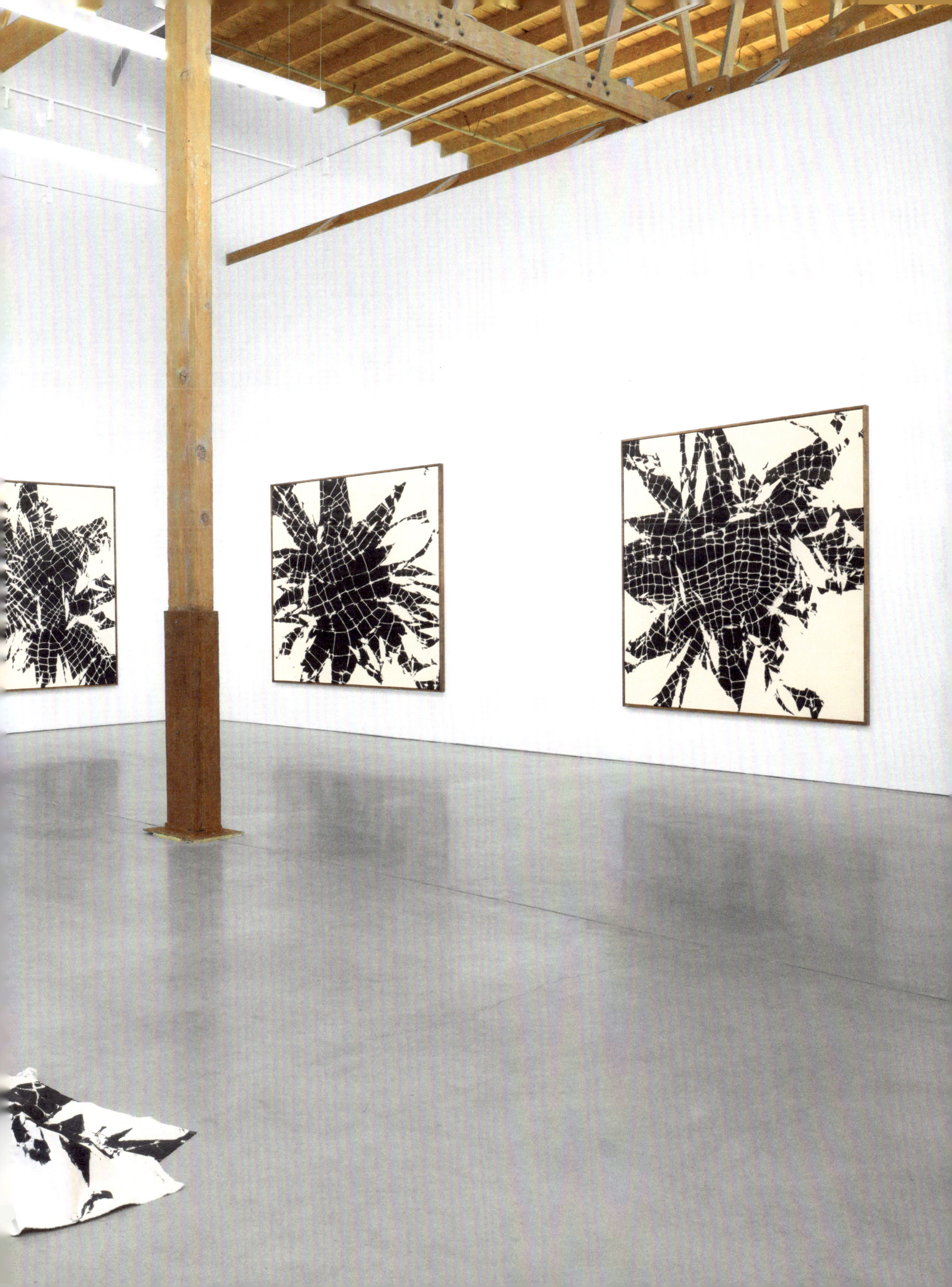

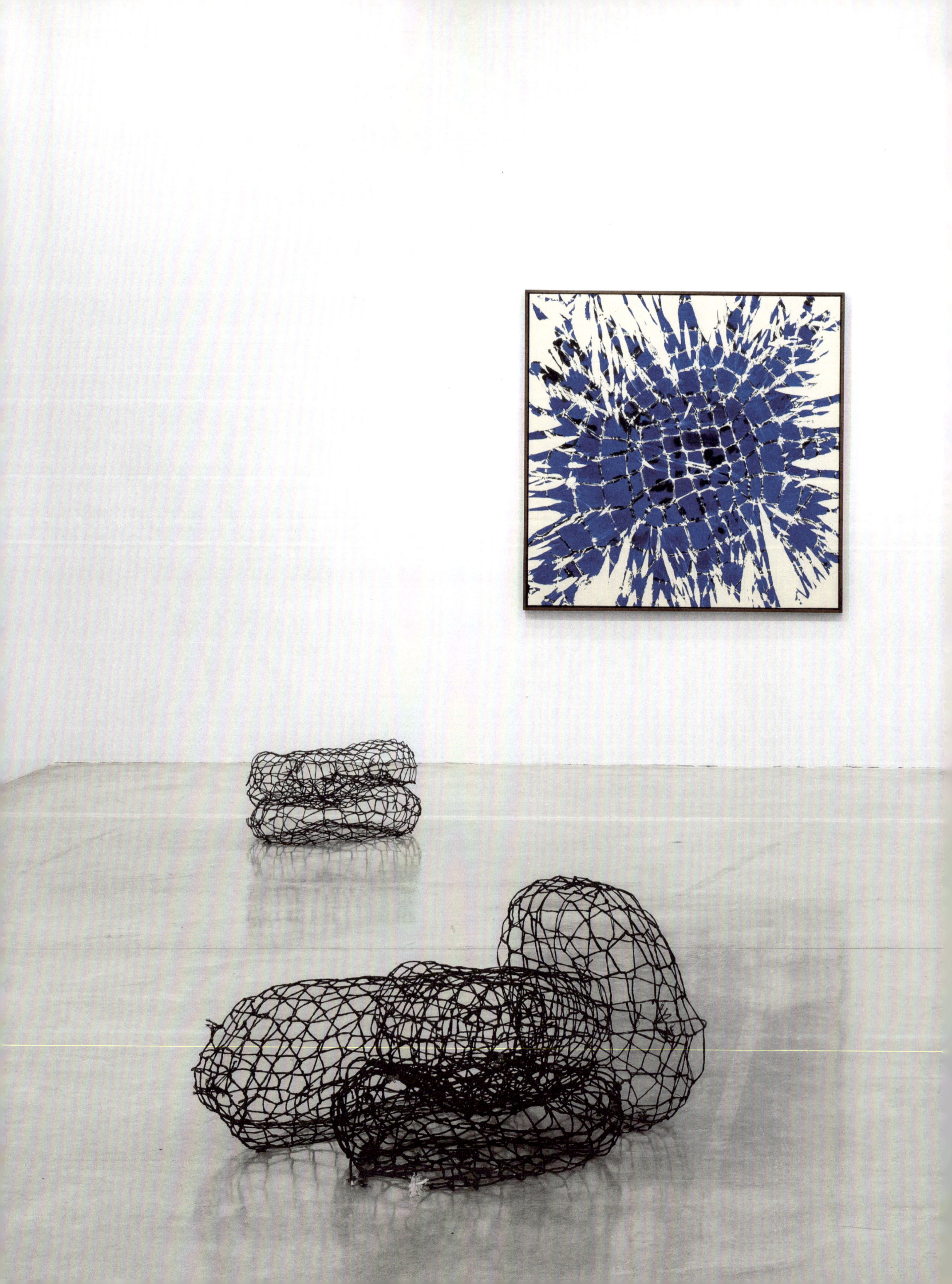

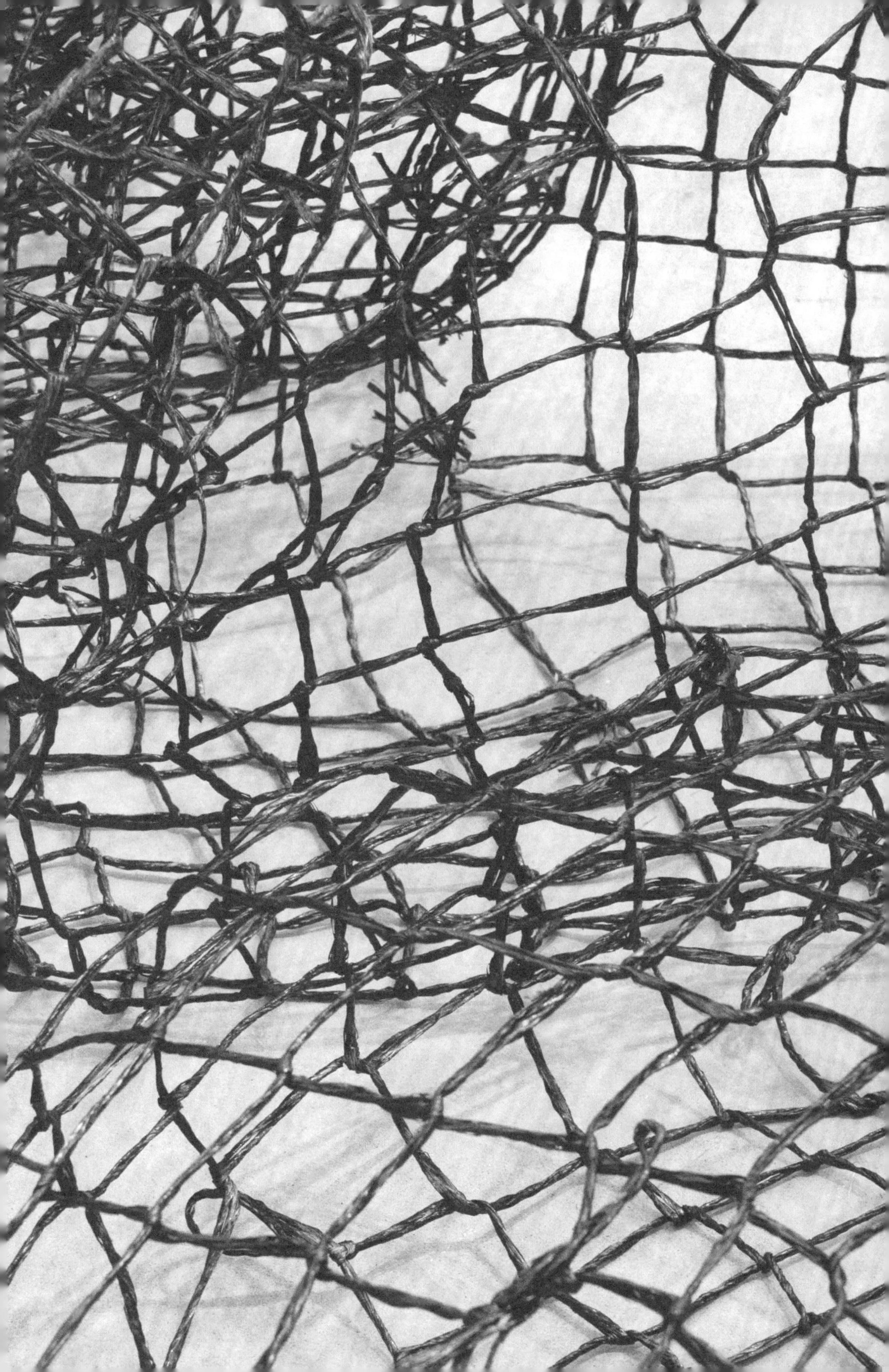

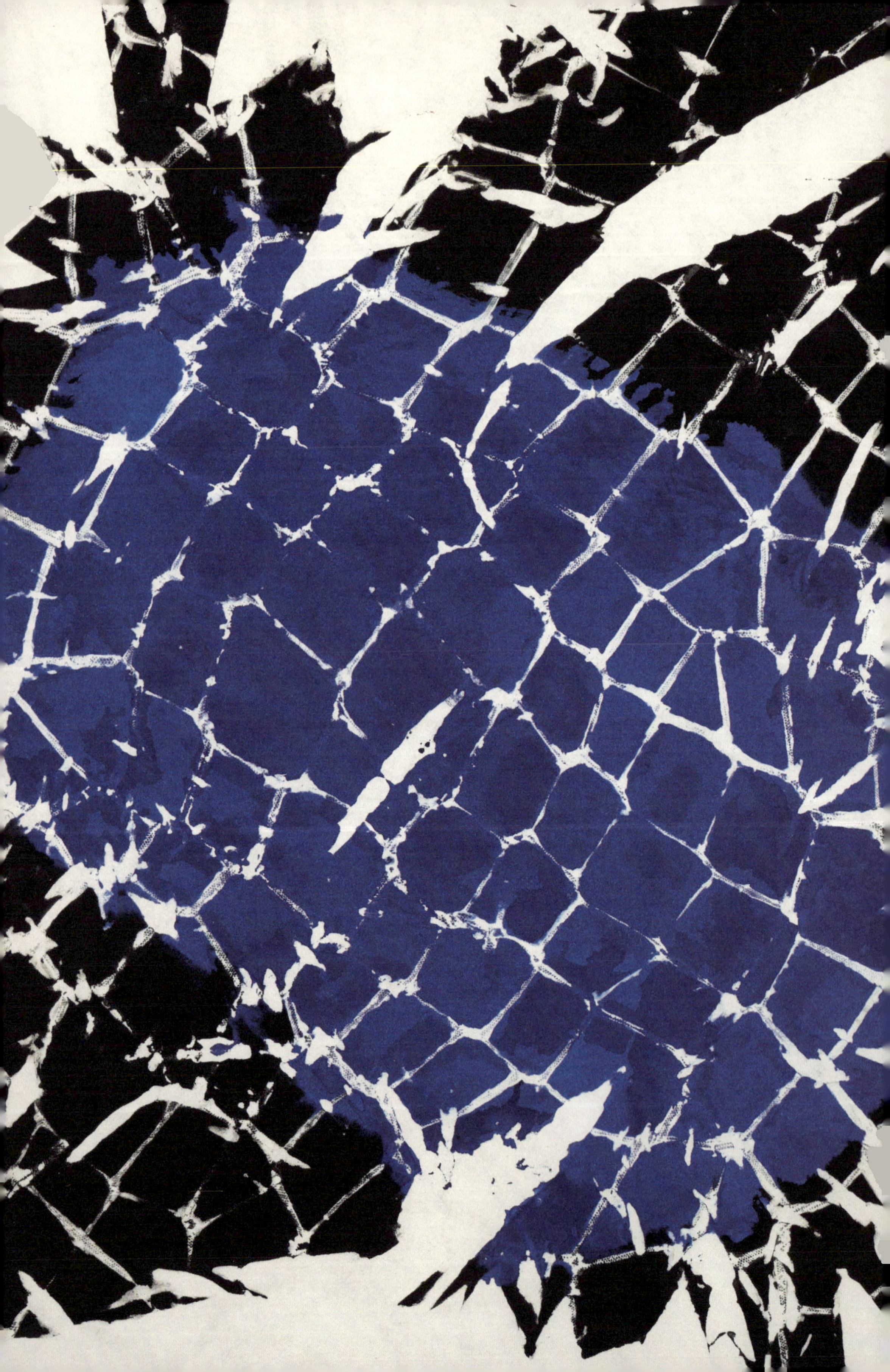

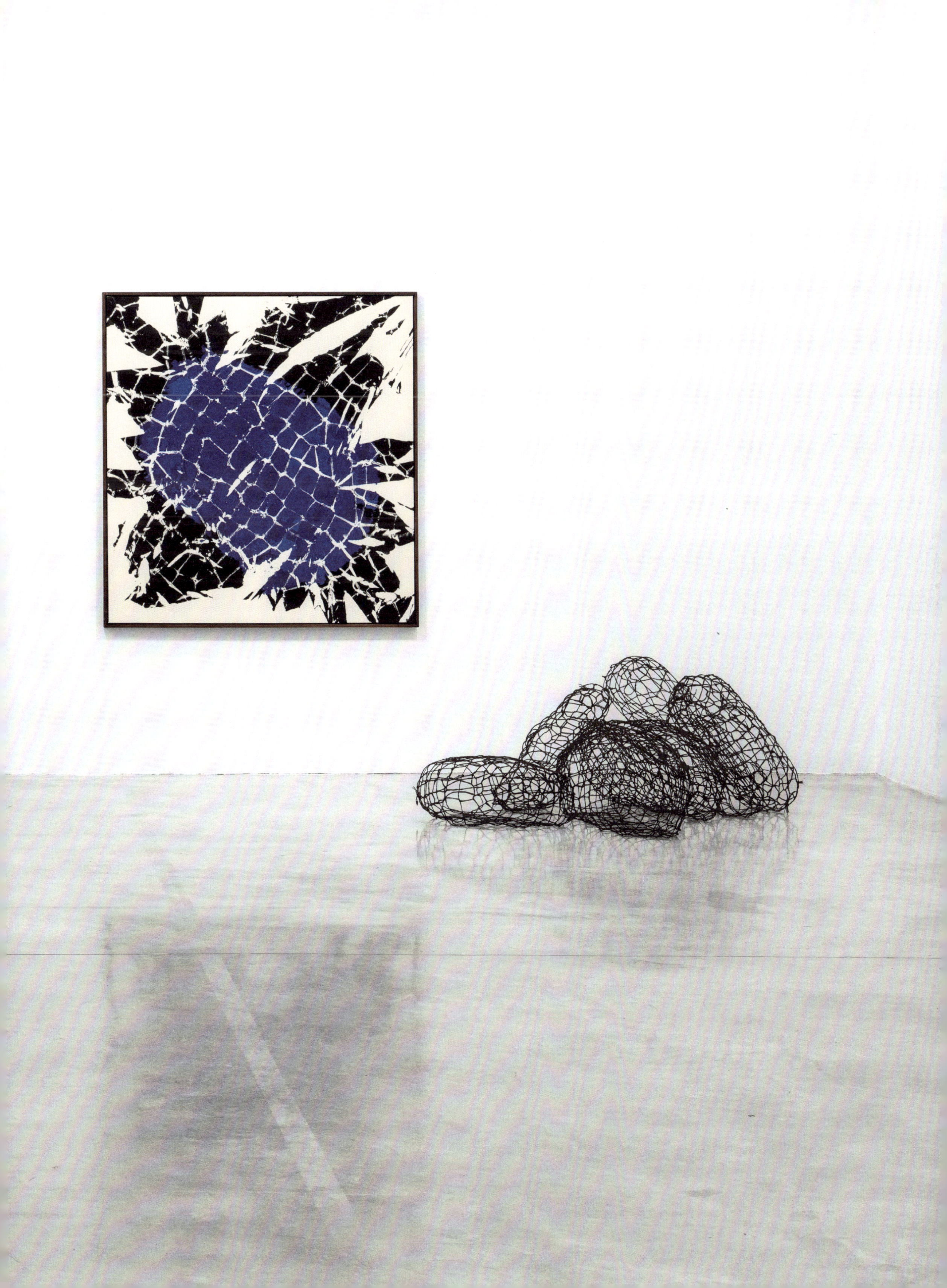

PAGES 36–37:

INSTALLATION VIEW OF **MAIA RUTH LEE: MIGRANT READER**
François Ghebaly, Los Angeles, 2022
courtesy of the Artist and François Ghebaly, Los Angeles and New York
photo: Paul Salveson

PAGES 38, 41:

INSTALLATION VIEW OF
MAIA RUTH LEE: THE SKIN OF THE EARTH IS SEAMLESS
Tina Kim Gallery, New York, 2023
courtesy of Tina Kim Gallery
photo: Charles Roussel

PAGE 40:

B.B.M. COBALT UMBRA 1-23, 2023
India ink and acrylic ink on canvas
62¼ × 60 × 2 inches (158.1 × 154 × 5.1 cm)
courtesy of the artist and Tina Kim Gallery
photo: Charles Roussel

OPPOSITE:

BONDAGE BAGGAGE LIFT, 2022
aquatint on Hahnemühle bright white paper, 350 gsm
36 × 42 inches (91.4 × 106.7 cm)
courtesy of the artist and Harlan + Weaver

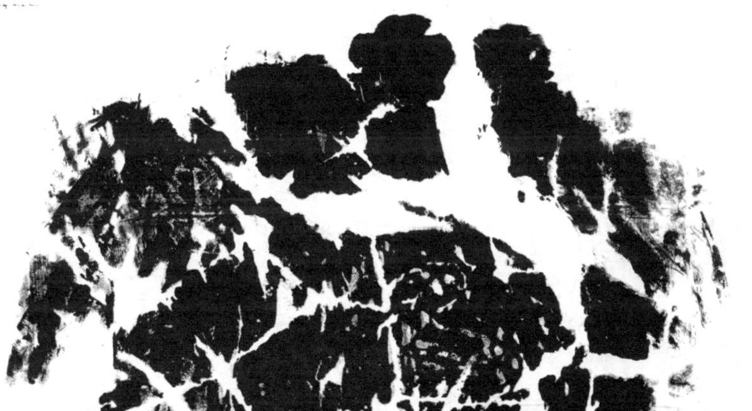

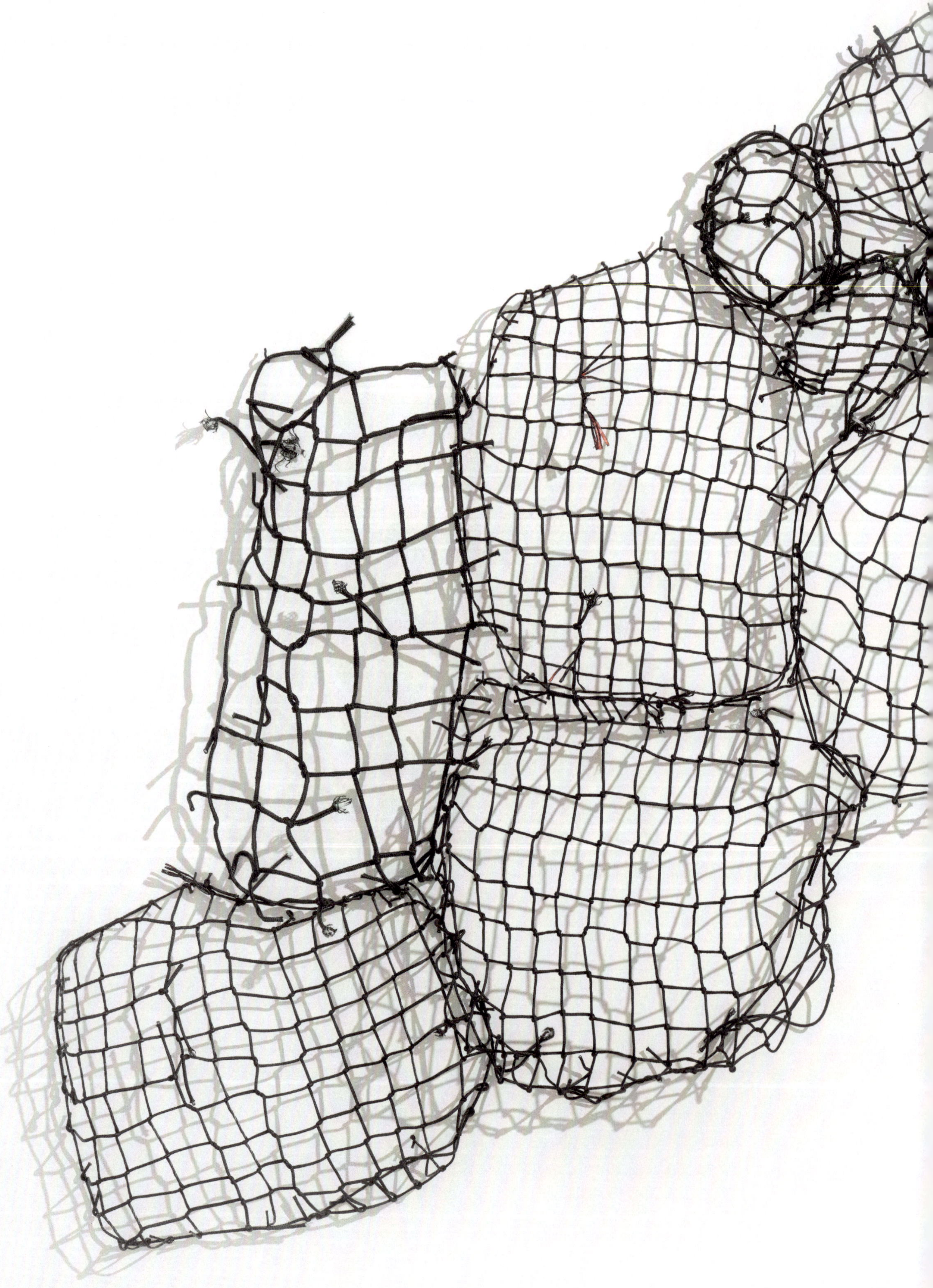

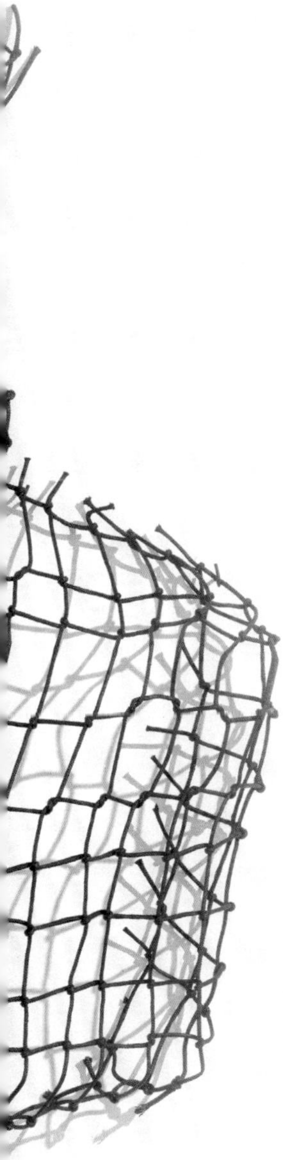

May 30, 2017

A repeating dream, I'm in my schoool (highschool) and I have no idea which class I'm supposed to go to θ I've accidentally missed out on an entire semester of classes, my fear of failing takes over and I'm frantically running around endless corridors and classrooms to find my firneds.
Is there a Timetable?I ask. Nobody knows. Time escapes me, the concept doesn't stick and I'm perplexed.

~~For the first time of my pregnancy I'm anxious~~

Becoming receptive. and adaptive. and accepting.

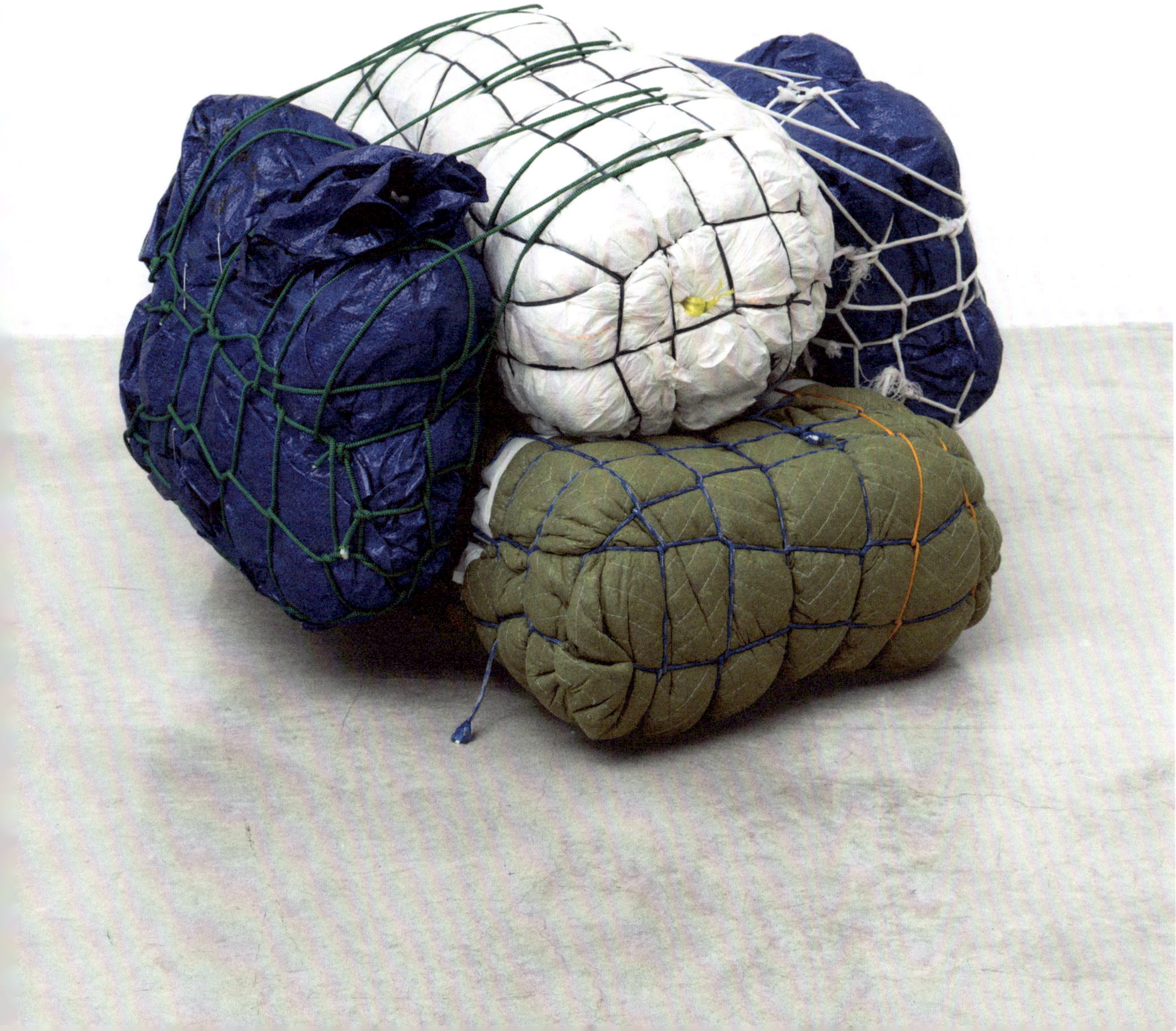

PAGES 44–45:

BONDAGE BAGGAGE ATLAS II, 2022
rope and India ink
64 × 61 × 5 inches (162.5 × 155 × 13 cm)
courtesy of the artist and François Ghebaly, Los Angeles and New York
photo: Paul Salveson

PAGE 47:

B.B. 23-4, B.B. 23-2, B.B. 23-16, 2023
tarp, burlap, rope, tape, luggage, used clothing, bedding
21 × 32 × 37 inches (53.3 × 81.3 × 94 cm)
courtesy of the artist and Tina Kim Gallery
photo: Charles Roussel

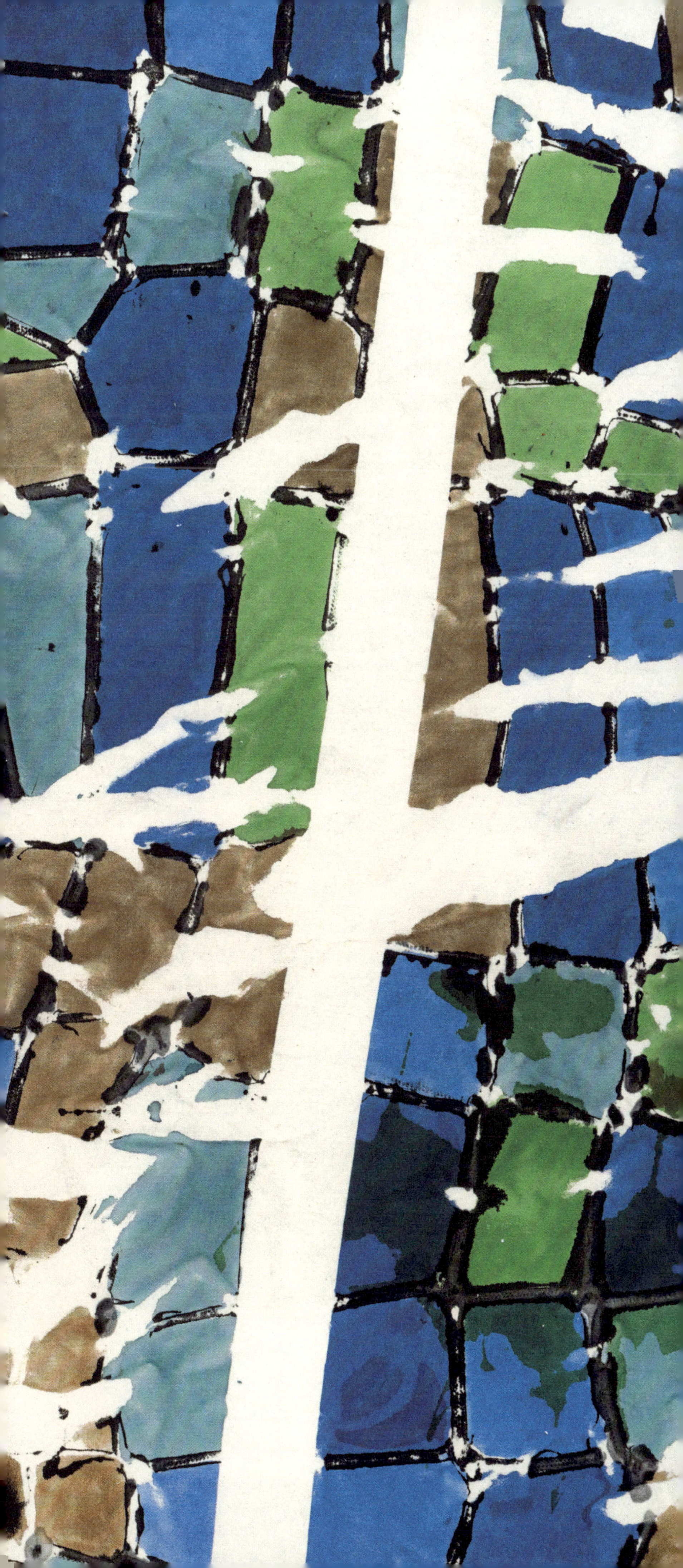

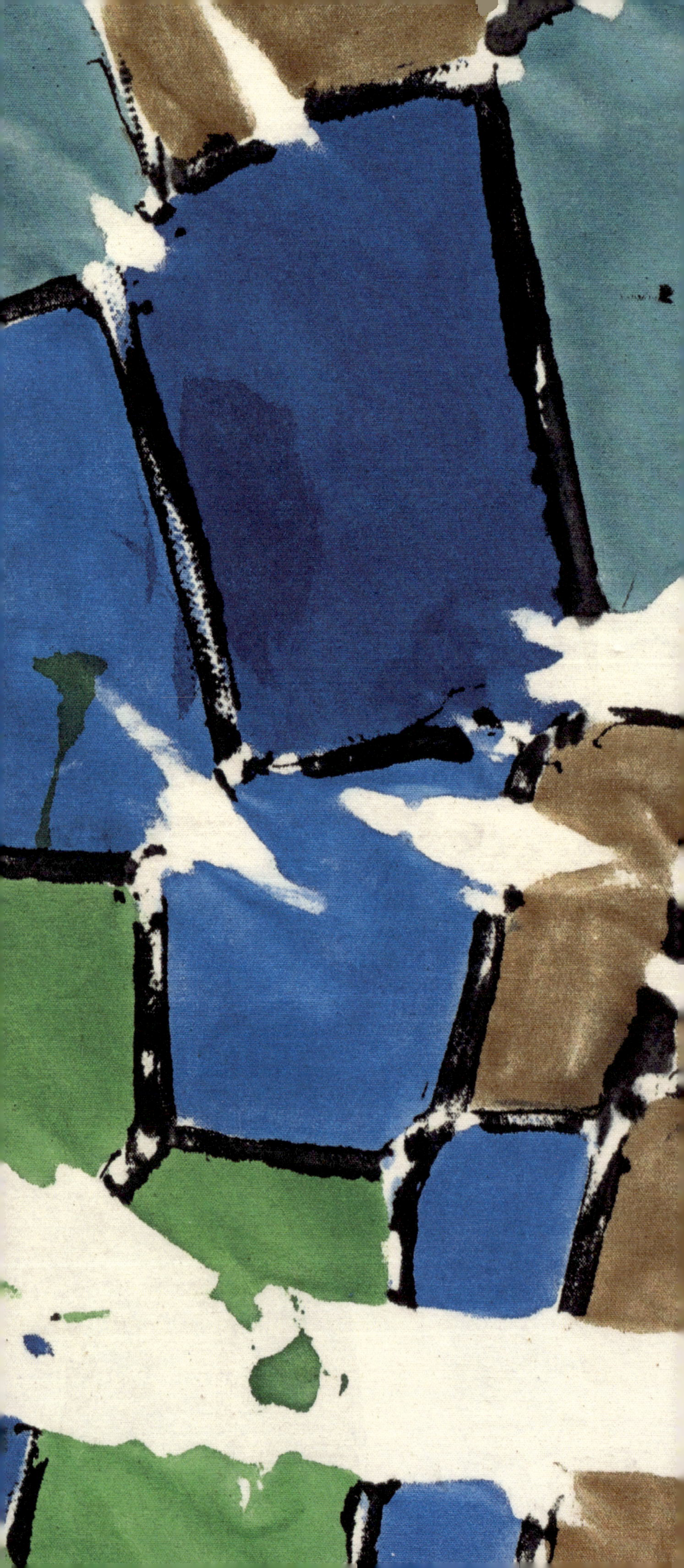

young

FRESH WATER

Lim

FOREST

my mother dreamt of a young deer drinking from
a stream

            in the forest

when she conceived me -

taemong

a pbhoto of a young deer drinking out of a storm
drain

twenty seven years later i am here

young

FRESH WATER

Lim

FOREST

my mother dreamt of a young deer
a stream

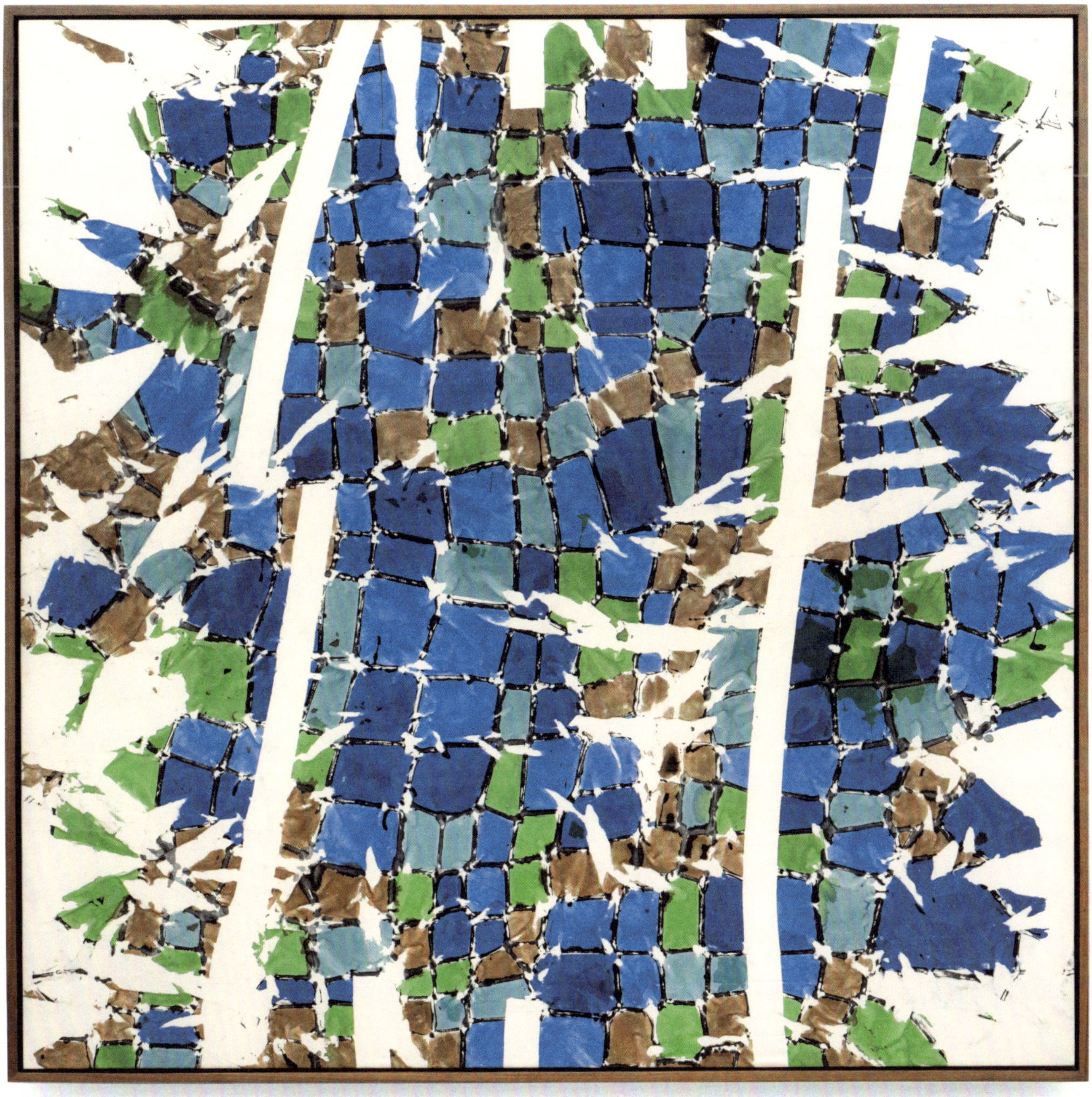

PAGE 49–50 [DETAILS], 53:

B.B.LATTICE 1-3, 2025
acrylic ink on canvas
61½ × 60 inches (156.2 × 152.4 cm)
courtesy of the artist and Tina Kim Gallery
photo: Hyunjung Rhee

OPPOSITE:

BONDAGE BAGGAGE PROTOTYPE 5, 2018
tarp, tape, rope, cardboard, used bedding
44 × 19½ × 21½ inches (111.8 × 49.5 × 54.6 cm)
courtesy of artist and Jack Hanley Gallery

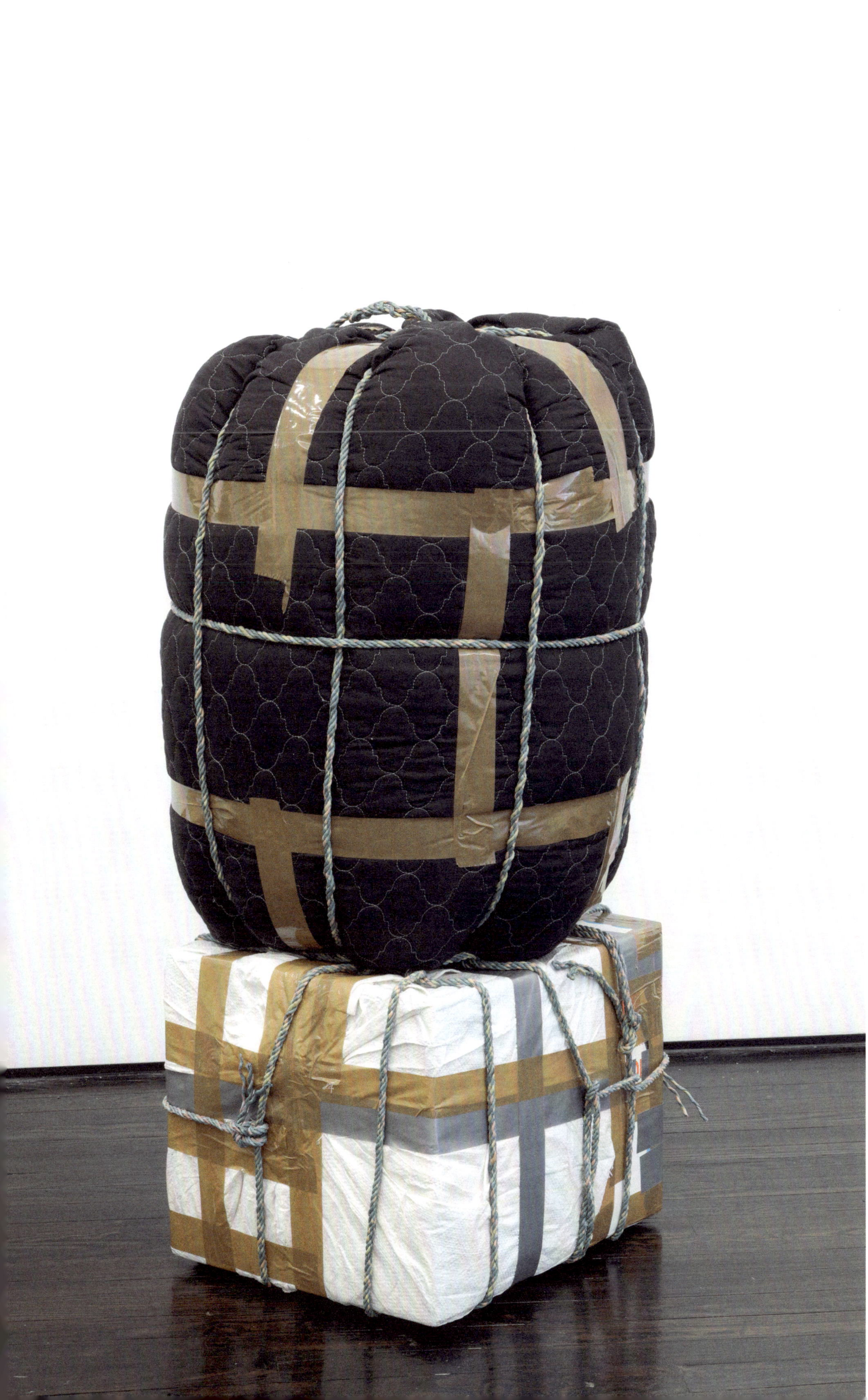

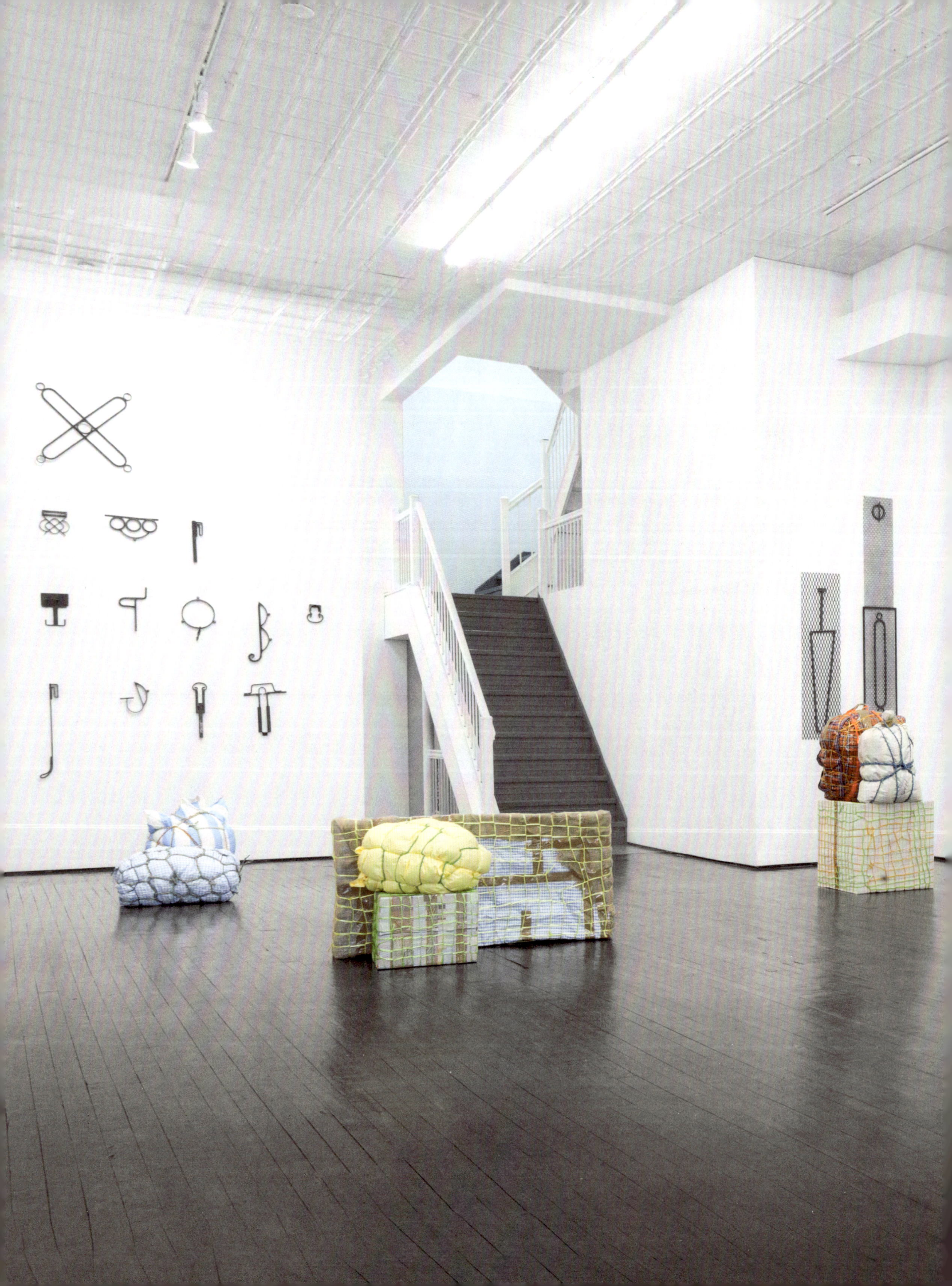

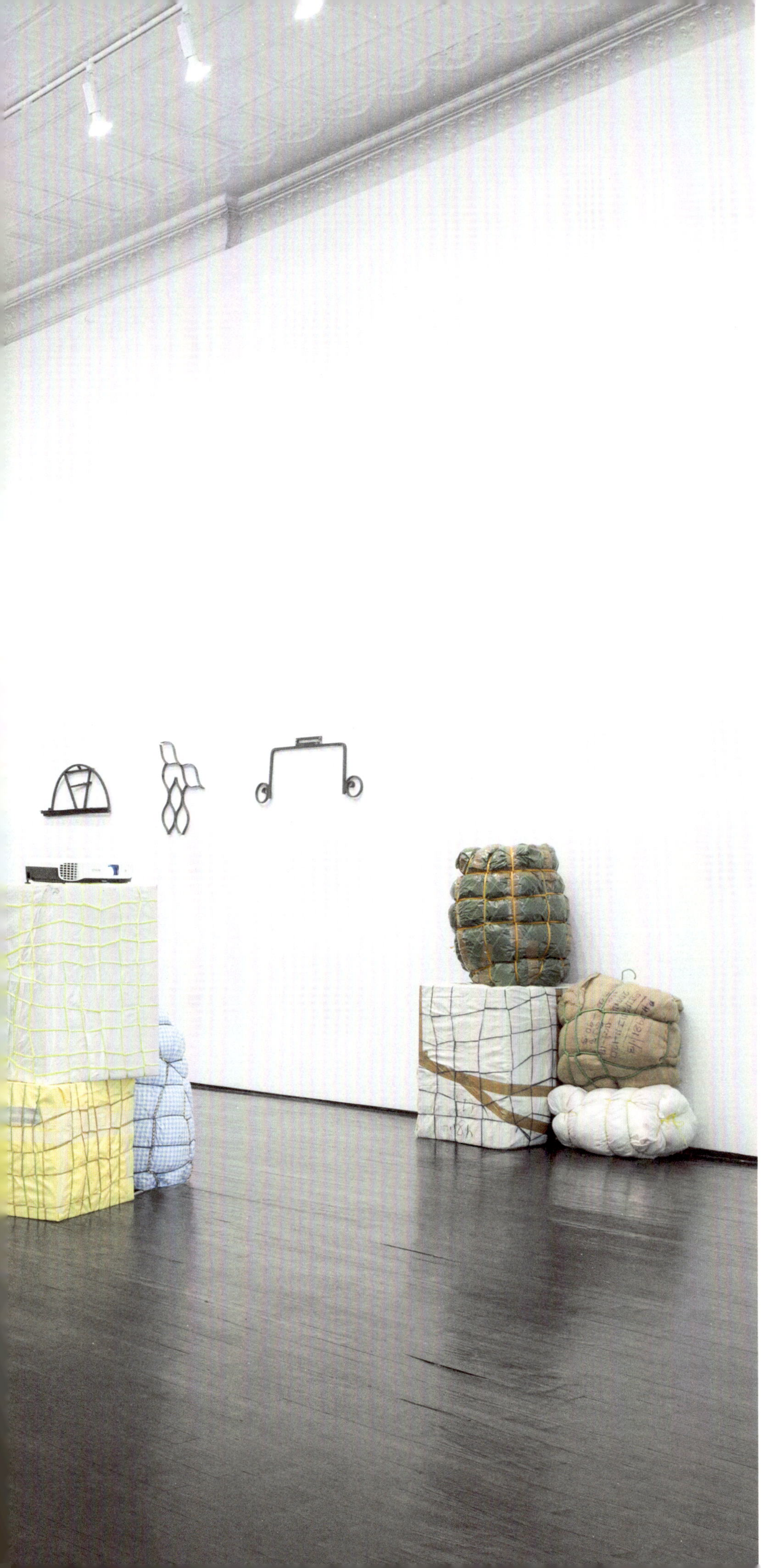

PAGE 56-57:

INSTALLATION VIEW OF **MAIA RUTH LEE: ACCESS TO TOOLS**
Jack Hanley Gallery, New York, 2018

OPPOSITE:

B.B.M. 2-1, 2023
India ink and acrylic ink on canvas
60¾ × 30¾ inches (154.5 × 78 cm)
courtesy of the artist and François Ghebaly, Los Angeles and New York
photo: Paul Salveson

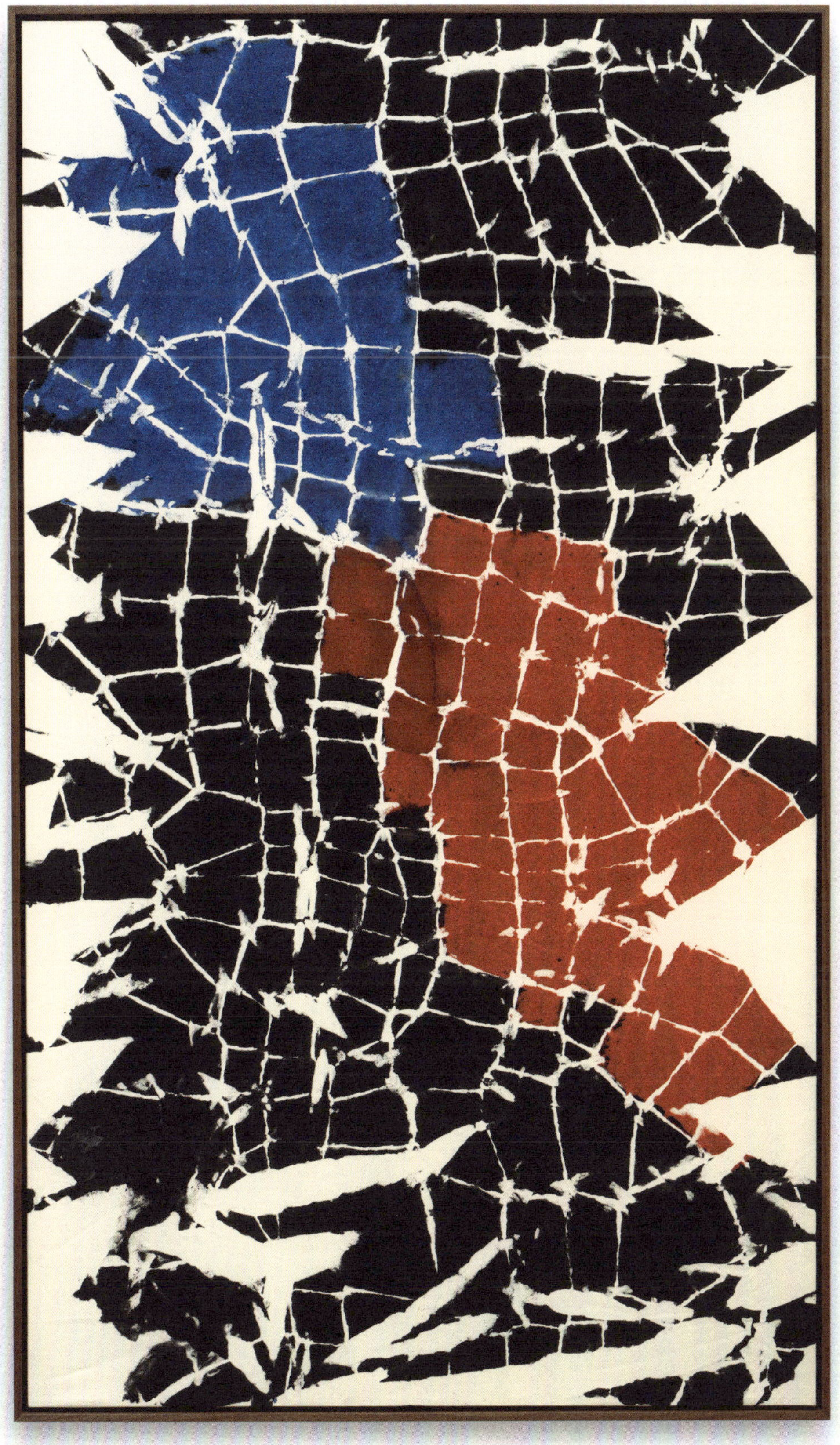

How to be sensitibe:
(without taking it personally)
Put yourself in the position of others, how does it make youv-feel?
Discrimanated? Abandoned? Criticized? Abused? Sad? Jealous? Envious?
Lonely? Afraid? Guilty? Victimized? Misunderstood?
All of these emotions are not yours, but the feelings of others. Take a s back. Even if they are not asking for help, be ready to listen. A good listener is a good friend.Sometimes it is unbearable and boring, but remem not to take it personally. Set some boundaries -- these are sometimes usu tools, but more likely will keep you sane.
Being sensitive doesn't necessarily mean you are weak. From sensitivity co true strength and endurance. Even the toughest of men are sensitive, and e one of us have been vulnerable infants. Interdependance vs. Independance.

How to be confident:
(without being vain)
There is no one else like you on this planet. This is terrifying yet ultin refreshing. Not even your parents are you, your siblings will never be yo Your are one of a kind, and that is extraordinary, in and of itself.
Confidence comes from experience, adversities and overcoming these advers: When you are still dwelling on the past, unable to move past obstacles - will then become obstalcles that keep you from being who you are destined Every single human has their own potential. When you are unsatisfied with life,it is perhaps because you are not living to your fullest potential. will make you unhappy and resentful of others around you. The key to full confidnce is within each and every one.

----
side track:
I dreamt of the sky - the sun rose bloody red, coming past the clouds tha dark and gloomy, but only to rise again seconds after. The sun kept risin repeatedly through the clouds, then the clouds parted and behind it a hug blue moon appeared, as the main act - the ta-da moment encaptured, my bre was taken away.

----

cont'd.. (How to be confident)
True confidence comes from the beleief that you will no matter what surviv The small things remain small, and the big things are the ones you will b concerned about. Change of perspective, and a chance to move away from th that are insignificant. Do not be phased by fortune, fame, popularity, th but focus on the things/peiople you need in your life. Manifest what is im for you, and experience them coming your way. Set your blueprint, walk th

Have I unknowingly tapped into some truths? I feel no agency in this world Home doesn't mean anything, how I float through this world I don't know what kind of pathway I've chosen, but it is 'taking' me. Since Nima a part of me has shut off. A valve that controls emotions, it feels jammed.

Perhaps because the emotions a child brings into the world is overwhelming, perhaps because I am afraid. Afraid to fully feel and accept what Nima means to me. It is so easy for Peter to love him and express his love for him, I findmyself sometimes having to edit my thoughts and feelings towards him in order to not 'over-do'. Was this how I was loved by my mother? But Nima is me, how I used to be - expresses with freedom and non judgemental and he is kind. He is gentle, his love succeeds. I see all of these traits clearly, but yet I sometimes stop myself from giving that back to him.

The love he receives from the world is enought I sometimes think. Can some-one be 'over-loved'? Does that harm?

What is my intention in this world/? I look back at old writings and I have now EVERYTHING i have asked for, it is uncanny it is wild. I am in denial of my own happiness, and this year I have to conquer that denial and accept what I have been given.

What is my inward realm? This Labyrinth I am working on should be my template.

Blue Template
Ripening
Pathway

CONTROL is restraint upon movement - a movement forwrd, upward, sideways. Letting go of control is infact a boost of motion, letting elements vibrate and navigate. Old particles stay static and die away, new particles evolve and grow. I have ultimately no control of this universe, except to control my inner growth - which is counter productive. I must remember this, letting go of restraint is blind faith, an intuitive understanding that the unknown is safe.

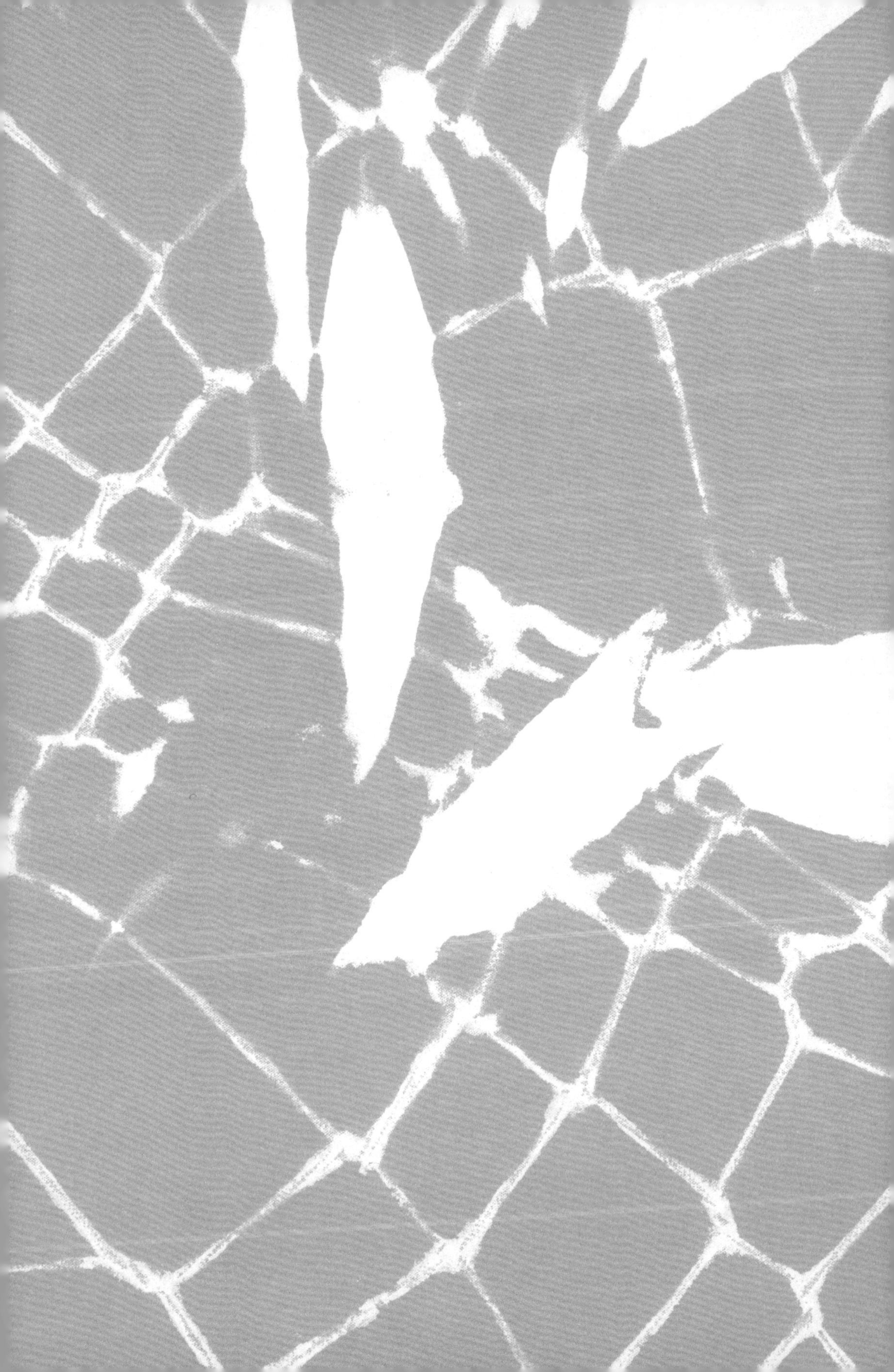

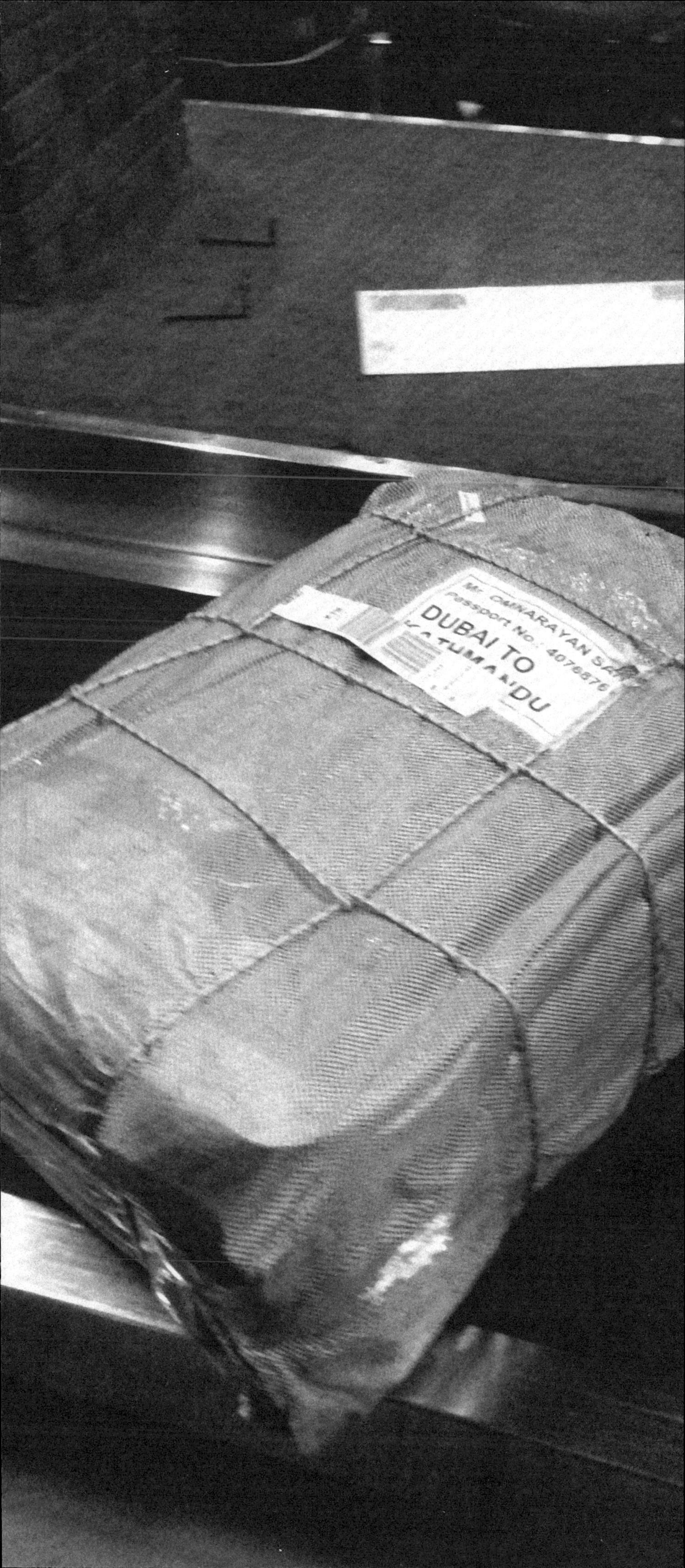
DUBAI TO

January 15th 2019

Focusing is my main agenda this ye
being present for the people aroun
intently, breathing, setting reali
and mostly following up with thing

TO DO

1. Get my drivers licence
2. Get my health insurance
3. Do a great job at WB.
4. Write more, read everyday.
5. Speak Korean to Nima.
6. Be less on the phone.
7. Be more organized with stduio/C
8. Make new work.
9. Learn how to play the cello.
10. Make more video work
11. Spend less money.

Only I will ever remember my pain.
broke, tearing into shards of glas
with a sledge hammer. My eyes desp

'The uncreative sense of guilt'

Obligation vs creativity

the labyrinth, a unicursal pathway
The way in and out. The labyrinth

Existence not only ceases to be a

Transparency; a window into clarit
Every year I wish upon an intentio

2013 I wished for financial gain,
2016 I wished for family and so it
This new year in 2019 I wish for l

In order to gain happiness, one ne
others but to myself. Maintaining
feel it. Remembering what makes ou

Breaking habits, breaking depressi

Shanwn has entered back into my li
Michelle Murphy is a medium I have

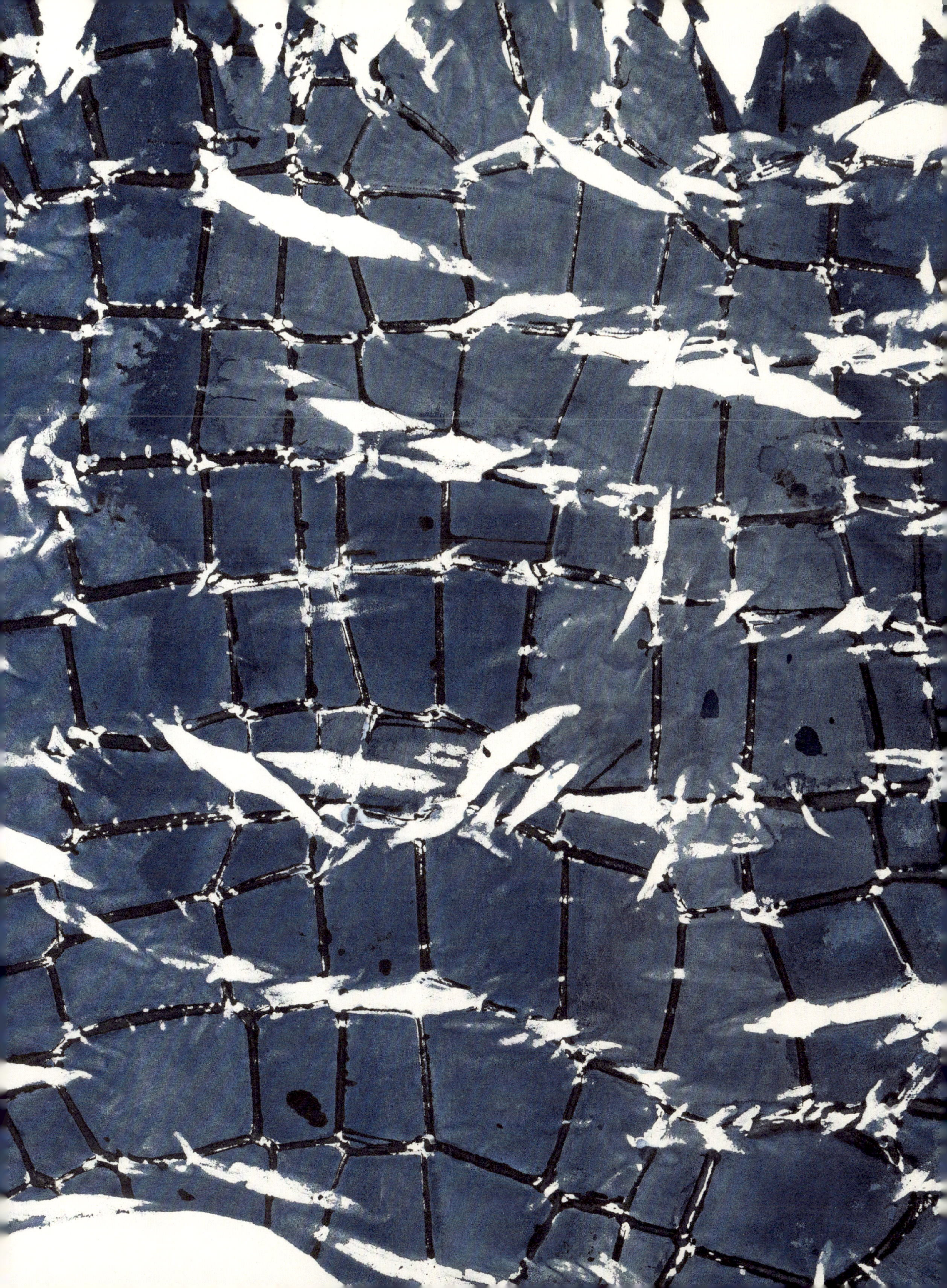

PAGE 65:

B.B.M. 2-16, 2023
India ink and acrylic ink on canvas
62½ × 44 inches (158.8 × 111.8 cm)
courtesy of the artist and François Ghebaly, Los Angeles and New York
photo: Paul Salveson

OPPOSITE:

BONDAGE BAGGAGE RESIDUUM, 2022
four-color, hand-pulled screenprint on Coventry Rag
44 × 35 inches (111.8 × 88.9 cm)
courtesy of the artist and Kingsland Printing

PAGES 68–69:

B.B.CHECK-IN, 2023
tarp, burlap, rope, tape, luggage, used clothing, bedding
dimensions variable
courtesy of the artist and Tina Kim Gallery
photo: Lyn Nguyen

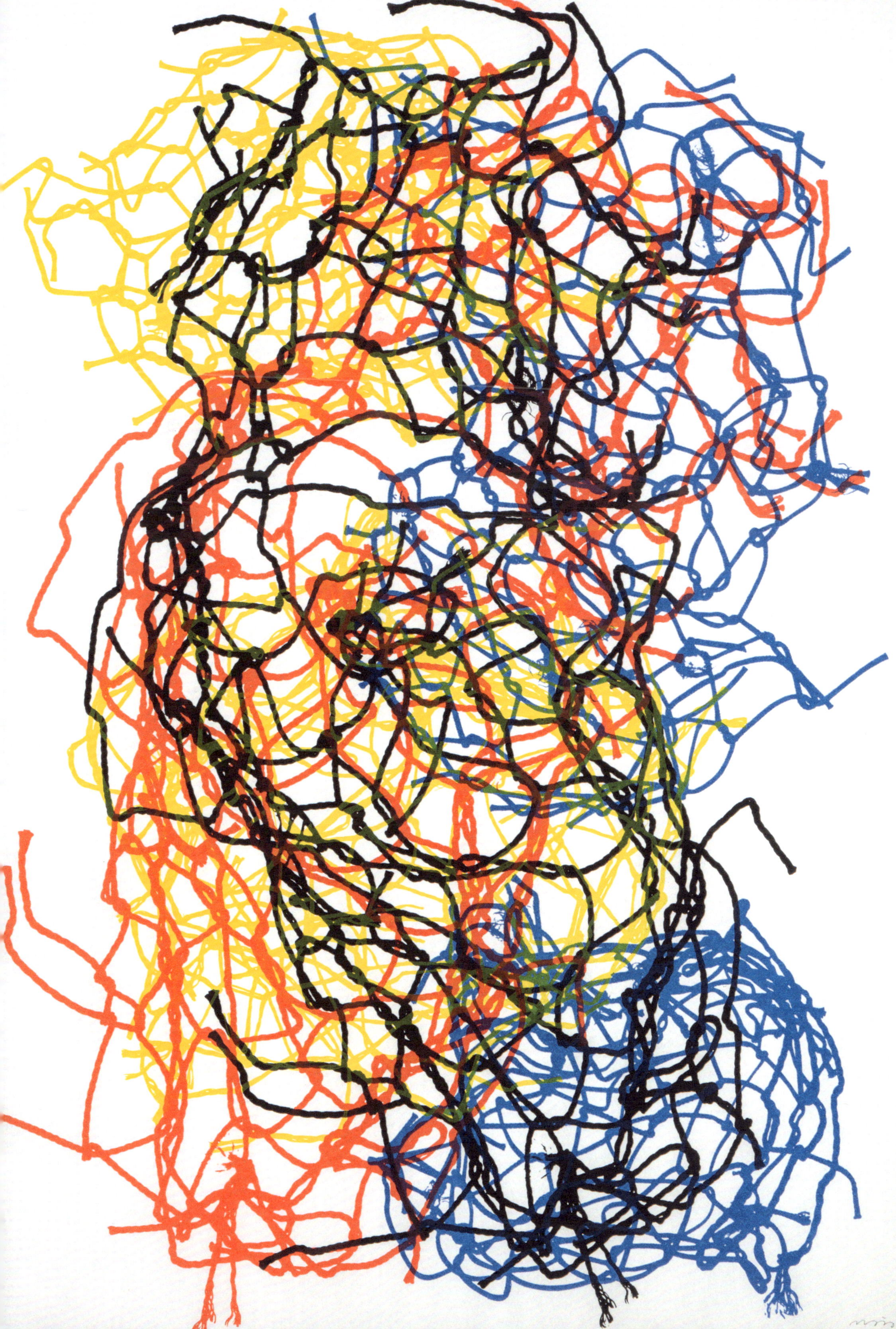

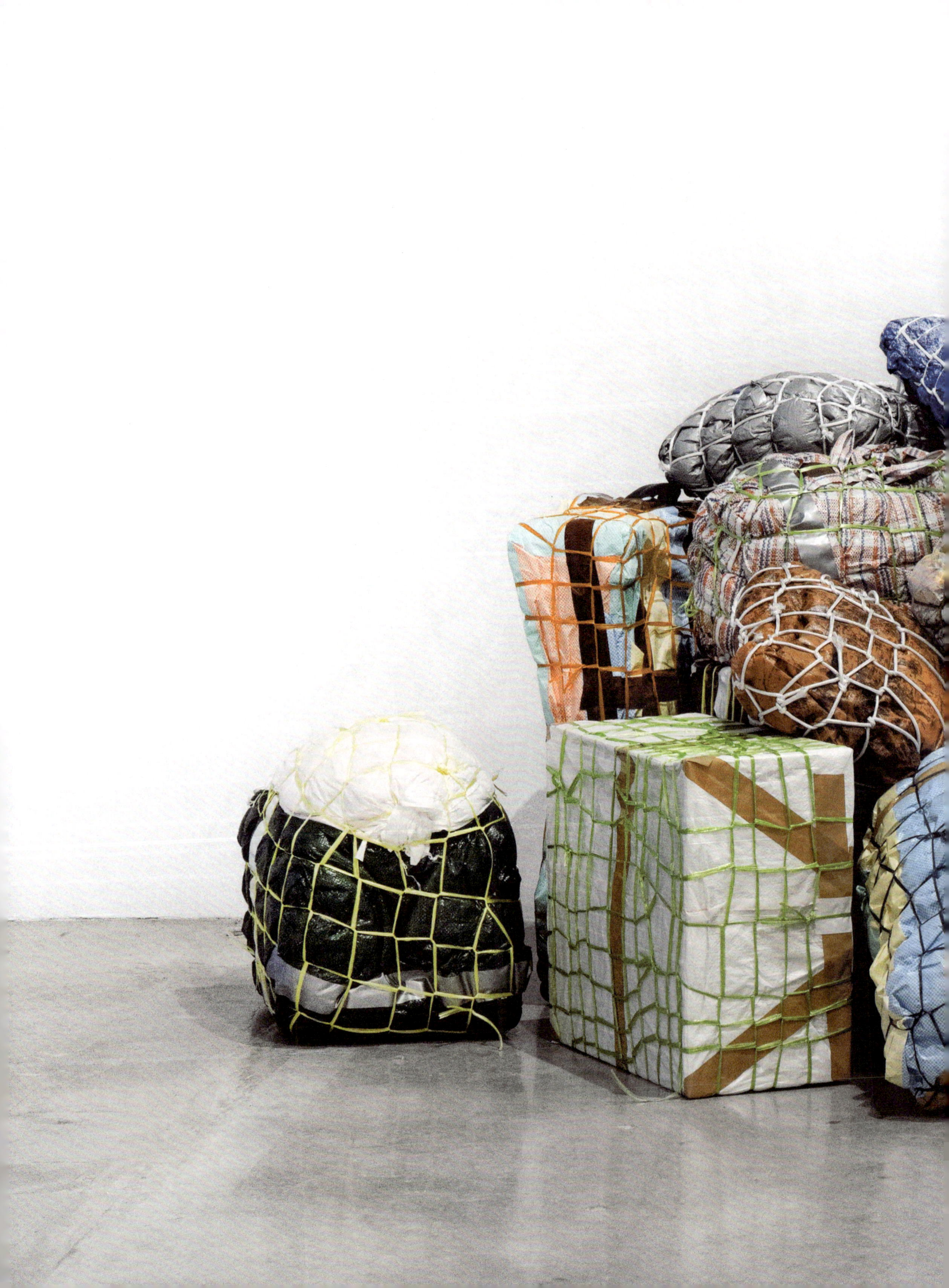

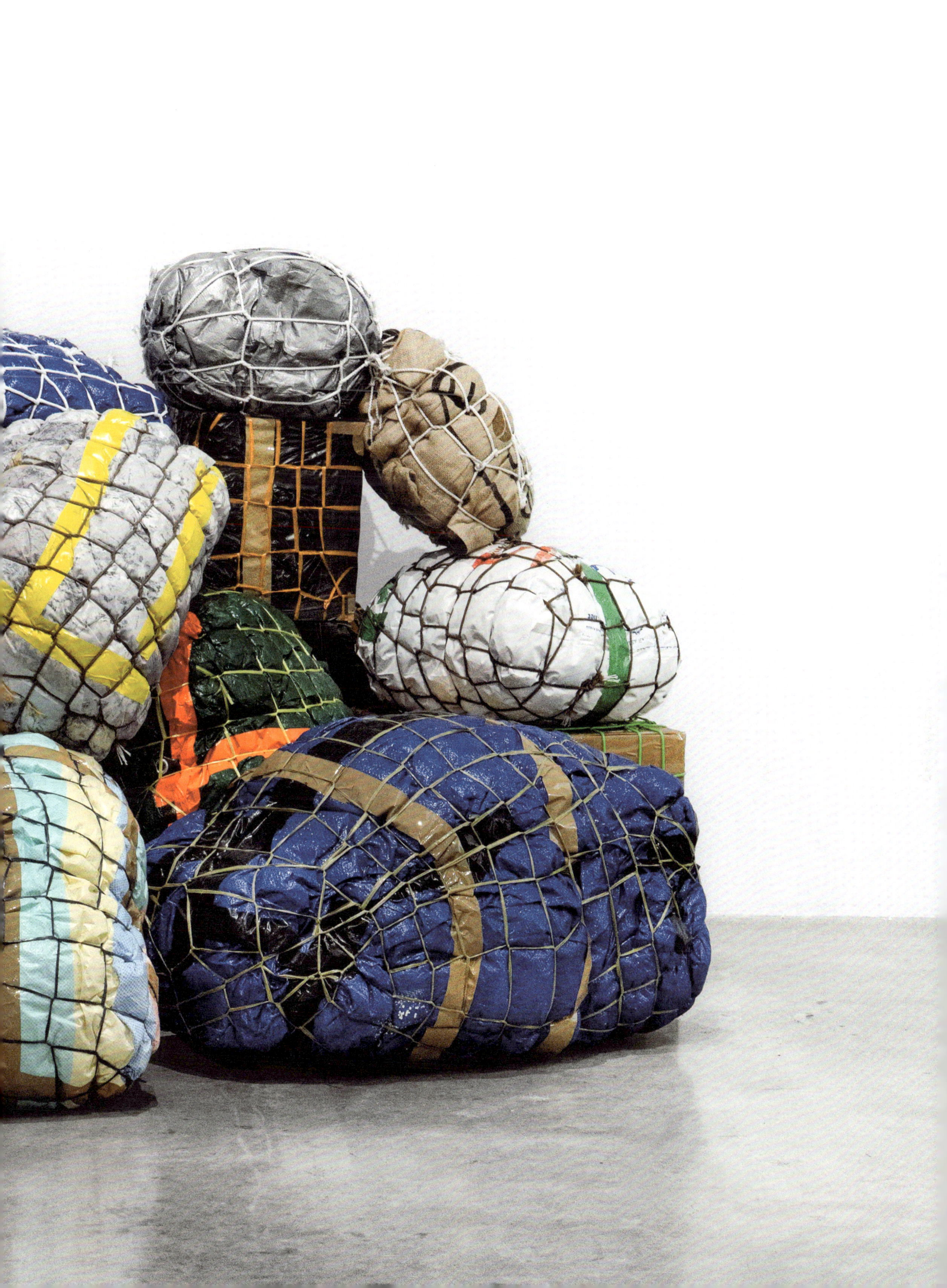

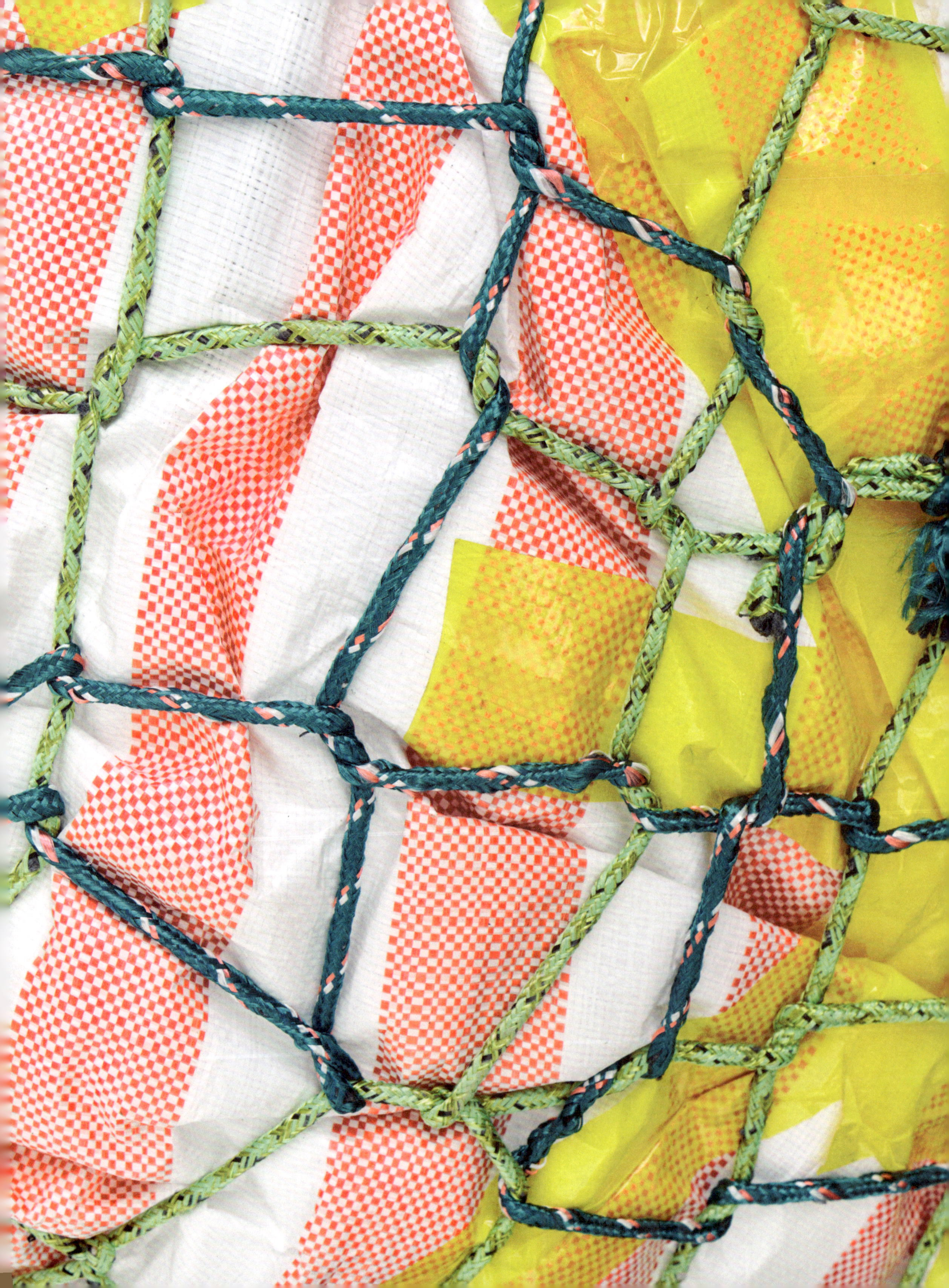

Friday, February 21, 2025
1:11pm EST

Dear Maia,

I stopped taking the peptides for now. All of them. Last week, another person I know had their ovaries explode. That makes five this month, including me. What's happening? Do our ovaries know something we don't?

I'm getting an ultrasound on Tuesday. What if the cysts started talking to me through the monitor? I wonder what they'd say. High-frequency sound waves yelling: *Protect your energy!*

I called My Peptide Dealer to get his doctor's phone number. It was awkward. I still love him, but I'll get over it. I tried to tell him that the juice is making me sick, and he kept saying that I looked good. And that it could be a number of factors. He didn't know I'd been hospitalized twice. Our Mutual Friend hadn't told him, which pissed me off. If I'm dying, everyone should know, right? At least it's not cancer. You were/are right. This is the end of that cycle. How come it doesn't feel like an end then?

The Disaster Movie didn't feel like an end either, though it most certainly is. The weight of it is hitting everyone as the new reality settles. My own grief and despair rise in stillness. Tears rolled down my face as my French manicure dried under the fan at Jade Nails & Spa. The tech wiped my eyes with tissue paper. I couldn't get "thank you" out of my mouth, so I smiled. On the way to Pittsburgh, a wave knocked me over. My face was wet, and my lips were trembling so hard. I'm glad the woman next to me didn't ask if I was okay. I'm doing my best to be actively optimistic and receiving of love/support. Feel much stronger and less afraid on the other side.

I'm too high functioning. I think I really need to show people I'm not okay. I'm going to get a dog, a gun, start an experimental shoegaze band, start doing stand-up comedy, and start doing heroin. Then we start the cult. You in?

Love,

Martine

PAGE 70:

HUMAN LIFE IN MOTION [DETAIL]

curated by Jade Foster, Primary, Nottingham, UK, 2025

courtesy of the artist and Primary, Nottingham, UK

Explanation.

This medicine is composed of the oriental Medical Herb.

This medicine does good at circulating of blood, increasing immunocompetence.

The contents of this oriental Herb Medicine is as follows.

① 香附子 Cyperi Rhizoma.

② 白朮 Atractylodis Macrocephalae Rhizoma.

③ 甘草 Glycyrrhizae Radix

④ 厚朴 Machili Cortex

⑤ 陳皮 Aurantii nobilis Pericarpium.

⑥ 半夏 Pinelliae Rhizoma.

⑦ 枳実 Ponciri Fructus

⑧ 砂仁 Amomi Semen.

⑨ 川芎 Cnidii Rhizoma.

⑩ 蒼朮 Atractylodis Rhizoma.

2022. 9. 5

Explanation.

This medicine is composed of the Oriental Medical Herb

This medicine does good at circulating of blood,

increasing immune competence.

The contents of this Oriental Herb Medicine is as follows.

① 香附子 Cyperi Rhizoma.

② 白朮 Atractylodis Macrocephalae Rhizoma

③ 甘草 Glycyrrhizae Radix

④ 厚朴 Machili Cortex

⑤ 陳皮 Aurantii nobilis pericarpium

⑥ 半夏 Pinelliae Rhizoma.

⑦ 枳實 Poncíri fructus

⑧ 砂仁 Amomi Semen.

⑨ 川芎 Cnidii Rhizoma.

⑩ 蒼朮 Atractylodis Rhizoma.

2022 9 1

[illegible]

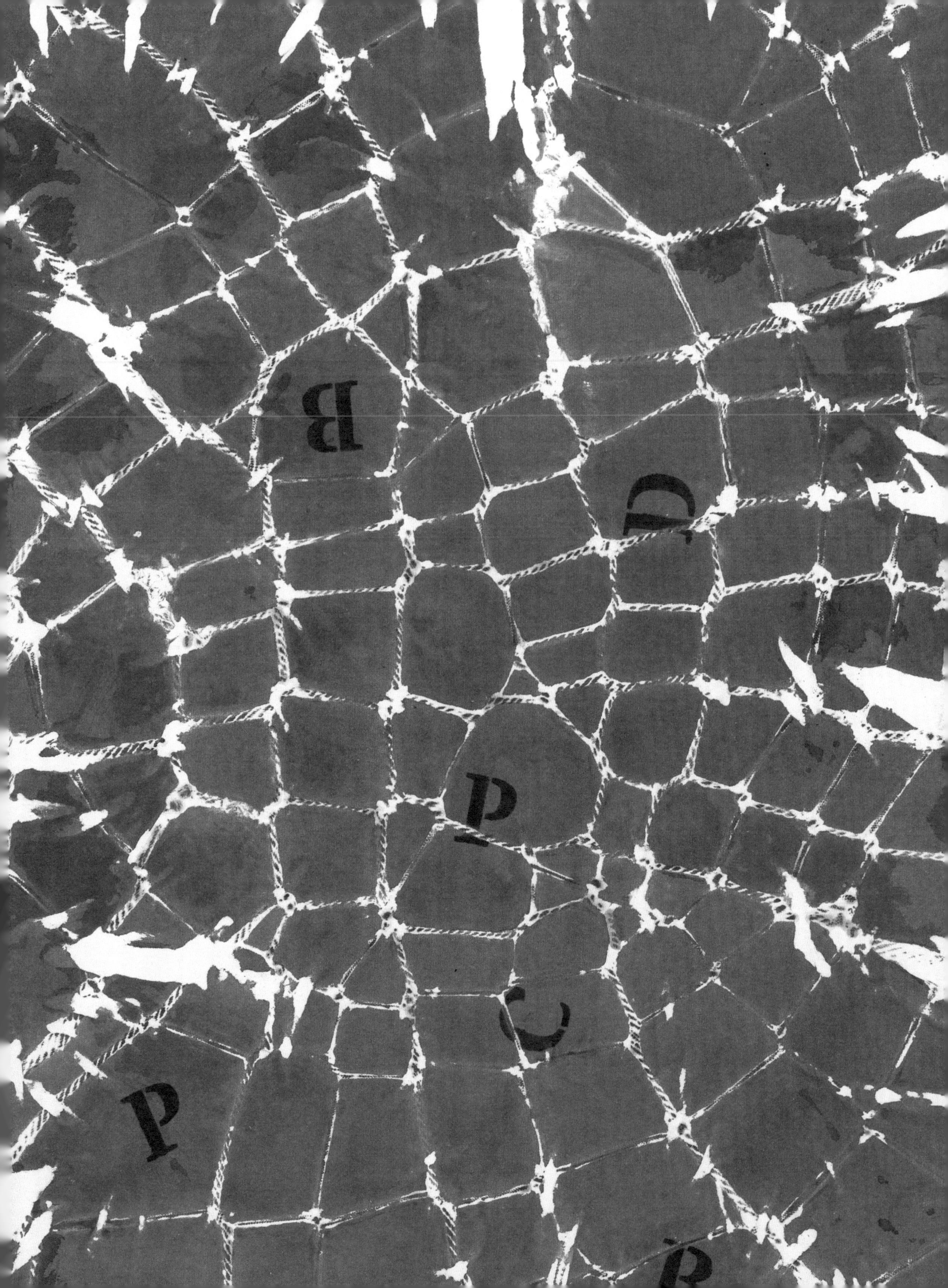

PAGE 77:

B.B.LETTER 1-3, 2024
acrylic ink and oil on canvas
60½ × 68 × 2 inches (153.7 × 172.7 × 5.1 cm)
courtesy of the artist and Tina Kim Gallery
photo: Hyunjung Rhee

OPPOSITE:

SELF PORTRAIT IV, 2022
pigment print in artist's walnut frame
7 × 5 inches (18 × 12.5 cm); framed: 20½ × 20½ inches (52 × 52 cm)
courtesy of the artist and François Ghebaly, Los Angeles and New York
photo: Paul Salveson

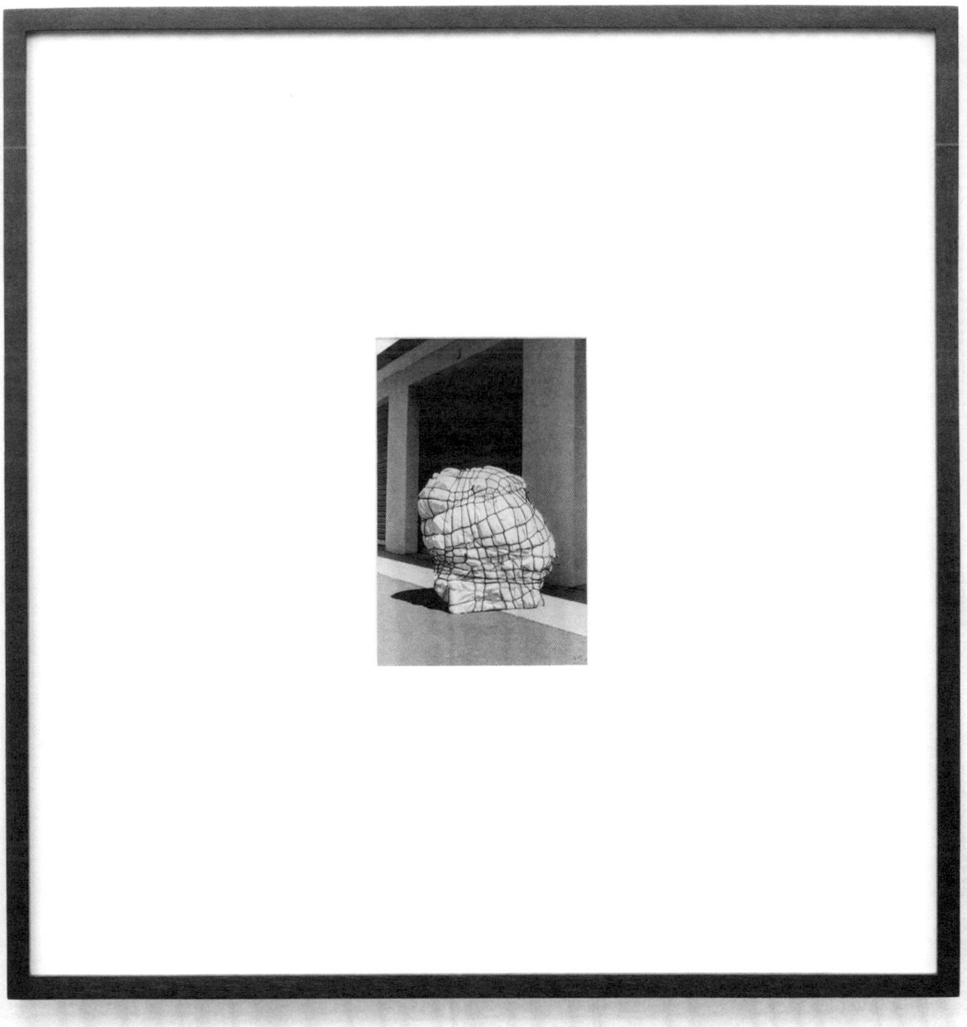

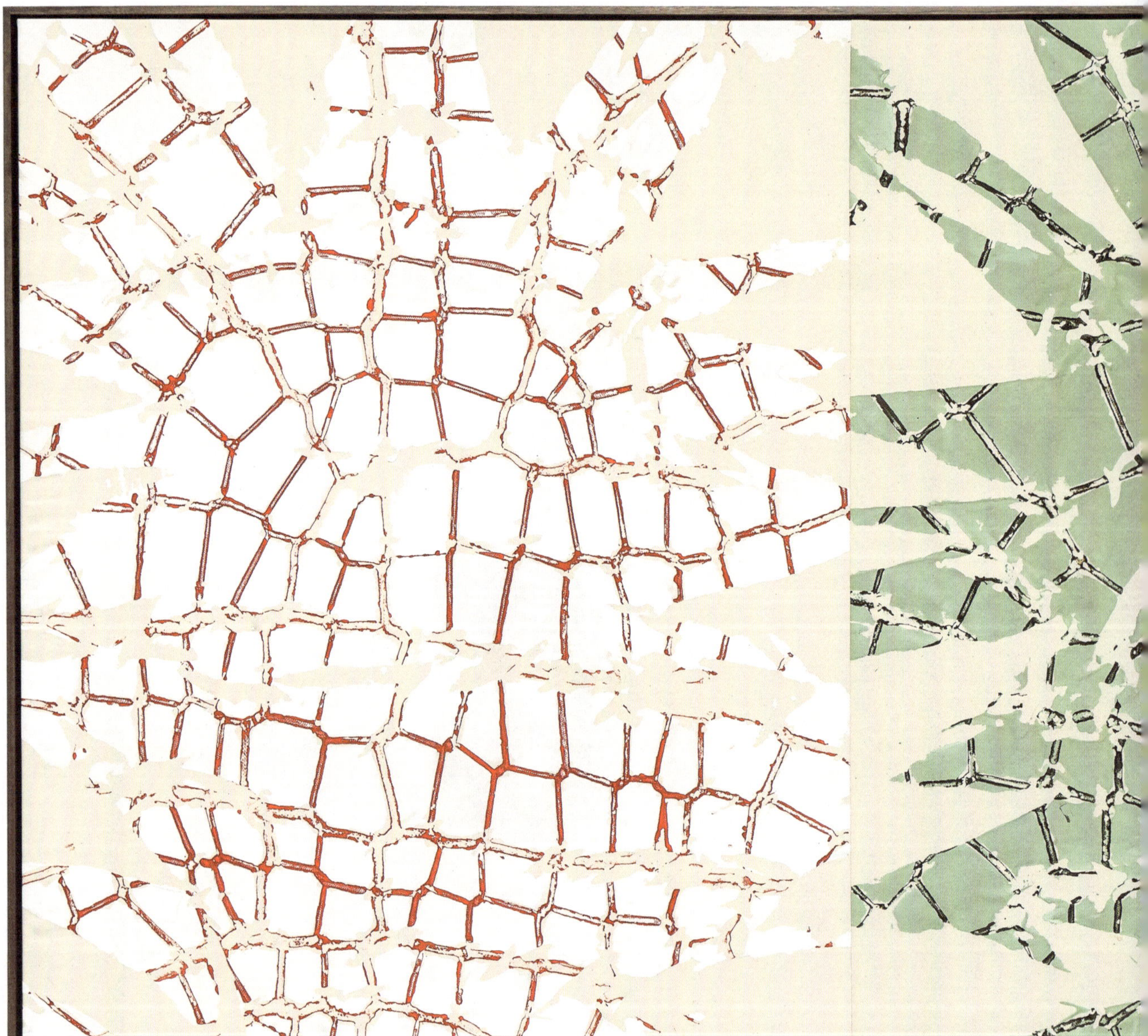

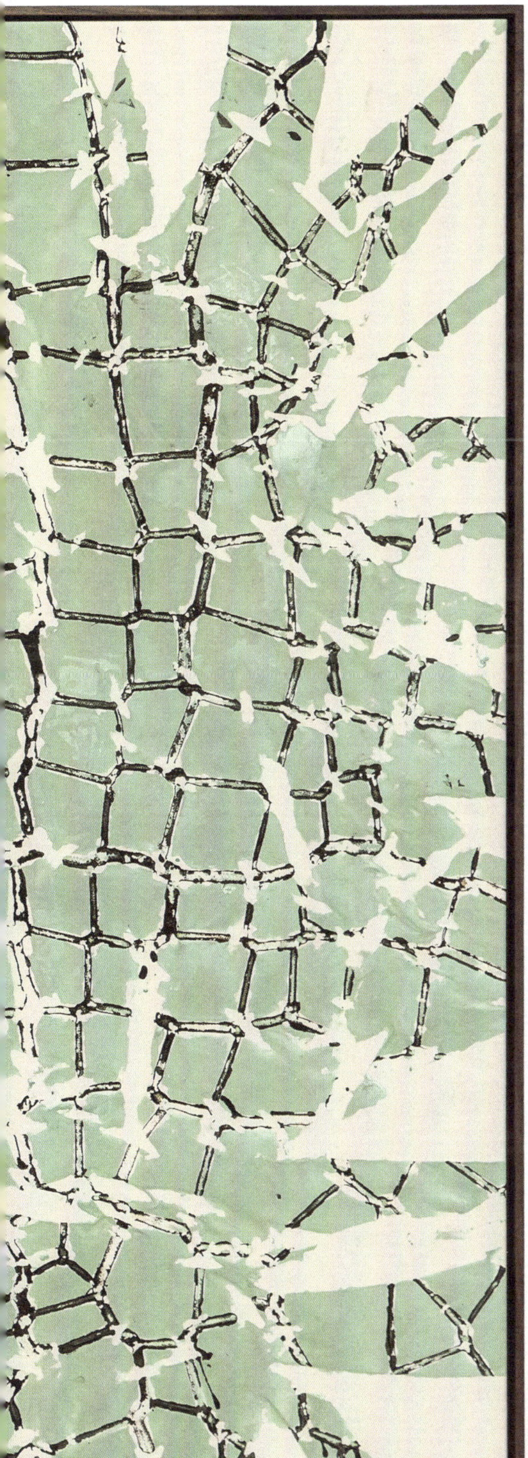

OPPOSITE:

B.B.NEARING 1-10, 2025
acrylic ink on canvas
56 × 69 inches (142 × 175 cm)
courtesy of the artist and Mai 36 Galerie, Zürich, CH

language of grief

the look of your partner as you give birth
waiting at a stop sign with no other vehicles in sight
all the books on your shelf you have not read
the rotting onion in your refrigerator
the toenail that is still purple from dancing 9 months ago

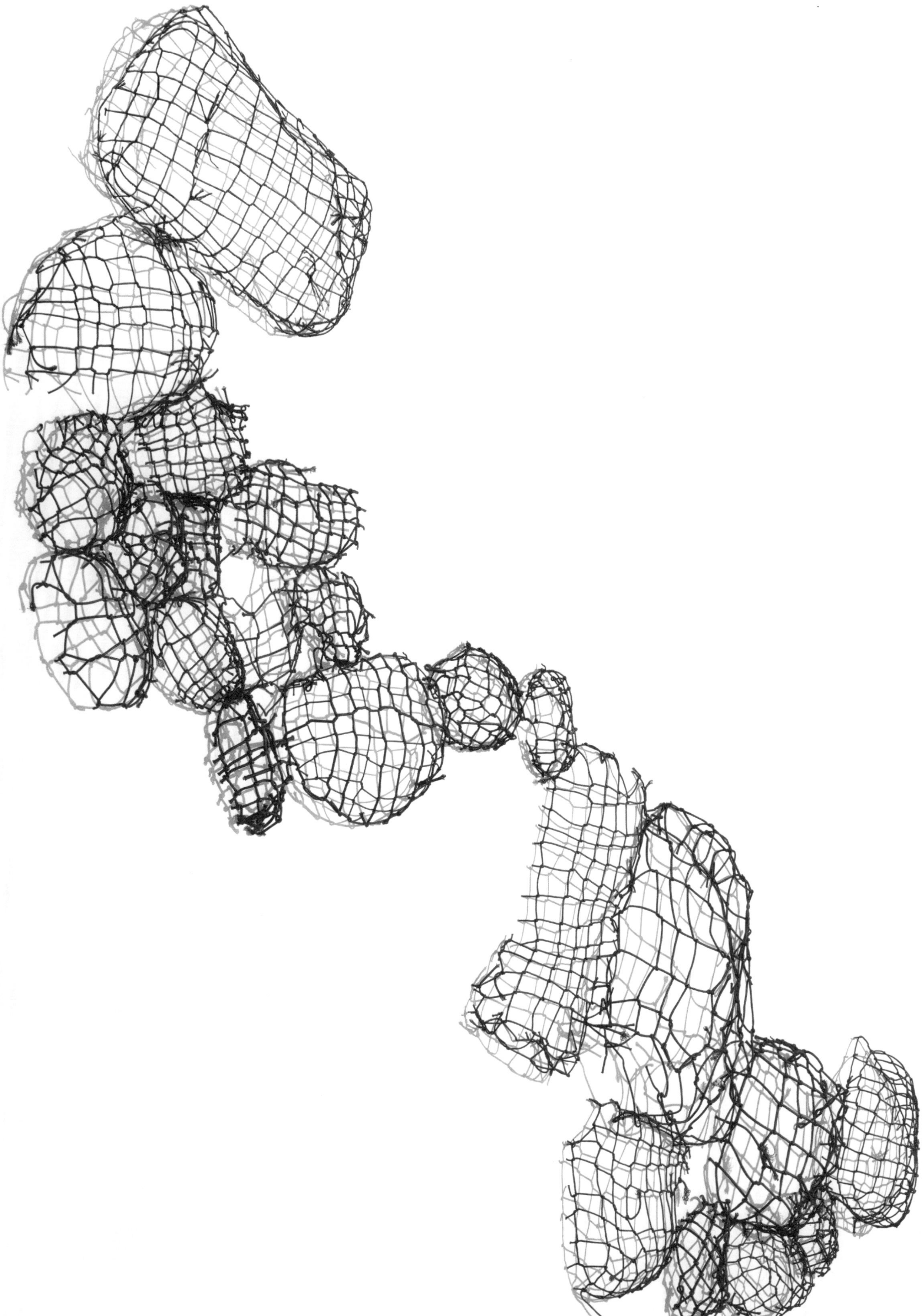

PAGE 83:

BONDAGE BAGGAGE ATLAS VI, 2022

rope and India ink

112 × 118 × 6 inches (284.5 × 300 × 15 cm)

courtesy of the artist and François Ghebaly, Los Angeles and New York

photo: Paul Salveson

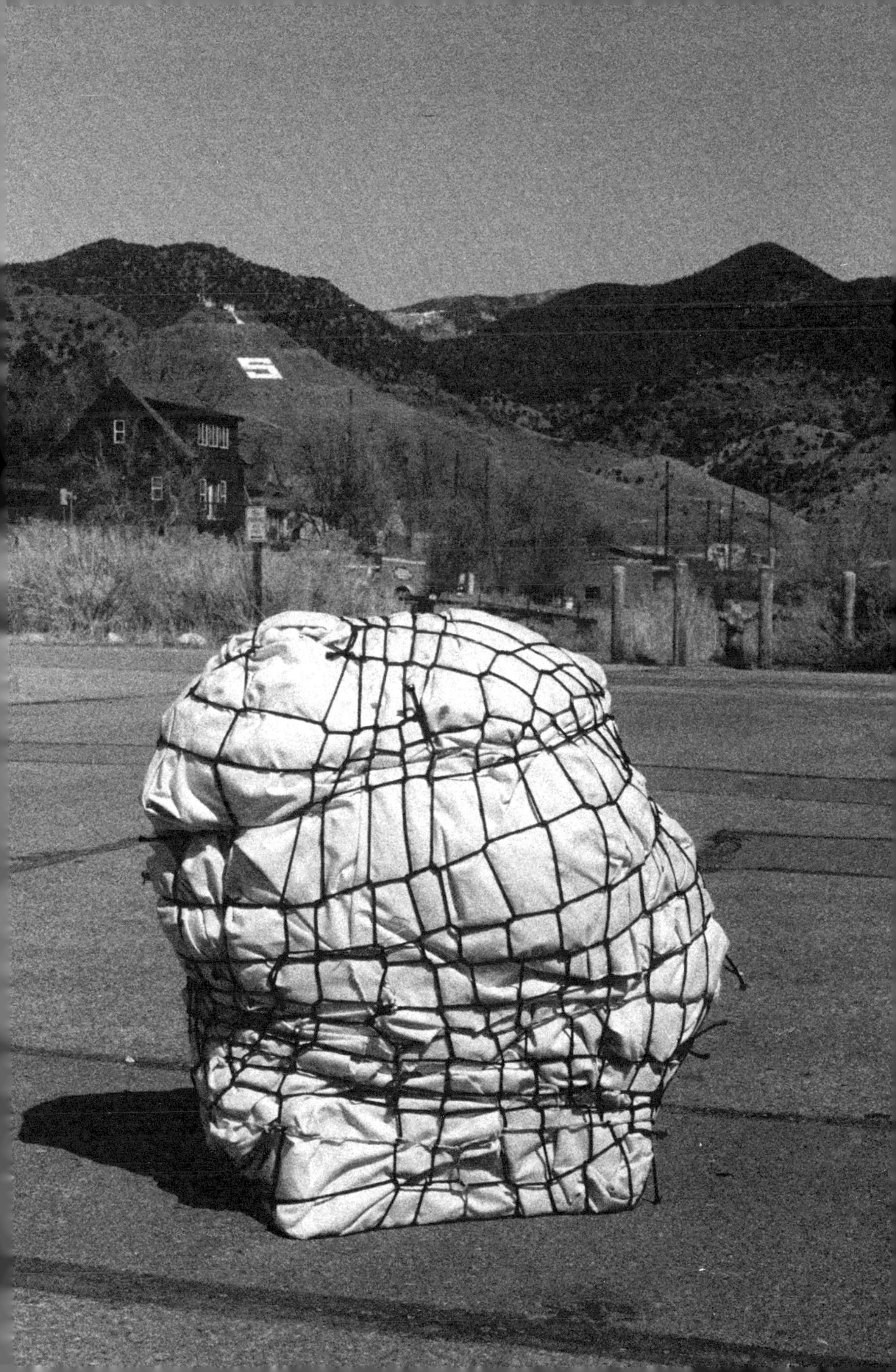

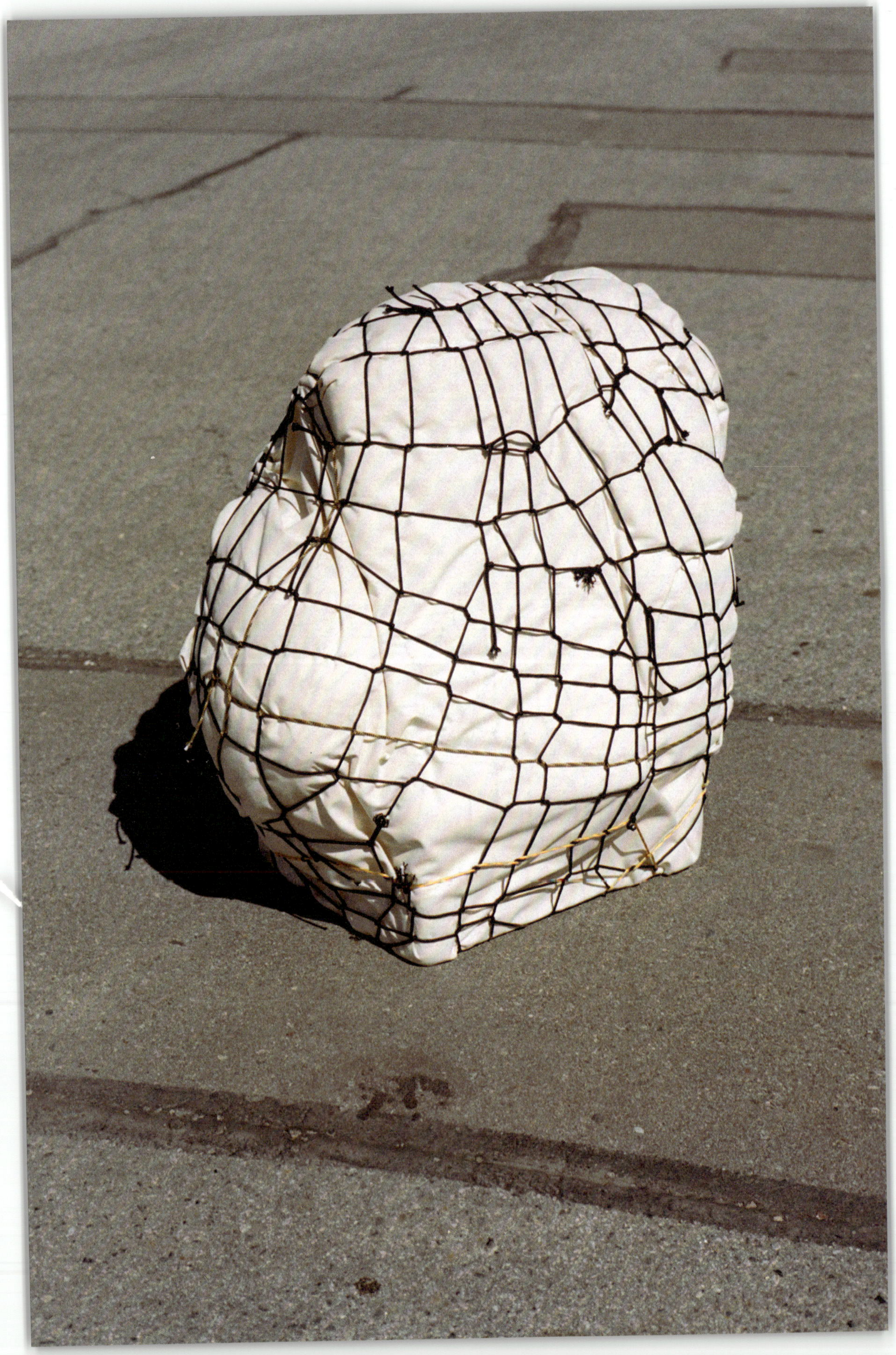

dear ellie,

it was so lovely to receive your letter and two books last night!
it was allso funny to re-read myt letter to you, it reminded me
but also resonated with me in a different way, it is true that
tiem heals, and in the past year we have all grown so much i feel
i've peacefully moved on despite the lingering feelings of resent
-ment that comes up once inca whiel, but now it is more like a whi
ff i get in the air, and i can keep going. the resentment i think
largely comes from feeling disappointed with myself, but that too
i know is past and there is not much i can do, nor much we couldn
have done differently at the time but at the end of the day my
heart is so full, i have safely walked away from a situation that
coudl have been far worse and could have escalated into a more
negative outcome, but now i feel i have more positive things i
can cherish. mainly that is my friendship with you and the group,
i have such love for you guys, and that will never go away.

today nima is back in school after the week long scare, he was
so excited to be back to see his friends, he didn't even look
back to wave at me. it's so interesting to watch him grow
especially out here where i feel we have the space and time to
really expreience one another and observe. i can see that he's
becoming a good kid, and maybe he always was, but he is gentle, co
-nsiderate and caring. even on days where he can realy get on
my neveres i can really not be mad at him. i'm so blessed ellie,
to be out here, to have my own space that i'd longed for, to have
the time to appreciate everyone in my life. it feels good to be
able to sit down and write a letter. it is precious to have these
moments to myself, but also share that space with freinds who are
so far, the distance doesn't bother me., i don't feel the distnace
at all really.

the studio is a big mess right now, all my materials are strewn
all over the floor, i've procrastinated in not only creating work
but cleaning as well. everything is getting picked up next week, a
and i think i'll be able to complete in time. making work during
these times feel silly, but i am glad, that we have htis outlet.
to keep ourselves a bit more sane. my show is titled language of
grief, an d if griefis the most universallanguage we are speaking,
we are all becoming fluent in it, effortlessly straight fromt he
heart. iv'e been thinking about how self expression is intricately
linked to our minds and feelings, but sometimes overlooks how we
physically expreince life, i think grief can be one of those thing
-s, there is so much our body goes through without knowing, withou
-t computing, and that abstractness of expreience, a lot can be
lonst-in that forever. grief is like the oxygen we breathe maybe,
as we are completely surrounded by it. i want to think thatn, then
grief might be something that completes our lives, rather than
taking away from it, i don't know. there is much to explore.
i hope your injury is healing well, i can'timagine the frustration
having to walk around in crutches, how we take walking for granted
i'm glad mcckever is taking good care of you, and i'm sending you
much love,
xo maia, salida, feb 10, 2021

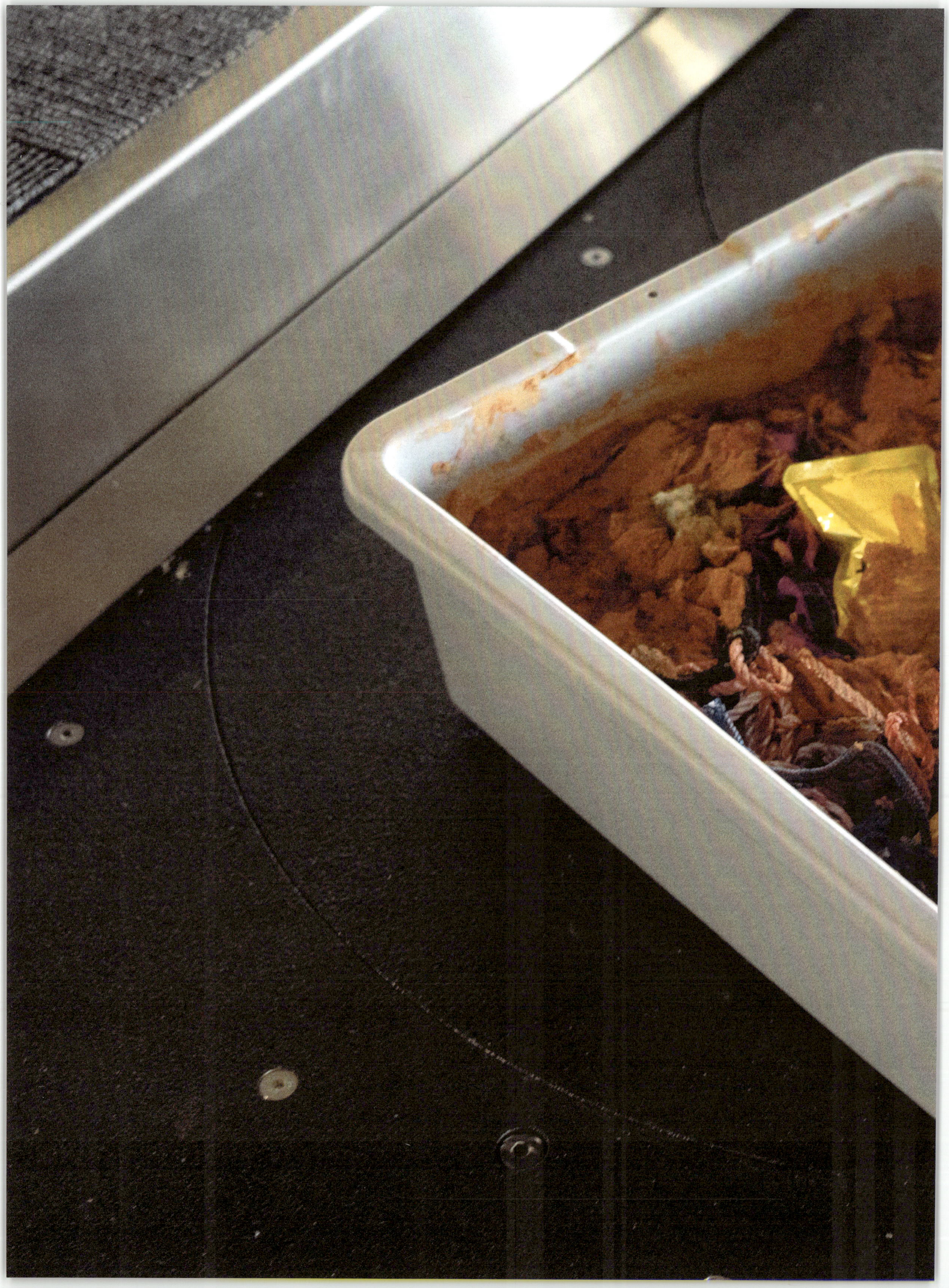

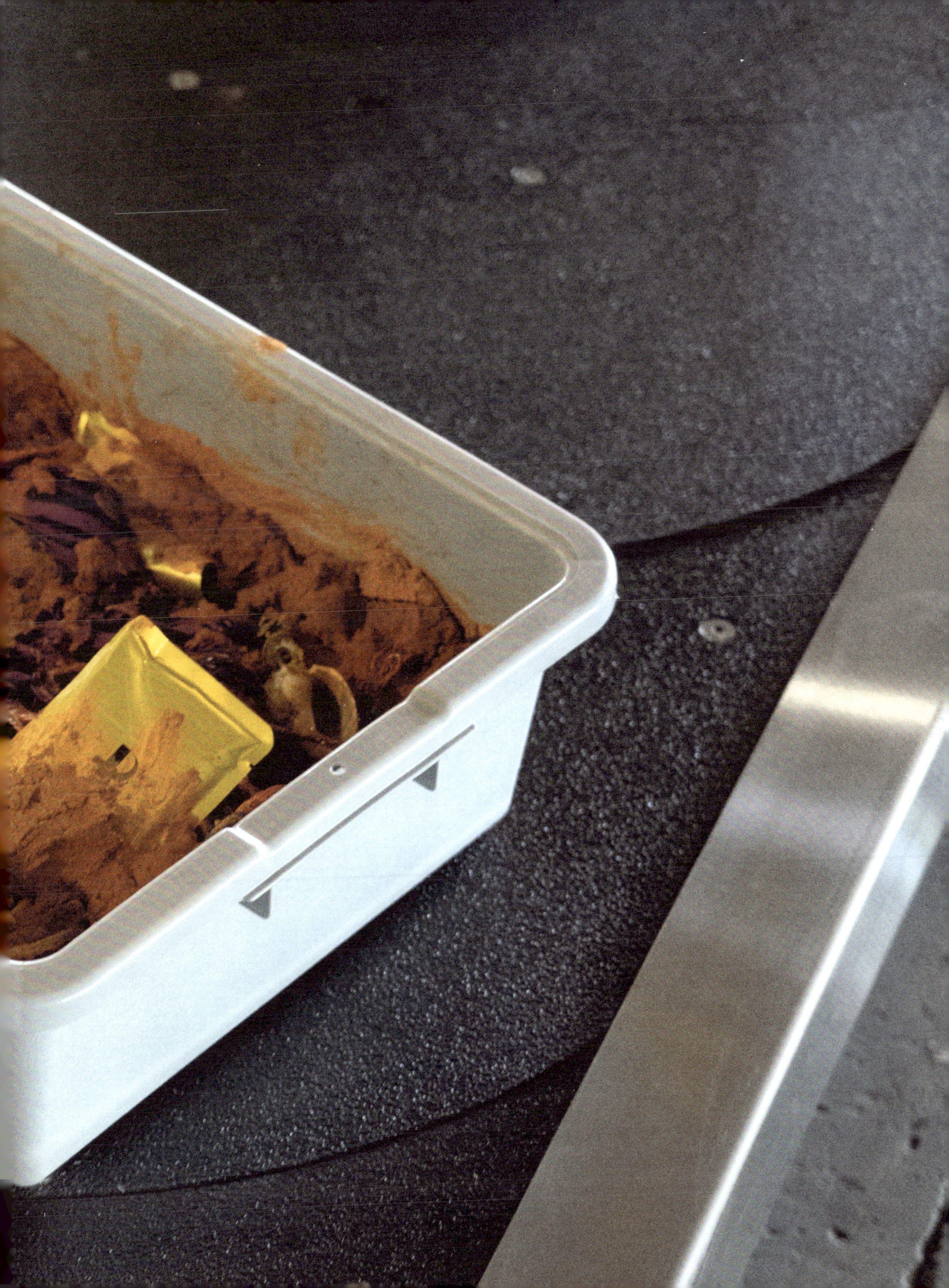

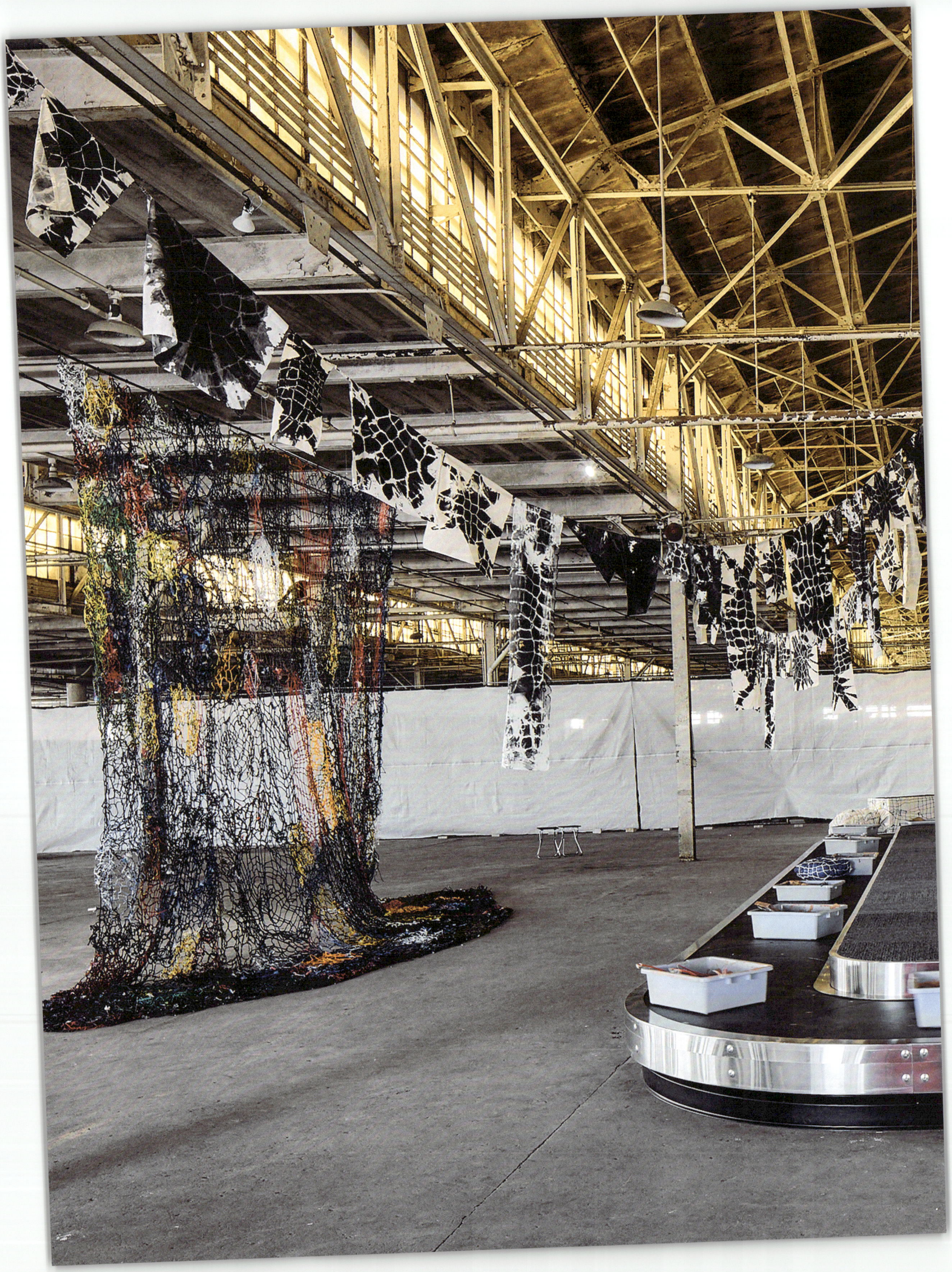

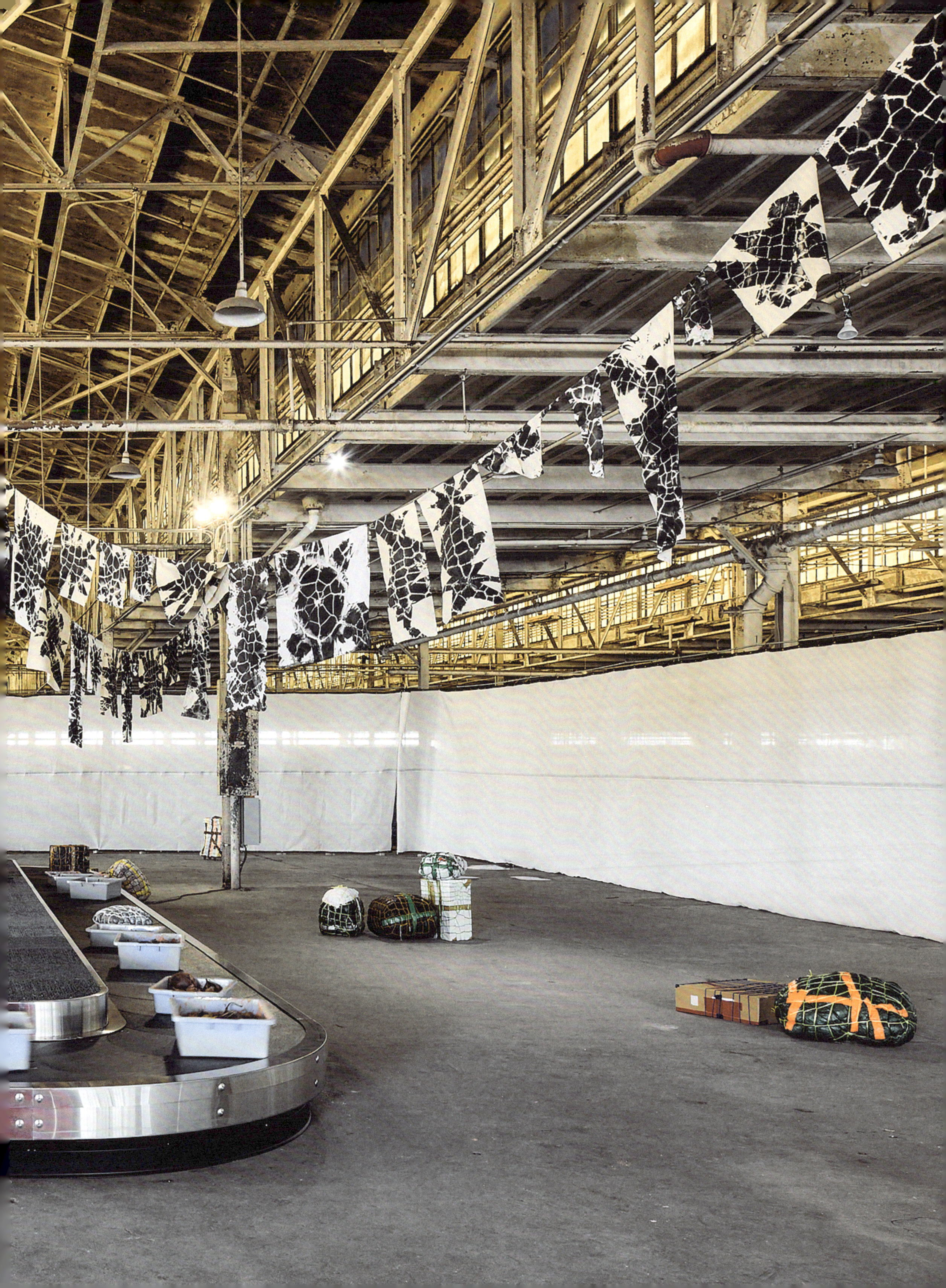

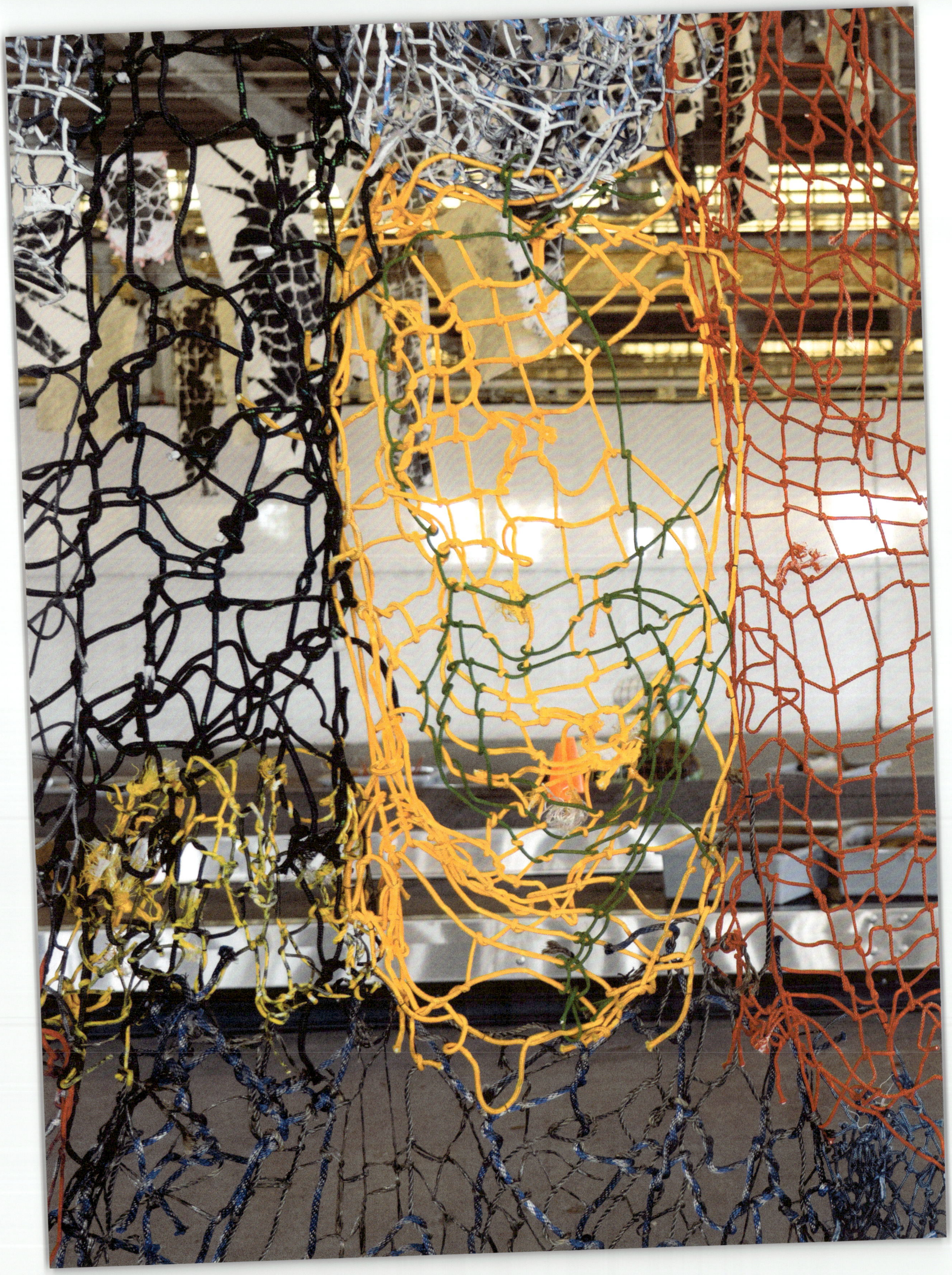

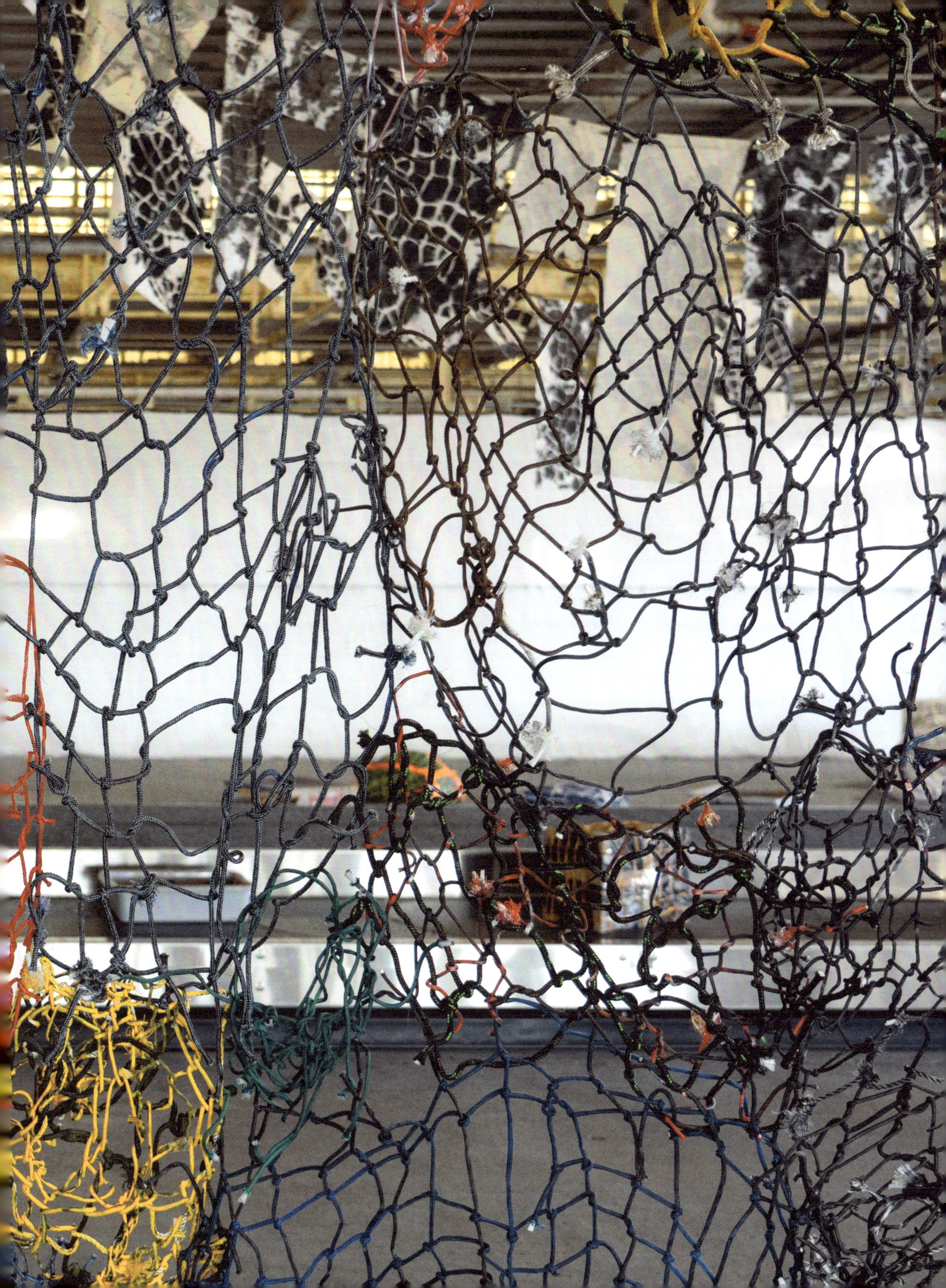

PAGE 89:

SELF PORTRAIT V, 2022

pigment print in artist's walnut frame

7 × 5 inches (18 × 12.5 cm); framed: 20½ × 20½ inches (52 × 52 cm)

PAGE 90:

SELF PORTRAIT II, 2022

pigment print in artist's walnut frame

7 × 5 inches (18 × 12.5 cm); framed: 20½ × 20½ inches (52 × 52 cm)

PAGES 92–97:

INSTALLATION VIEWS OF **THE CONVEYOR**, 2024

in Prospect 6 Triennial, 2024

curated by Miranda Lash and Ebony G. Patterson

supported by Art Production Fund, Ford Motor Plant, New Orleans, LA

courtesy of the artist and Prospect 6

photos: Hyunjung Rhee (PAGES 92–93, 96–97) and Alex Marks (PAGES 94–95)

ne change:
SN (cañon city) ✓ March 20.
assport
Insurance
Tax
Driver's license ✓ April 20.

✲ cancel subscriptions!

팔레스타인은
해방되리라.

once an hour
every hour
on the hour
everyday
every hour you're awake
even in a whisper
say it with me
free Palestine

sept 26, 2022

numbness keeps presenting itself to me in different ways,
anumbness is active, an active agent - that is capable of
infiltrating almost anything. when numb i'm not sure how
to actually make new work, how to investigate the unkown

my mother = numbness - = unkown
the emptying of oneself to fill up with something else / / possessed
my mother = empty vessel = possessed = numb

decluttering of dogmas ✲ Mother → keep her distracted.
- Understand better, people's blind spots.
- Trust what resonates most. / stay true to the art.
✲ Bodily knowing / prophetic skin

---

had a miscarriage on thursday during my lunch with cecily
not sure what i was thinking or expecti g but a glimmer of
hope was certainly on my mind and some exceitemty for the future
but now, i'm questioning everything. e again.

(2) Denver → (4) NYC
3:45 9:30
(1) Salida → (3) Denver
7:30 11?

what is intentionally positive
VS.
unintentionally damaging?

Death force VS life force
(death instinct) (life instinct)

separation / unification
individuality / survival systems
dynamic change / eternal return
↓ disruption / ↓ cyclicality/regeneration → unrecognized
→ valorized

let the disruption
awaken me, not
rattle me.
- Don't fear the "shock"
- The truth is coming into
a clean space

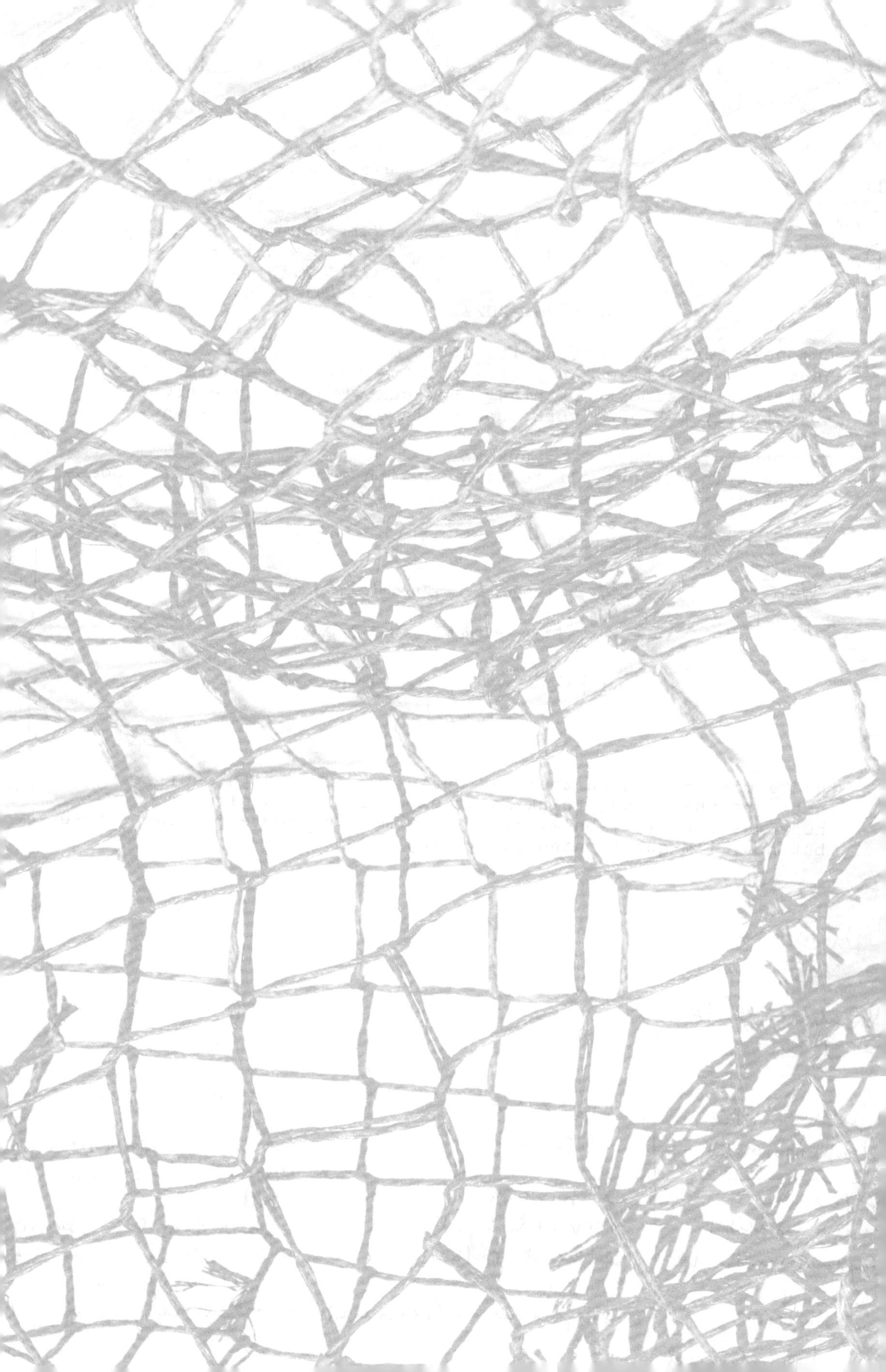

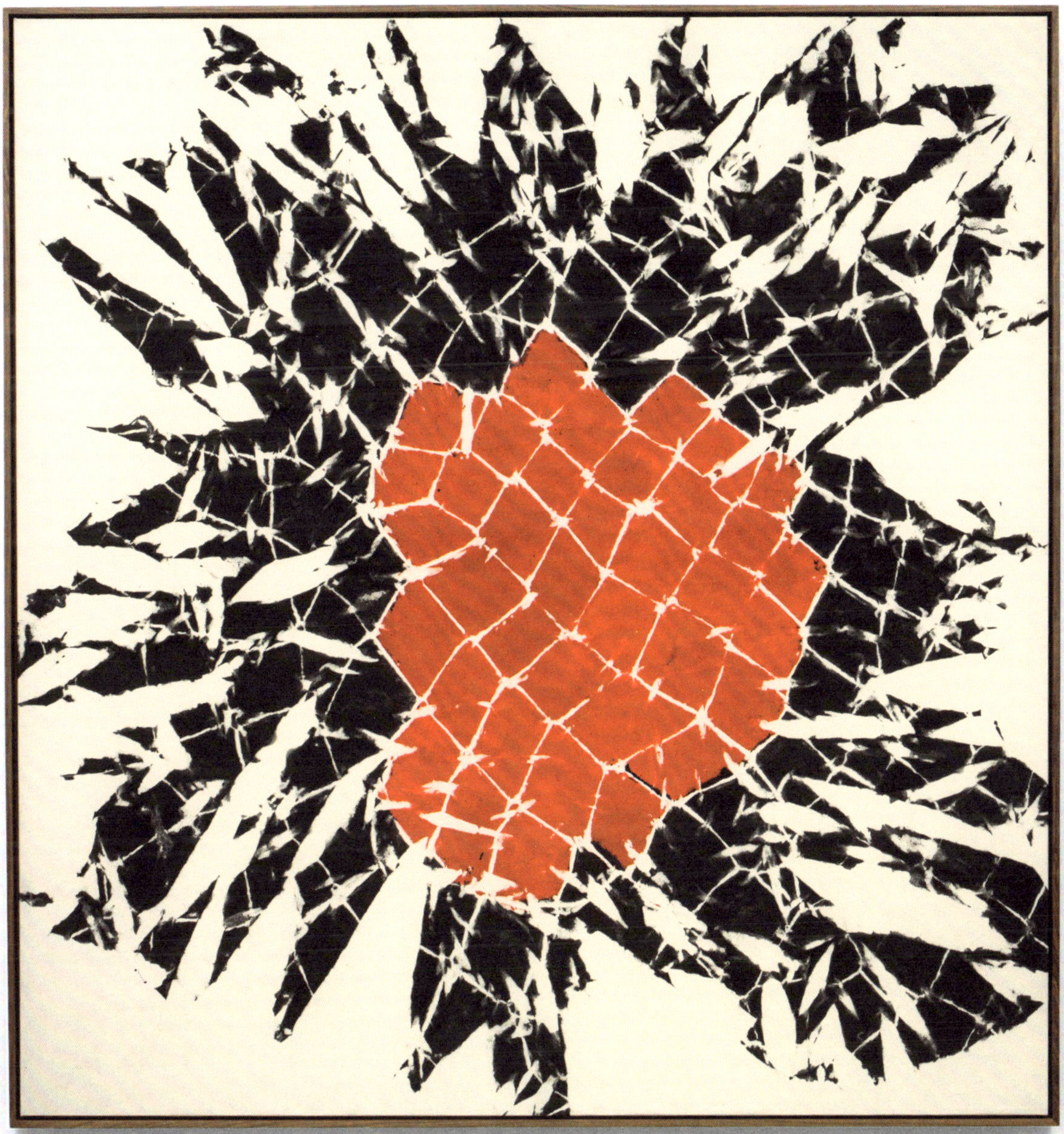

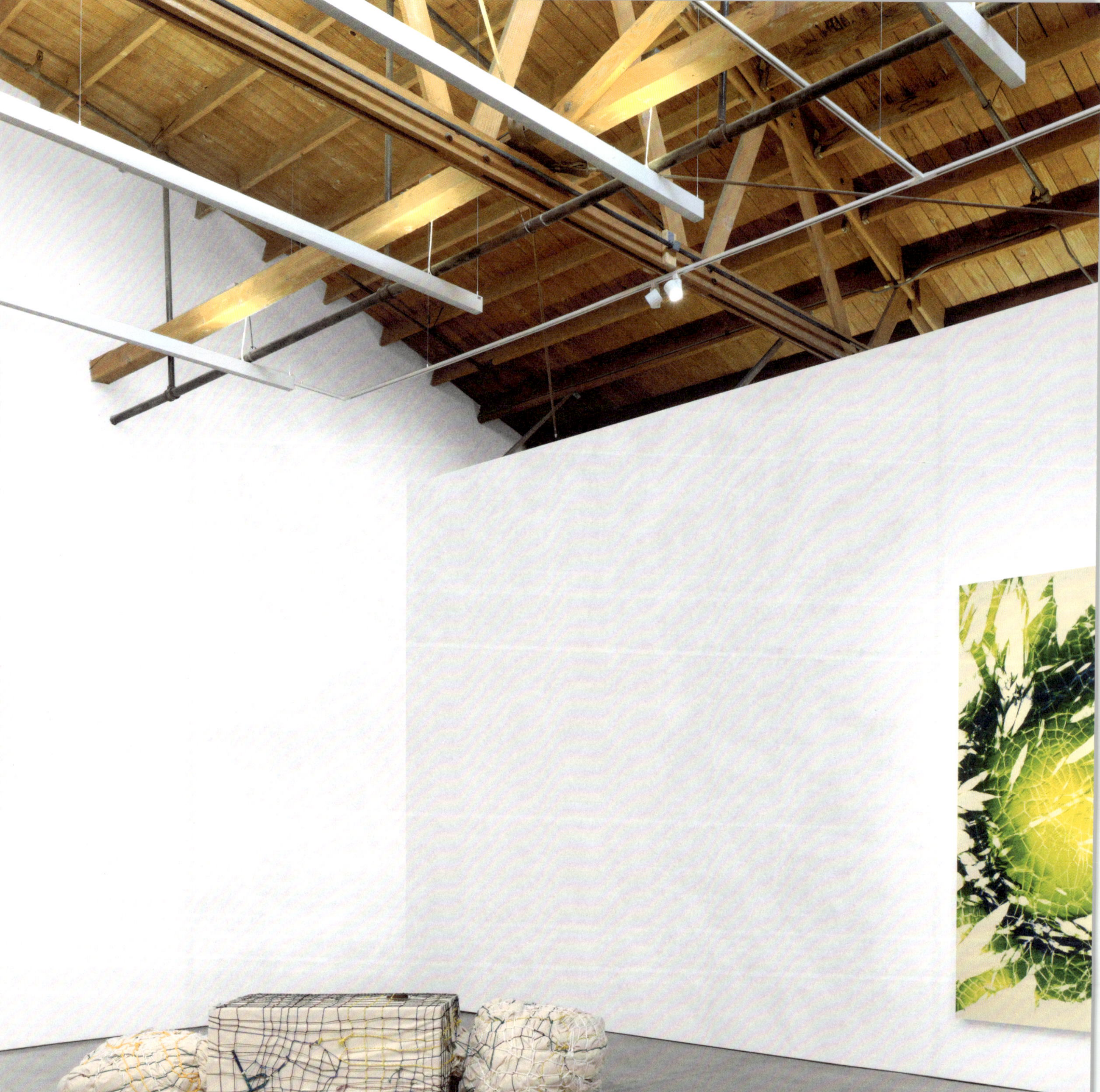

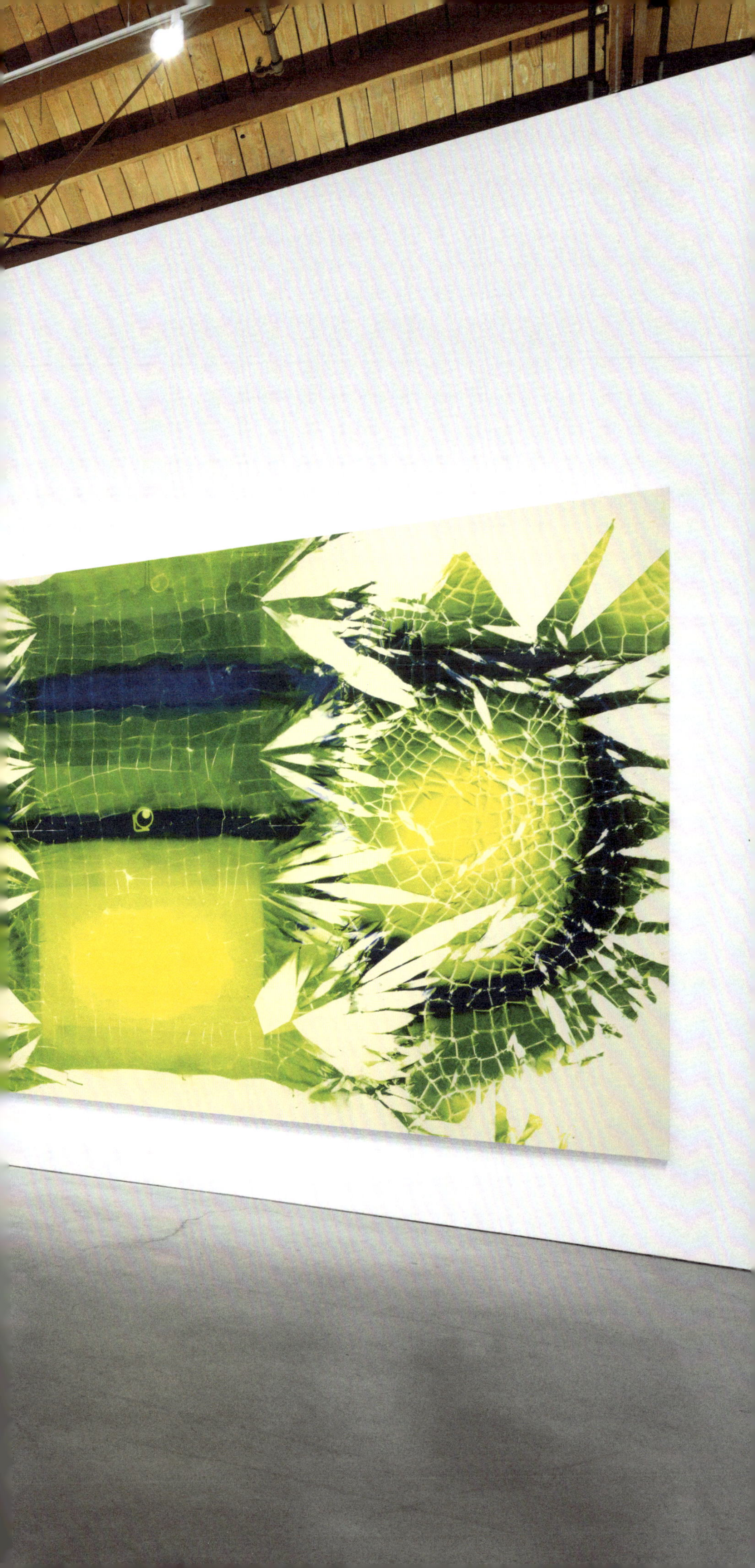

PAGE 101:

B.B.M. 2-4, 2023
India ink and acrylic ink on canvas
59 × 60½ inches (150 × 154 cm)
courtesy of the artist and François Ghebaly, Los Angeles and New York
photo: Paul Salveson

PAGES 102–103:

INSTALLATION VIEW OF **MAIA RUTH LEE: HOLD SHIMMER WIND**
François Ghebaly, Los Angeles, CA, 2024
courtesy of the artist and François Ghebaly, Los Angeles and New York
photo: Paul Salveson

OPPOSITE:

B.B.EARTH [DETAIL], 2024
acrylic ink on canvas
109¼ × 184¼ inches (277.5 × 468 cm)
courtesy of the artist and François Ghebaly, Los Angeles and New York
photo: Paul Salveson

PAGES 106–107:

B.B.TIME_UNTIL LIBERATION 1, 2024
cardboard, canvas, foam, rope, steel
26 × 107 × 28¼ inches (66 × 272 × 72 cm)
courtesy of the artist and François Ghebaly, Los Angeles and New York
photo: Paul Salveson

PAGE 108:

THE ENTRANCE, 2018
steel; 16½ × 14¼ inches (41.9 × 36.2 cm)

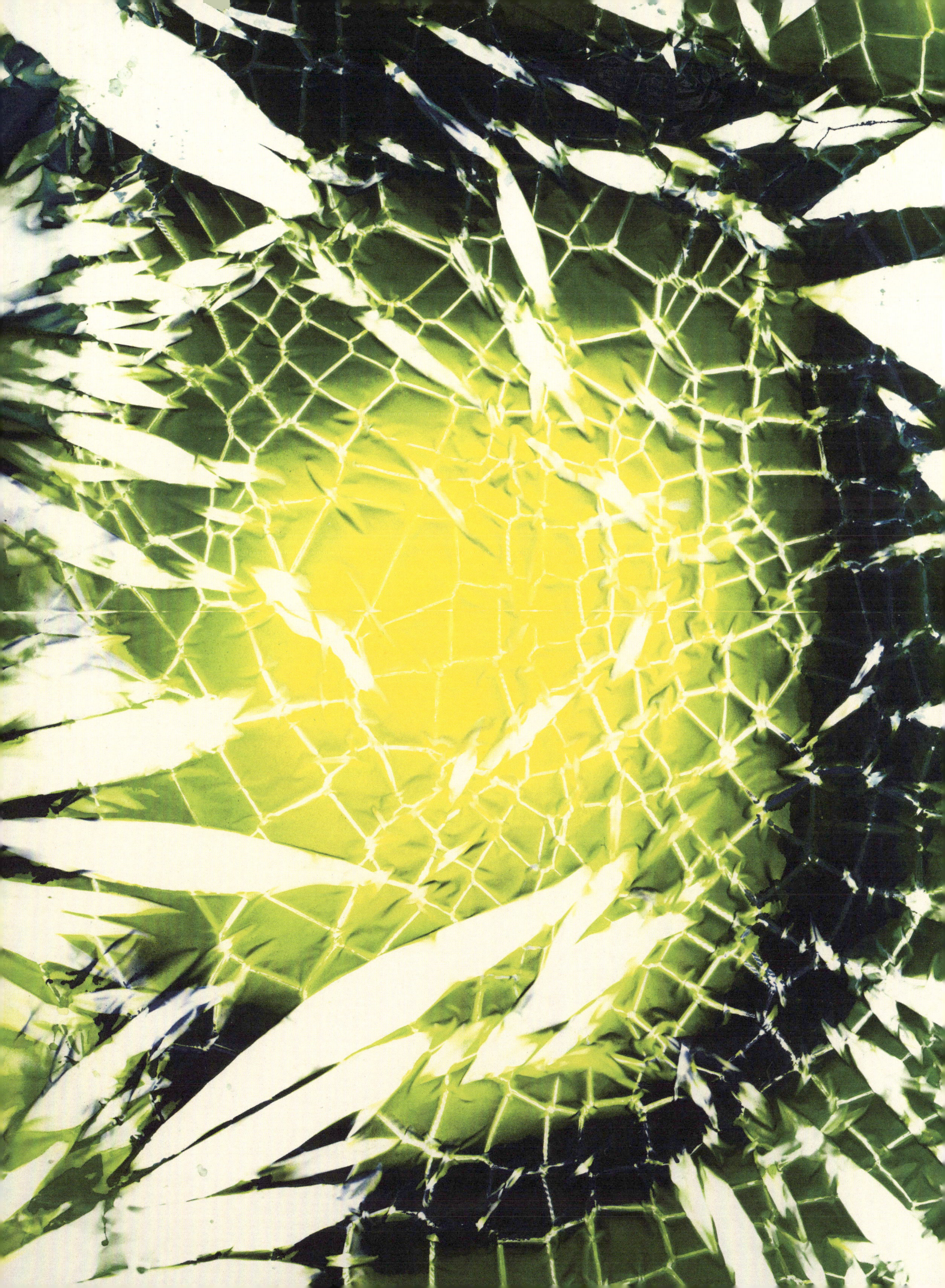

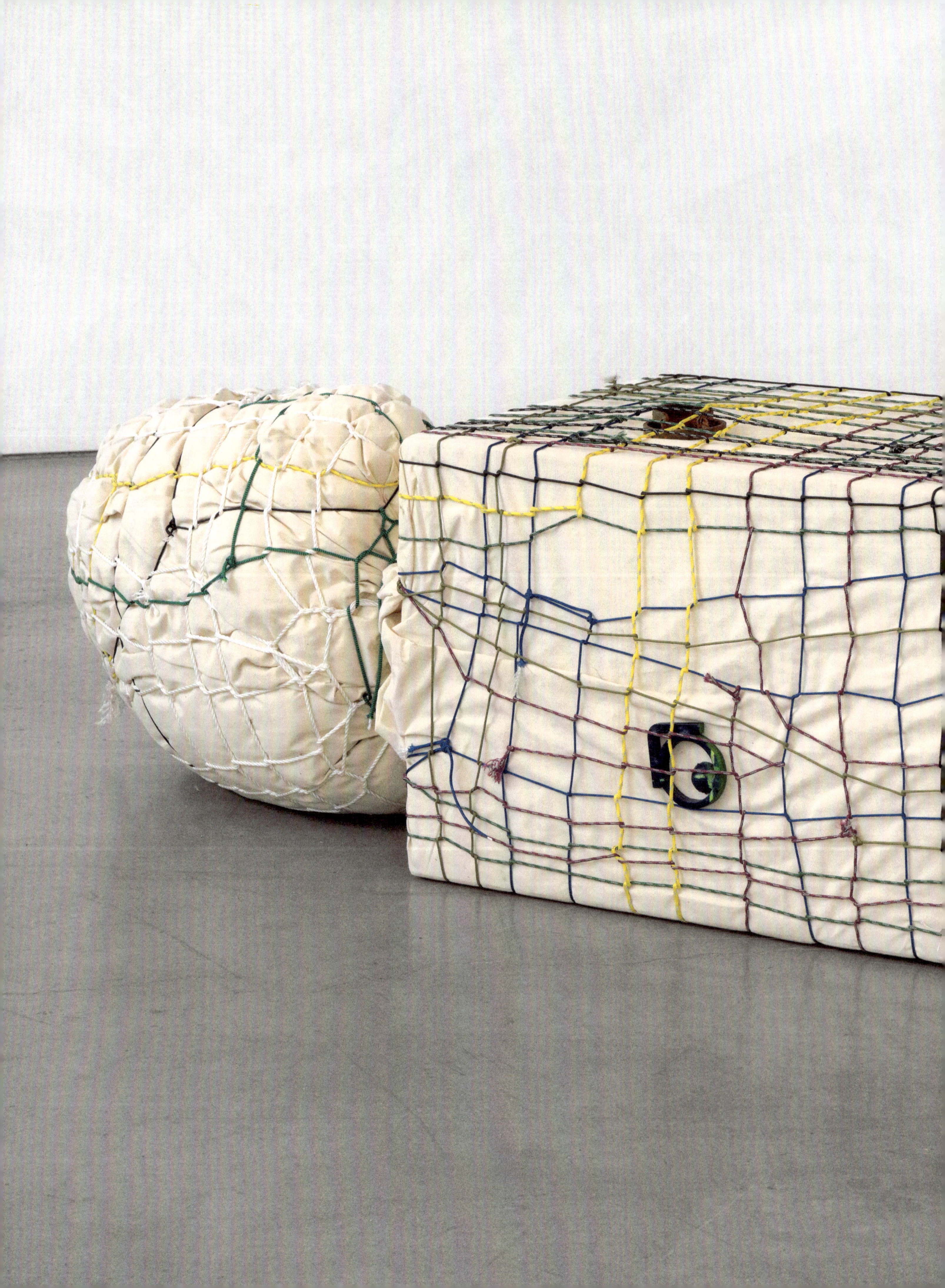

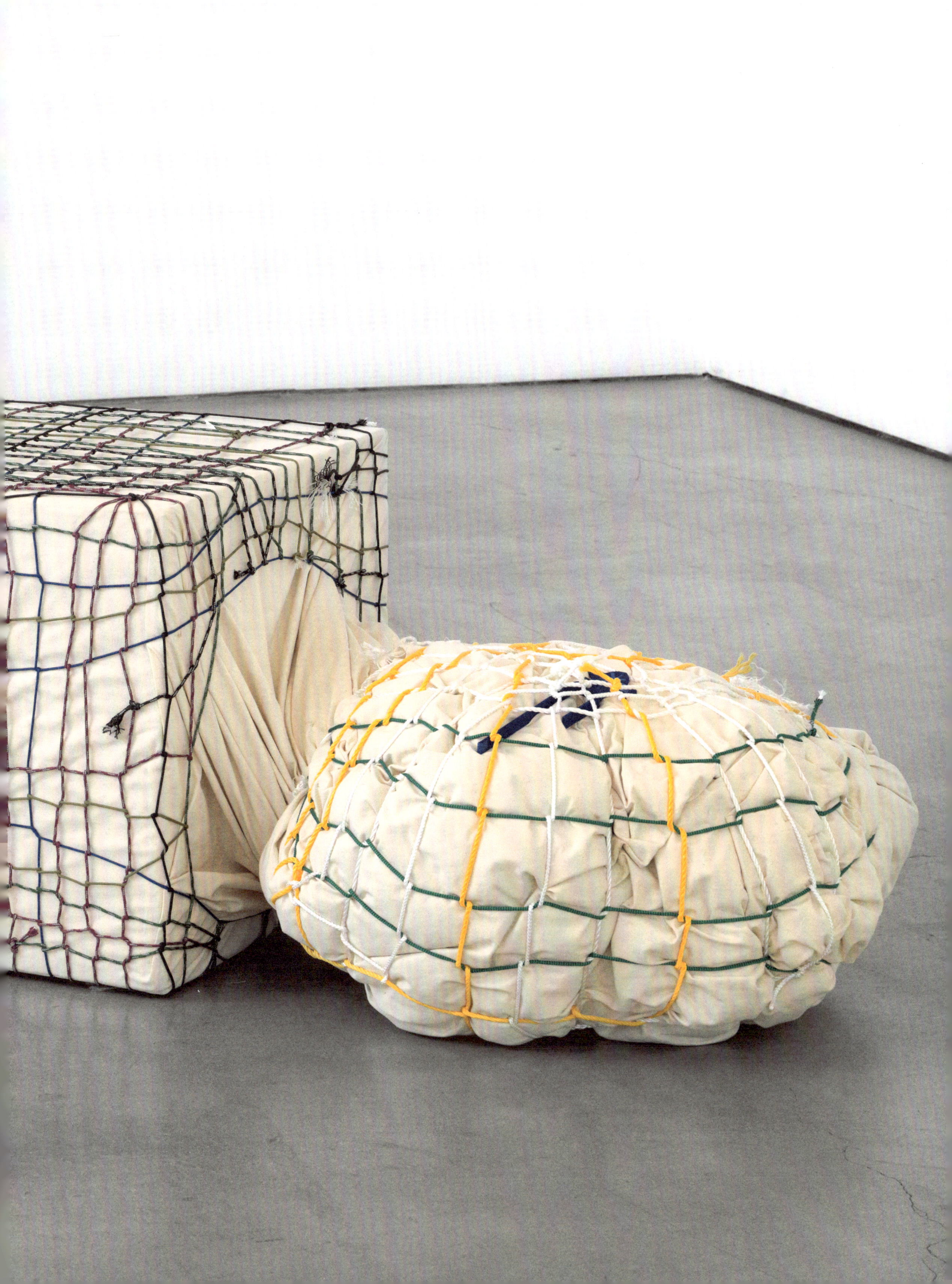

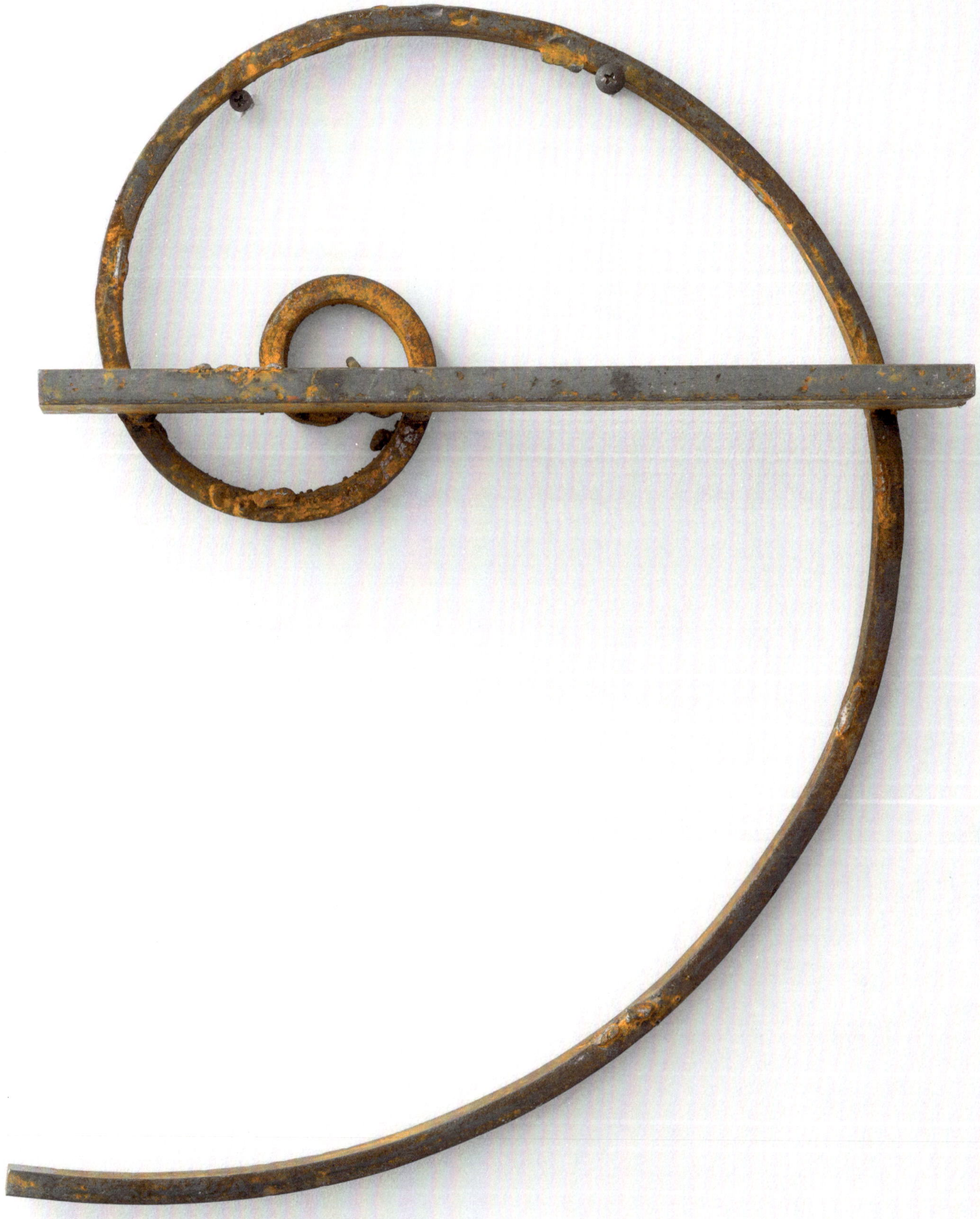

```
                            XXXXXXXXXXXX
XXXXXXXXXXX             XXXXXXXXXXXXXX        XXXXXXXXXXXXXXX
    XXXXXXXXXXXXX       XXXXXXXXXXXXXXXXXX XXXX   XXXXXXXXXXXXXX
XXXXXXXX      XXXXXXXXXXXXXX            XXXXXXXXXXXXXX     XXXXX
XXXXXXXXXXXXXXXXX    XXXXXXXXXXXXXX  XXXXXXXXXXXX   XXXXXXXXXXX
XXXXXX    XXXXXXXINTHISXXXXXXXXXXXXXLANDSCAPEXXXXXXXXXXXXXXXXXXX
    XXXXXXXXXXXX  XXXXXXXXXICANBEXXXXXXXXXXXXXXXXXXXXINVISIBLEXXXXX
          XXXXXXXXXXXXXXXXX    XXXXXXXX     XXXXXXXXXXXXXX

  XXXXXXXXX XXXXXXXXXXXX          XXXXXXXXXXXXXX XXXXXXXXXXXXX  XX
    XXXXXXXXXXXXX   XXXXXXXXXX   XXXXXXXXXX    XXXXXXXXXX  XXXX
XXXX   XXXXXXX  XXXXXXXXX   XXXXXXXXXXXXX  XXXXXXXXXX   XXXXX
   XXXXXXXXXXXXXXXXX XXXXXXXXX    XXXXXXXXXXXXXX   XXXXXXXXXXXXXX

==============================c=========================a========n===
=======y============o====================u=====s===e====e=======m====
```

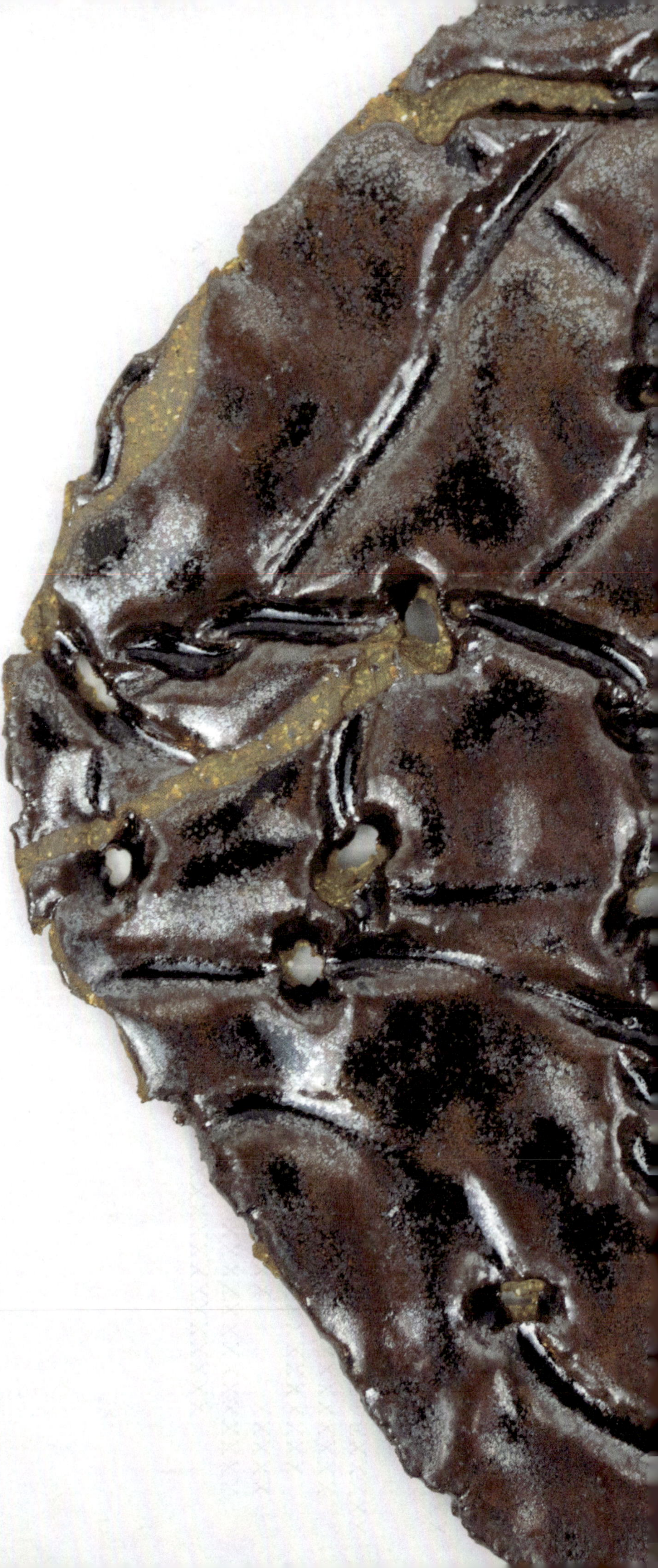

I BECAME an american today,

a certificate in a folder crunched under my
car seat, it's valuable they said

i held up my hand and pledged my allegience,
gave up my identity

and

bled all over my fancy dress

naturalization they say
of what i wonder

the fetus i was carrying didn't want any of it
escaped right out of my womb and onto the car seat

i gave up my korean name
it is a sad day

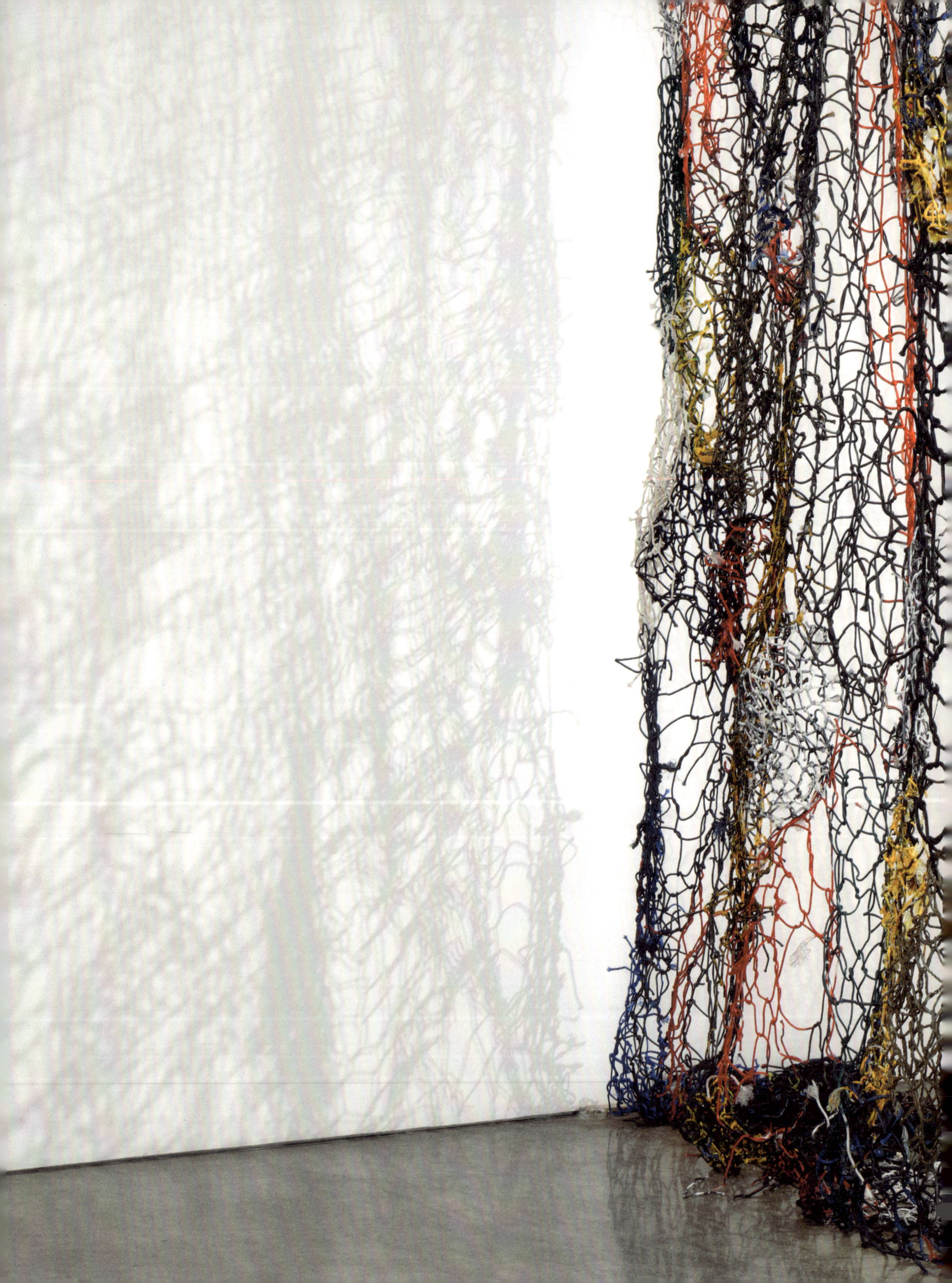

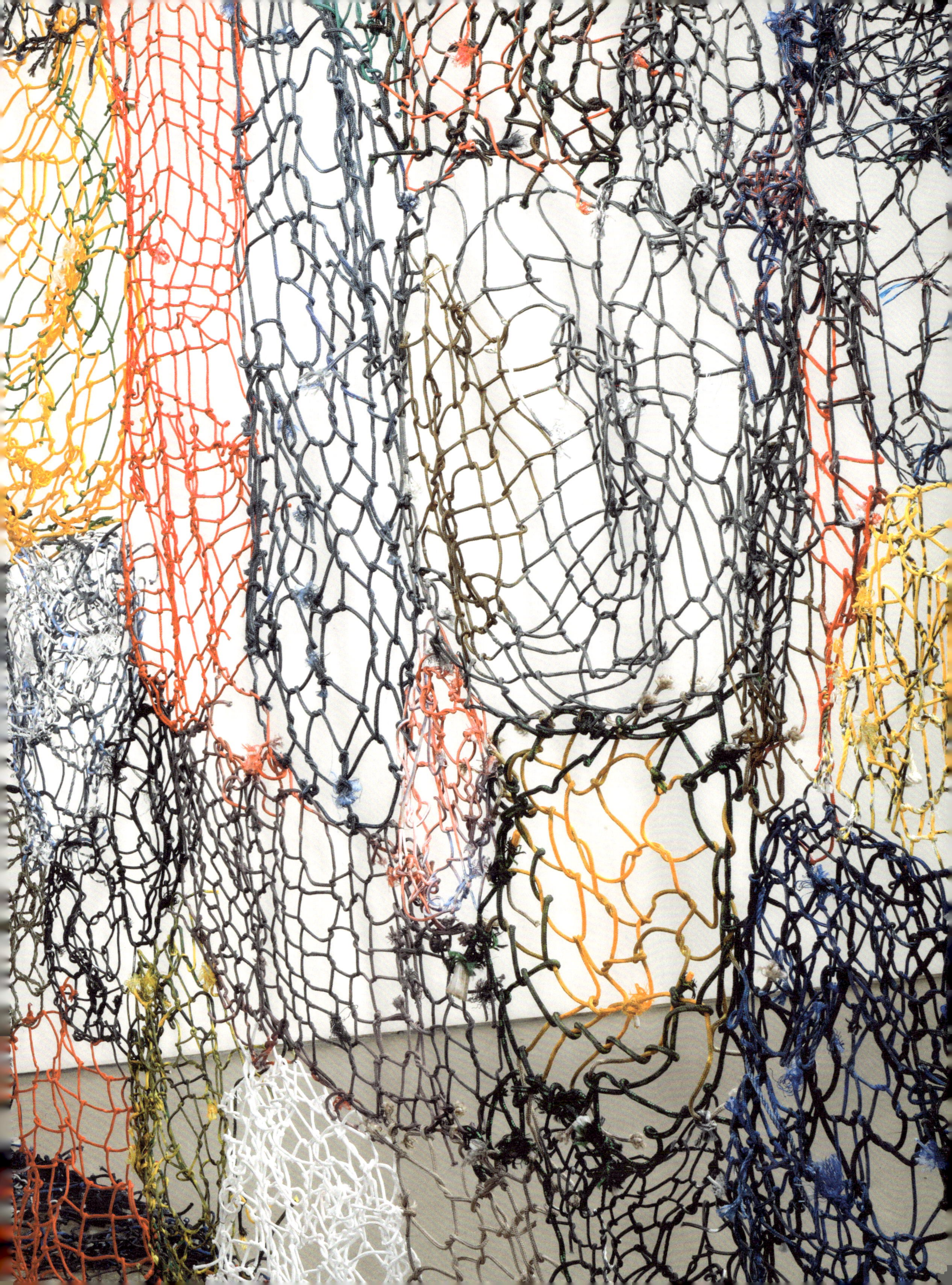

FEB. 2025

MRL,

The image pretty much went viral online, and it's forever seared into my mind. You were very pregnant, walking down a runway for Eckhaus Latta, wearing a dusty pink, ribbed dress with button details—except the dress was not completely buttoned up, leaving the belly part wide open. I first learned about you three months after I gave birth to Roux in 2017. I was so deep in my own world, struggling to breastfeed, figuring out how to be a mother, and learning to accept my postpartum body, that seeing such an image really yanked me out of it. I thought to myself, "This woman clearly knows what's up, and I need to meet her!"

Then, we showed together at the Whitney Biennial in 2019, and we've been great friends ever since.

I grew up in a rather extended, conservative Christian family, and my idea of *gyopo* was shaped by them. I was always too busy figuring out how to be Deaf and what that meant for me, so it wasn't until much later in my adult life that I realized I needed to reconnect with my Korean diaspora. This became especially true and urgent after moving to Berlin from the US.

As simple as it might seem, seeing your image made me rethink what it means to be a *gyopo*, a mother, and an artist—and you actually made all those things look cool.

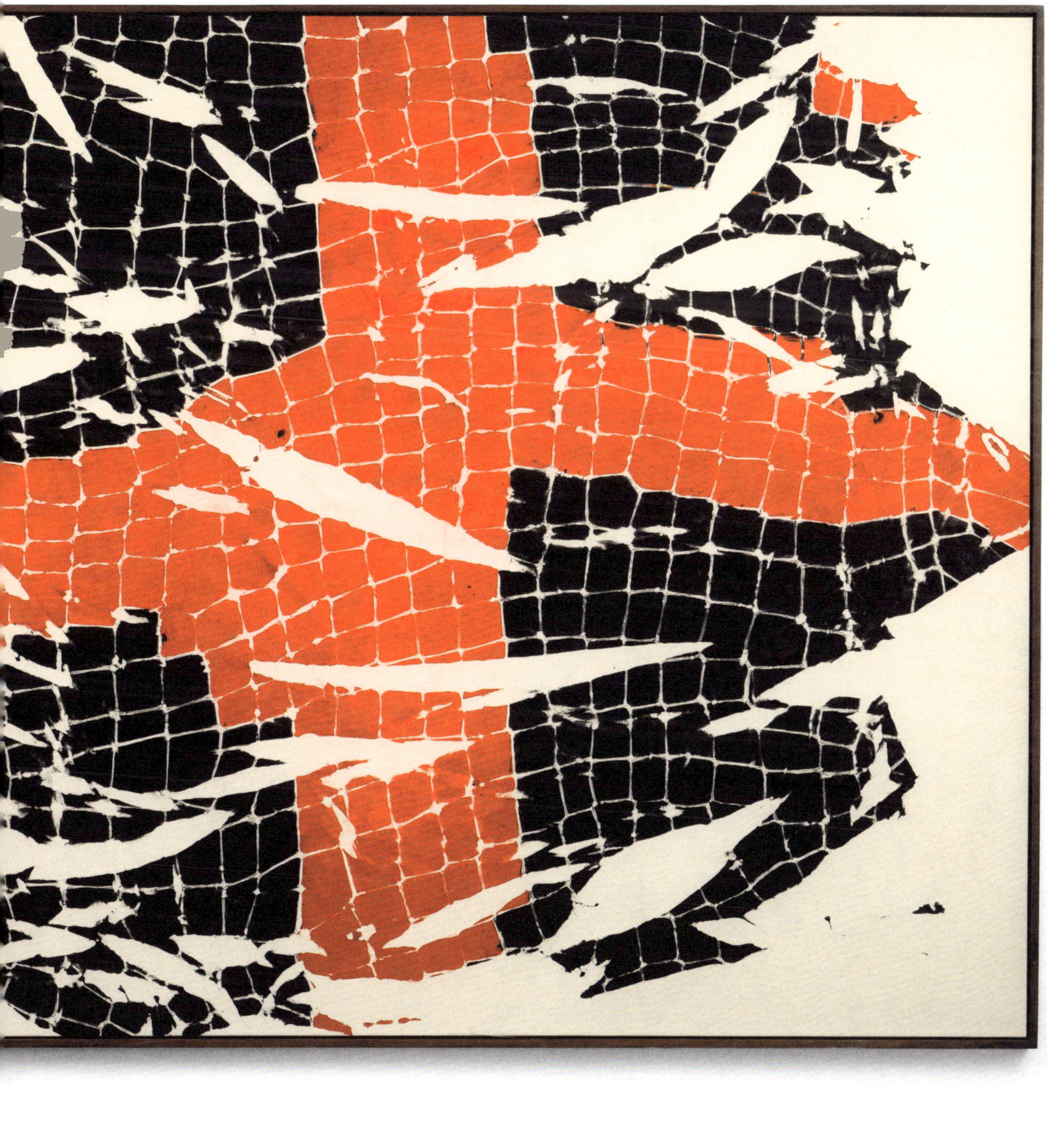

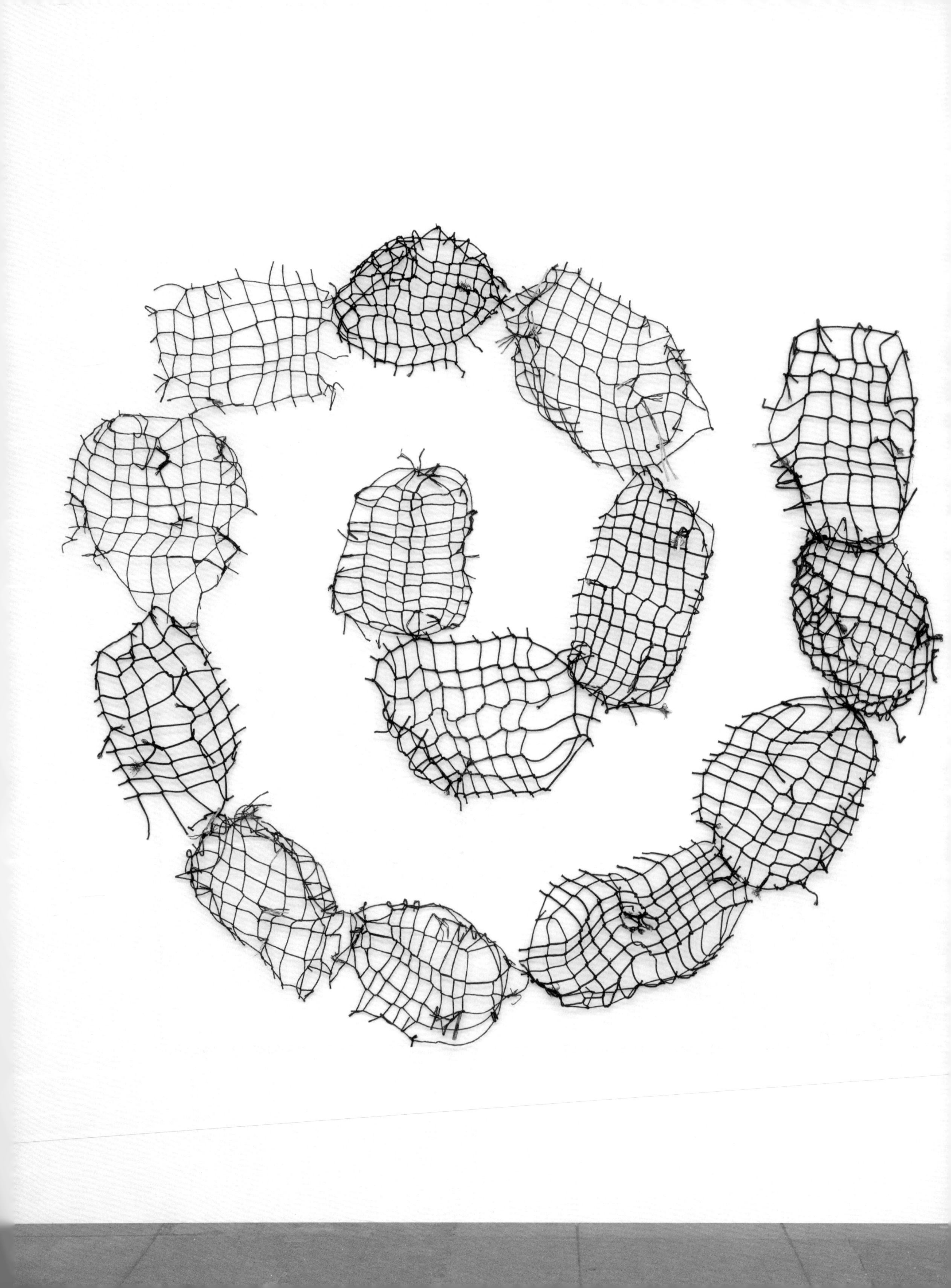

Watching you grow as an artist brings me so much delight. You are a living embodiment of what it means to truly communicate and to move ideas from one place to another, just like your diasporic family life. Your *Bondage Baggage* paintings are imprints of what's happening in the world right now: emigrating, migrating, and immigrating—constantly. Every single one of your art pieces holds such a weight of history. Mothers everywhere create new weight (literally!) and continue to carry and transport history through our children. The further you can go into the past, the more of the future you can see. The weight is full of old and new echoes.

Asking you to be Roux's godmother is one of the best decisions Tom and I have made as parents! I did not grow up with any godparents, and the fact that I am so far away from my parents, sister, and longtime friends—building my own family from afar—has constantly been on my mind. Watching the friendship between Roux and Nima grow is growing our friendship as well. I just showed Roux the runaway image and said, "That's Nima inside that belly!" and she responded, "So big!"

You're one of my favorite echoes. I love you so much.

— CSK

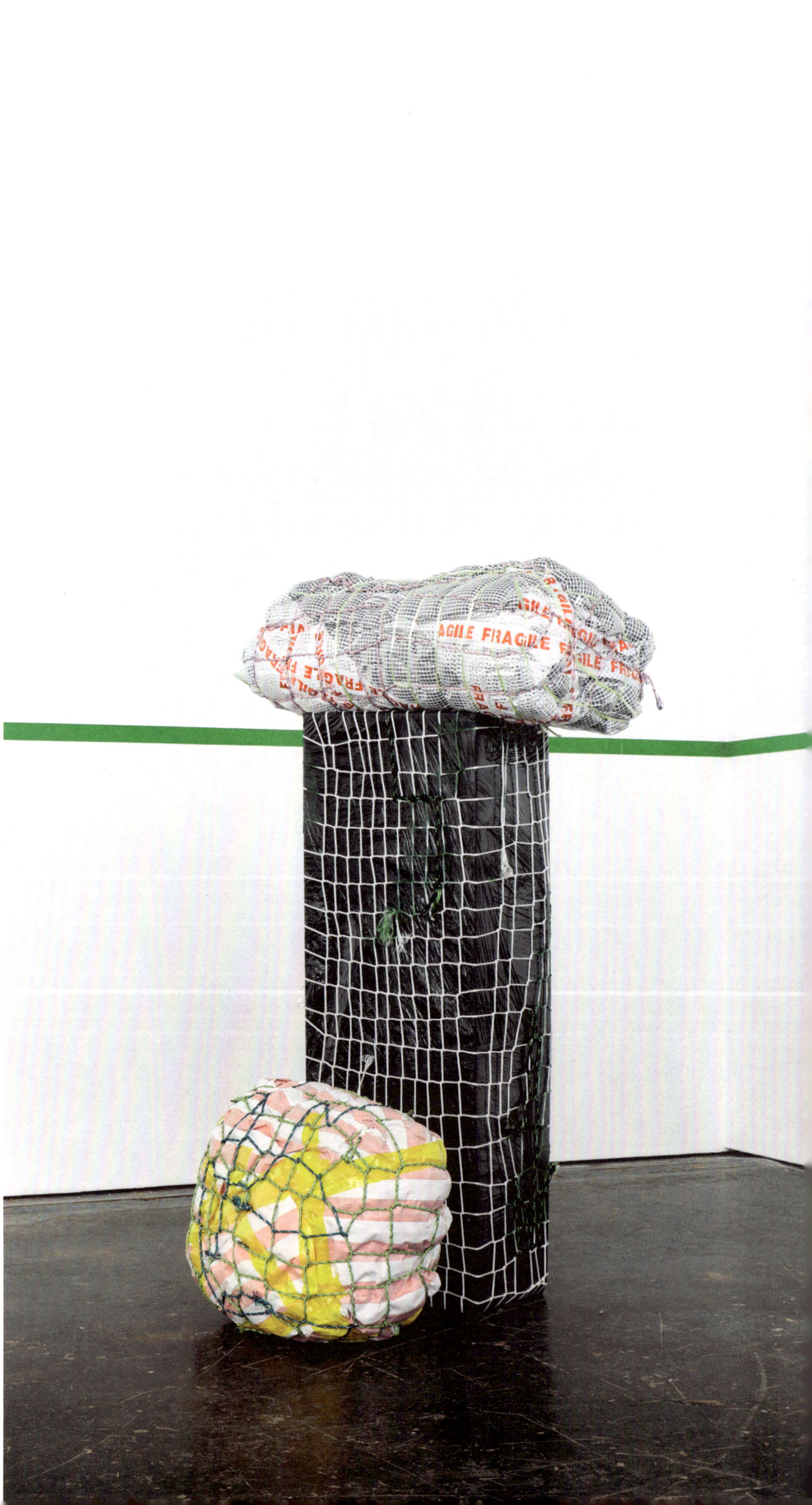
FRAGILE FRAGILE

Dearest Maia,

It's January 8th, the day I remember her more than the usual sum. Today, she dies, and I've woken up too late. In the bathroom, I fix my eyes so I can better see myself, though I never want to see it in a mirror. I look like him. Brows, nose, black hair narrowing from a double whorl; my scalp shines in the bathroom light. I make a face, and the horror animates. I make a face. And another. I make her face until I am enough her son. I write to you today as a son. I hope you read it as a mother to your own 니마. Read it as your own child-self, animating your face beyond the faces we inherit.

How is it we were both born—the same beginning—to leave our country—the same departure—to meet here? Can I write to you about my mother?

She was born in 1959, though, like most children of the post-war generation, the date is never entirely clear. I don't know how she was born. In a hospital, or at home, her mother biting down on a white fabric knot to push her into a life. Did it matter she didn't know her birthdate? Did it determine her fate to wander? To leave behind her infant children for six years, to build a life here, to die of a cancer her husband was too stupid to identify? When I was two, my mother went to see a 무당 who told her she must leave Korea in the next five days or be stuck forever. Did she want to go? Wouldn't she be happier with her children, her family, her own language? What does it mean to be migrant? I see her, in front of Buddha, holding its hand, rubbing small circles with her thumb against its gold hand. Isn't prayer permission to avoid disaster? Why did it lead her into another? In 1984, under Chun Doo-Hwan's dictatorship, she flew to Barcelona, to Alaska, to Mexico City, where a van would drive her to Los Angeles. The van left her at the border instead. She escaped border patrol hiding in the brush. She walked to a mechanic's garage, mimed a phone. A cab called for her to the airport where she would be deported. Except she wasn't. At twenty-six, she became illegal, mother of two but severed from it, wife, seller of counterfeit luxury goods in Fresno, California. Was she still herself? Or was she forced into becoming social history?

Isn't the work separate from the person? So, what is it about your artmaking that stirs my history, my mother's history, knots it into friendship? I am glad for it. When I see your art, I see you first, moving. Is it that the objects are too large, or I make you small in my imagining, your hands unfolding a room-sized tarp, ropes in eternal nylon turned eternal netting, the durable iron castings of your life's semiotics, the entirely too-large-not-large-enough canvases, the paints, the paints, colors into colors—blues, greens, yellows, oranges, black, reds—what is it you are covering? What is it you want to carry with you? What is it you want me to carry? All of us?

I see your work, and I see you carry it without worry of how much it bends you. I see you hook and tie a noose around your waist, a smaller noose looped on your sculpture. Your waist chokes, your entire physics at 30 degrees shuffling forward to tie on another package, another noose looped, another bondage to yourself. When I see you, I want to choke my own waist, yoke another sculpture, not to ease your burden but to walk next to you at the same angle, next to you.

Being in your life, I've come to understand we can't help each other carry our own weights—they will always and only be ours. We walk and work next to each other instead, filling the outlines between our weights, the outlines between our bodies, the shapes between our friendship with our languages, our silences, spoken from the faces we inherit. Speaking our histories, everything—our bodies, our weights—lightens.

To look into a mirror, to see only my own history, I hate myself. But I see your words, your history, your art, and it makes a shape between me and the world. Thank you, 친구야,

사랑한다

지민

PAGE 110:

B.B.TOGI V [DETAIL], 2022
glazed stoneware
8-inch (20.3-cm) diameter
courtesy of the artist and Picture Room

PAGES 112–113:

INSTALLATION VIEW OF **MAIA RUTH LEE: HOLD SHIMMER WIND**
François Ghebaly, Los Angeles, CA, 2024
courtesy of the artist and François Ghebaly, Los Angeles and New York
photo: Paul Salveson

PAGE 116:

INSTALLATION VIEW OF **HUMAN LIFE IN MOTION**
curated by Jade Foster, Primary, Nottingham, UK, 2025
courtesy of the artist and Primary, Nottingham, UK; photo: Reece Straw

PAGE 120:

DRAWING BY **NIMA LEE SUTHERLAND**, 2024

PAGE 121:

B.B.KUKKI 1-2, 2024
acrylic ink on canvas
60 × 44½ × 2 inches (152.4 × 113 × 5.1 cm)
courtesy of the artist and Tina Kim Gallery
photo: Hyunjung Rhee

ctobet 5, 2021
riting exercise, " write something about yourself"

have a constant fear of inadequacy, i always wonder who put me n charge? of my life? of my sons life? how can anyone take me eriously? i am an ocean, calm and tumutouous , affected by the 'eather perhaps, moddy at best
harp and round stones, as they grind down to sand towards the ater, i am a vsion when i'm calm, i try my best to savor those oments, i am a mother i am a monster.

octobetr 20, 2021

ancestral pulling
inter generational transmission
this year i found out my grandfather tried to emigrate us to dnever. my dogmatic grandmother wanted nothing to do with it and burned all the immigration papers in the kitchen fire. my grandfather, dreams crushed, kept on living out his life in korea, but i imagine with little passion, compared to what he felt in these mountians , trying to figure out his life best way forward, i also imagine with spite against myt ggradnmother who got her way, who kept her family together, kept her husband from wandering, i suspect she suspected that he had a wandering heart, my settlement, the settling of the heart, the settling of my wandering soul, found its place, by chance, or by pre navigatio -n, he led me here, if he has led me here, then is my behavior als -o in his steps?

does that mean we are intrinsically connected spiritually?
is he speaking to me.
am i being framed to

readch the next frame

we are descendants of people who survived,
it matters toknow where our forebearerss came from
body insticts brought us to where we are,

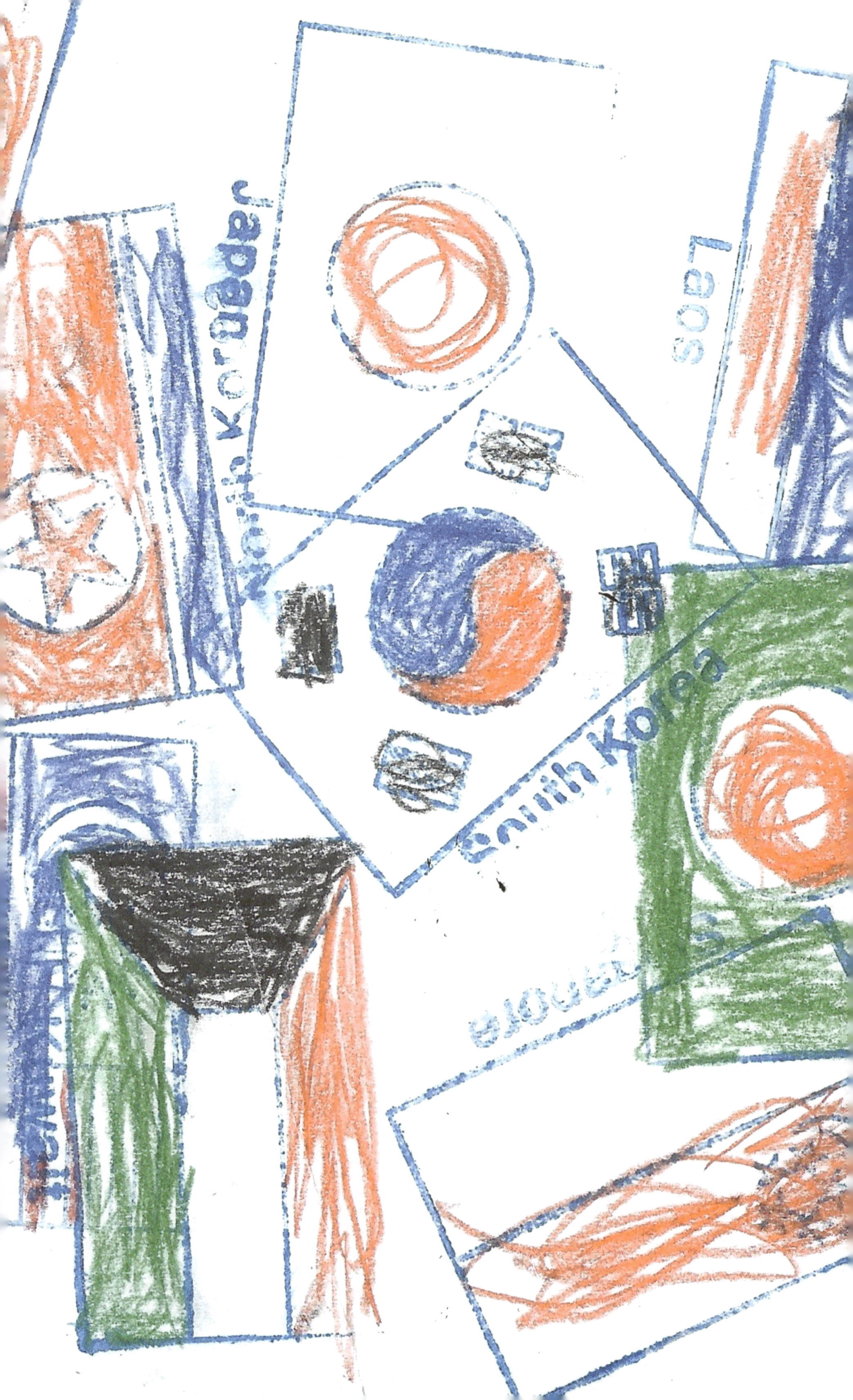
North Korea
South Korea
Laos

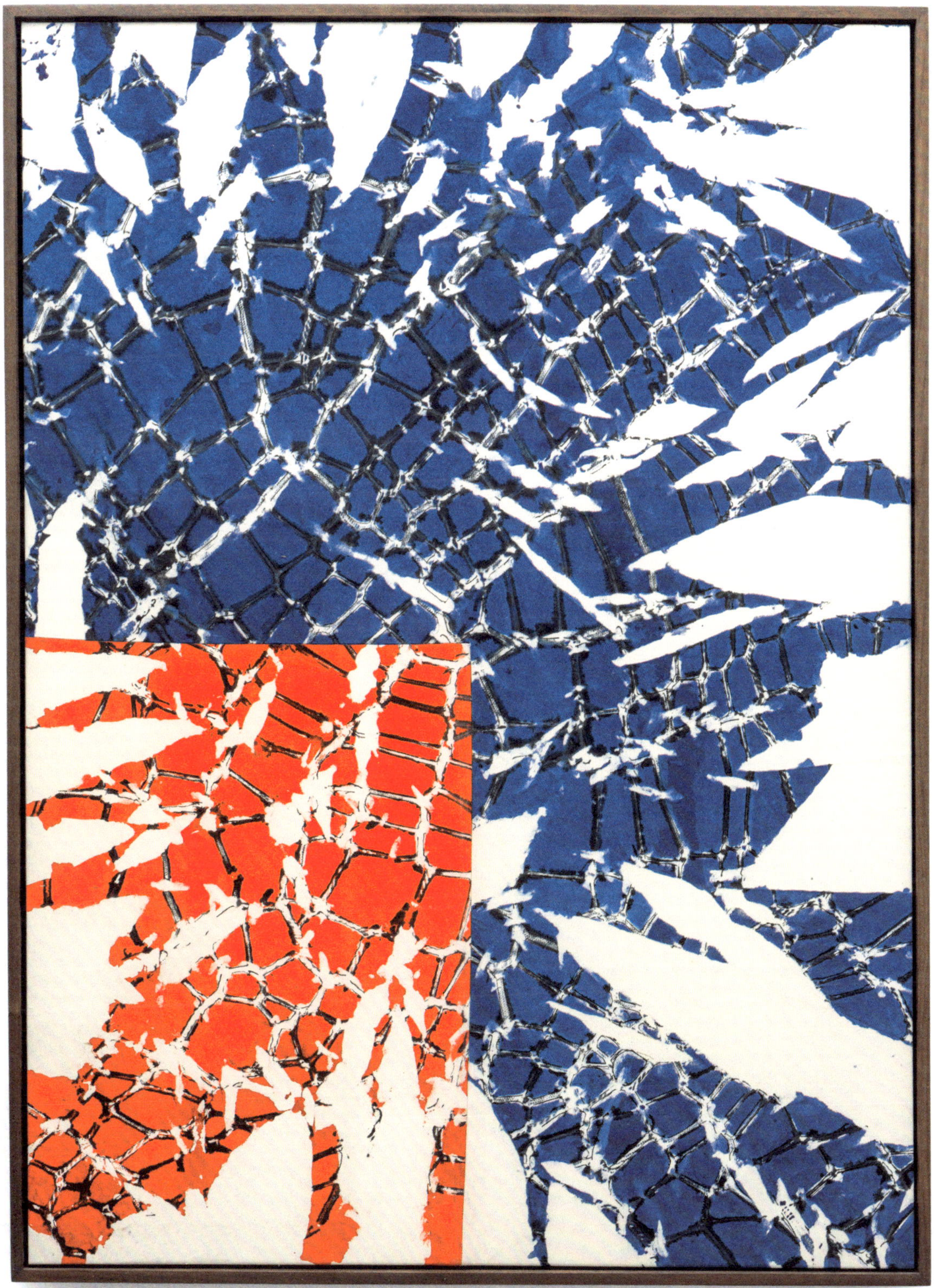

OPPOSITE:

B.B.L. RED UMBRA 1-41, 2023
acrylic ink and India ink on canvas
80¾ × 130¾ × 2 inches (205.1 × 332.1 × 5.1 cm)
courtesy of the artist and Tina Kim Gallery
photo: Charles Roussel

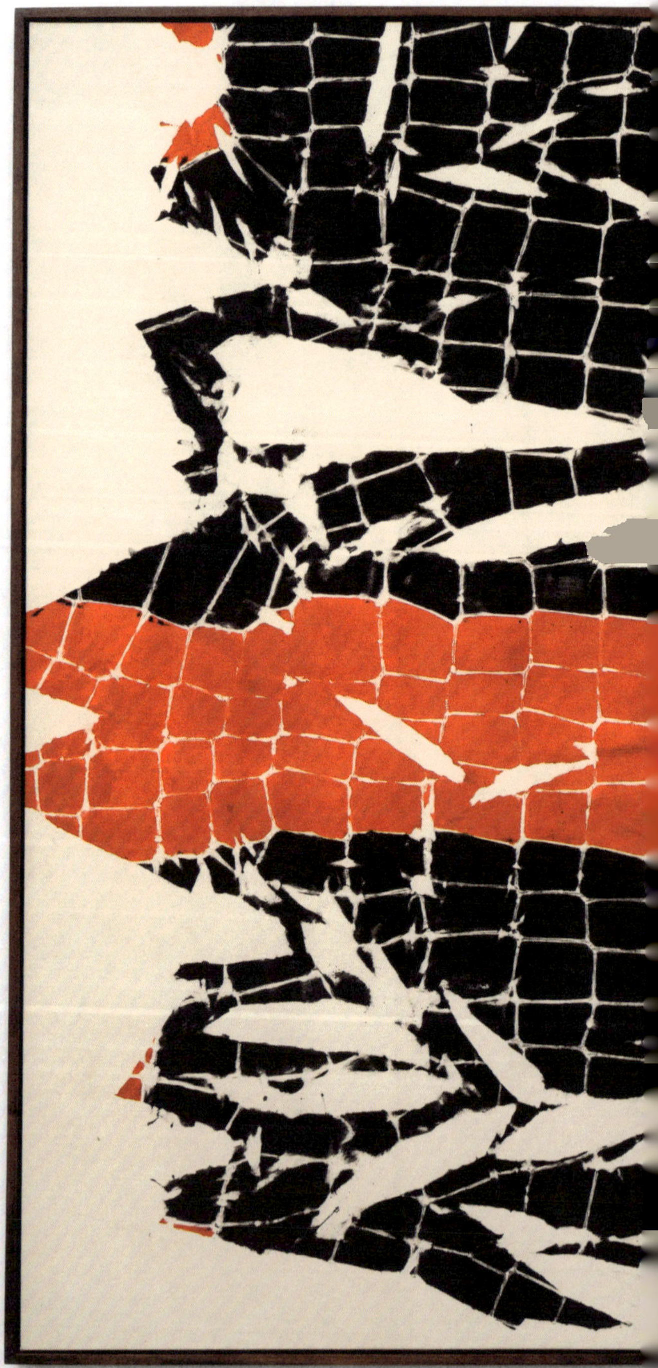

OPPOSITE:

"@", 2022
rope and India ink
96 × 108 × 6 inches (244 × 274.5 × 15 cm)
courtesy of the artist and Overduin & Co., Los Angeles, CA
photo: SEVLAS Photography

OPPOSITE:

INSTALLATION VIEW OF
ONCE WE LEAVE A PLACE IS IT THERE, 2023
curated by Malaika Newsome, Clarice Lee, Ruiqi Wang, and Fiona Yu
supported by ValeriaNapoleoneXXIFA
Institute of Fine Arts, New York University, New York, NY, 2023
courtesy of the artist, IFA NYU, and Tina Kim Gallery
photo: Hyunjung Rhee

PAGE 128:

SKETCH FOR **ONCE WE LEAVE A PLACE IS IT THERE**, 2023

PAGES 129, 133:

GLYPH SET 1 [DETAILS], 2016
steel

PAGE 131:

ONCE WE LEAVE A PLACE IS IT THERE [DETAIL], 2023
curated by Malaika Newsome, Clarice Lee, Ruiqi Wang and Fiona Yu
supported by ValeriaNapoleoneXXIFA
Institute of Fine Arts, New York University, New York, NY, 2023

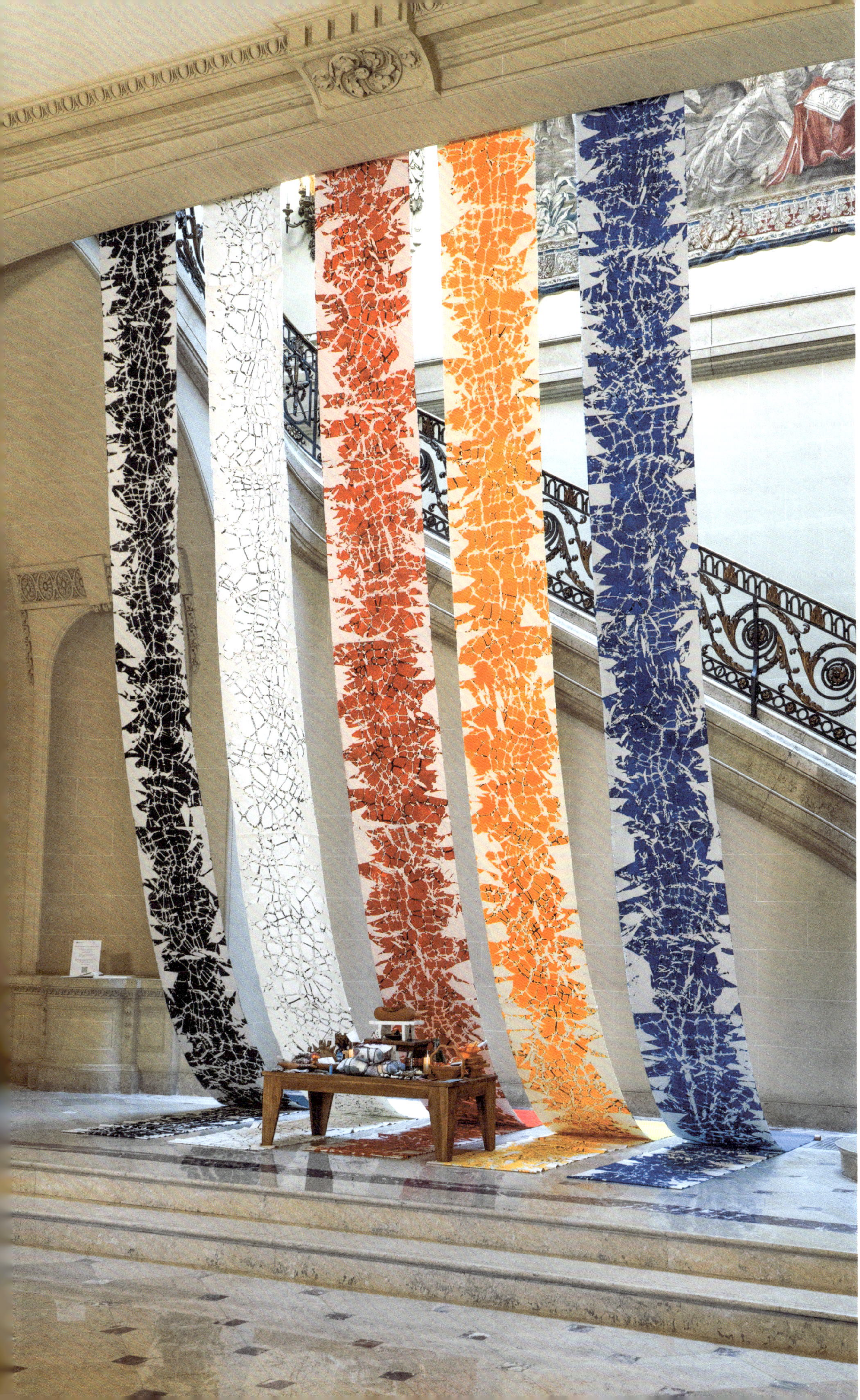

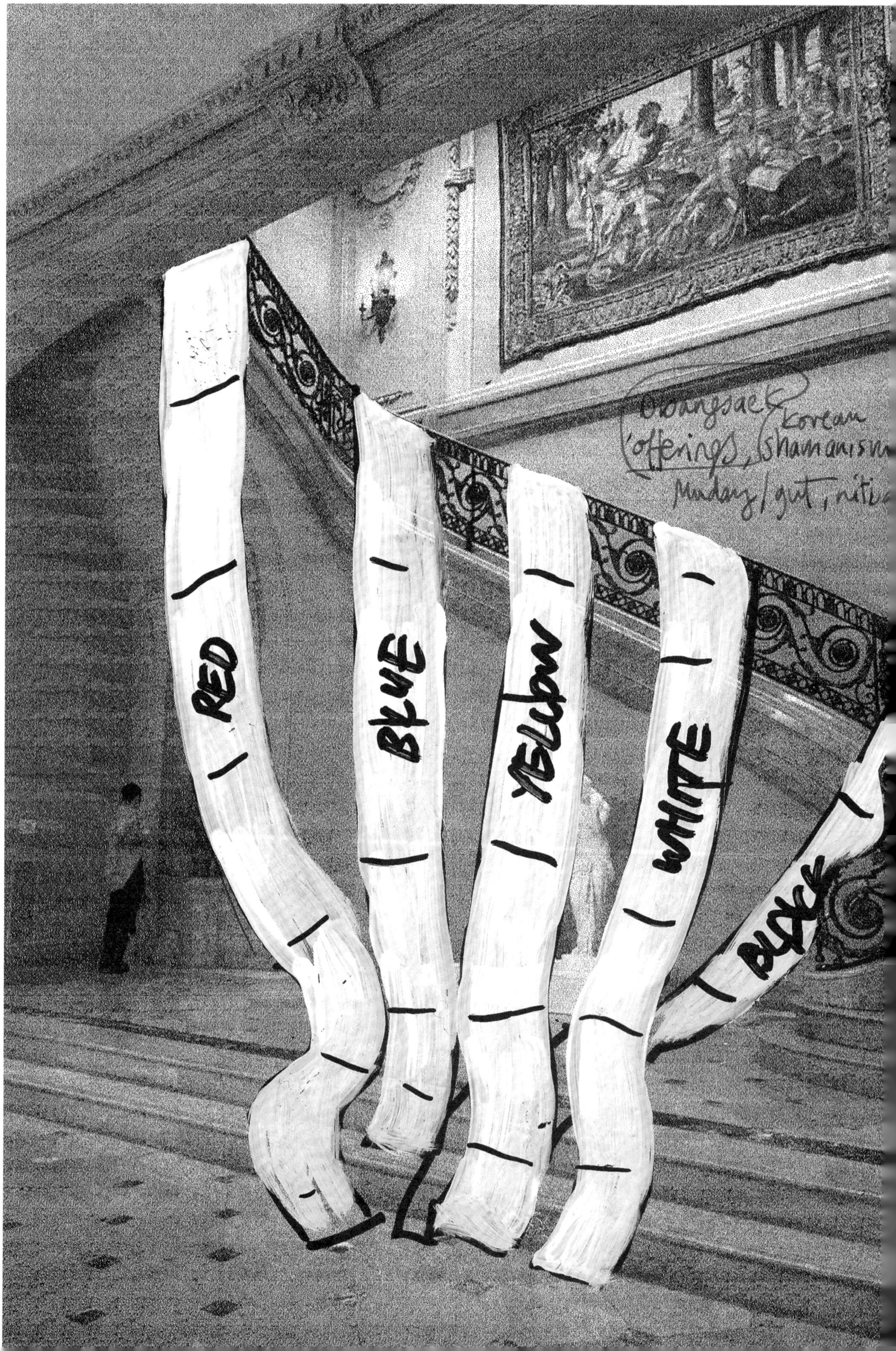
Obangsaek
Korean
'offerings,
Mudang/gut,
RED
BLUE
YELLOW
WHITE

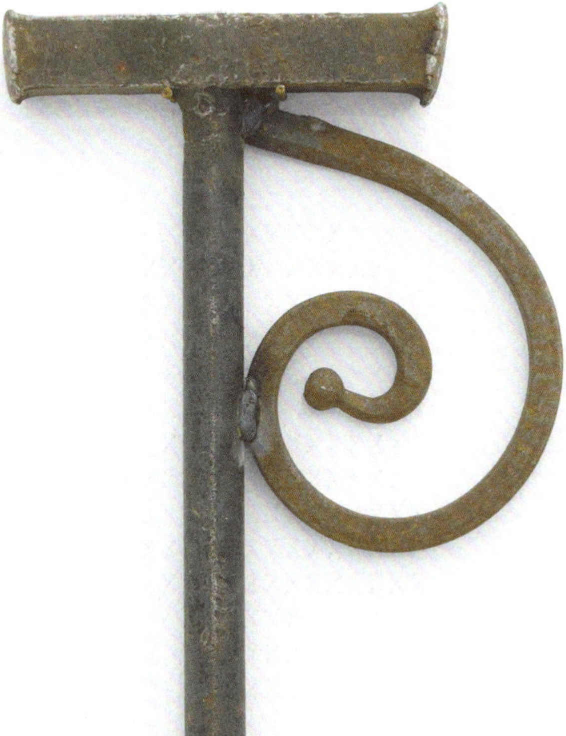

```
XXXXXXXXXXXXXXXXXXXXXXXXXXXXXXXXXXXXXXXX
XXXX                                XXXX
XXXX                                XXXX
 XXXX                              XXXX
  XXXX                            XXXX
    XXXX                        XXXX
       XXXXXXXXXXXXXXXXXXXXXXXXXX

        XXXXXXXXXXXXXXXXXXXXXXXX
         XXXXXXXXXXXXXXXXXXXXXX
            XXXXXXXXXXXXXXXX
                   XXXX
```

```
                XXXXXXXXXX
               XXXXXXXXXXXX
               XXXXXXXXXXXX
               XXXXXXXXXXXX
              XXXXXXXXXXXXXX
              XXXXXXXXXXXXXX
              XXXXXXXXXXXXXX
              XXXXXXXXXXXXXX
             XXXXXXXXXXXXXXXX
             XXXXXXXXXXXXXXXX
             XXXXXXXXXXXXXXXX
                 XXXXXXXX
                  XXXXXX
                    XX
```

```
XXXXX             XXXXXXX           XXXXXX
XX                 XXXXX                XX

XX                   XX                  X
XX                    X                  X
XXXXXXXXXXXXXXXXXXXXXXXXXXXXXXXXXXXXXXXXXX
```

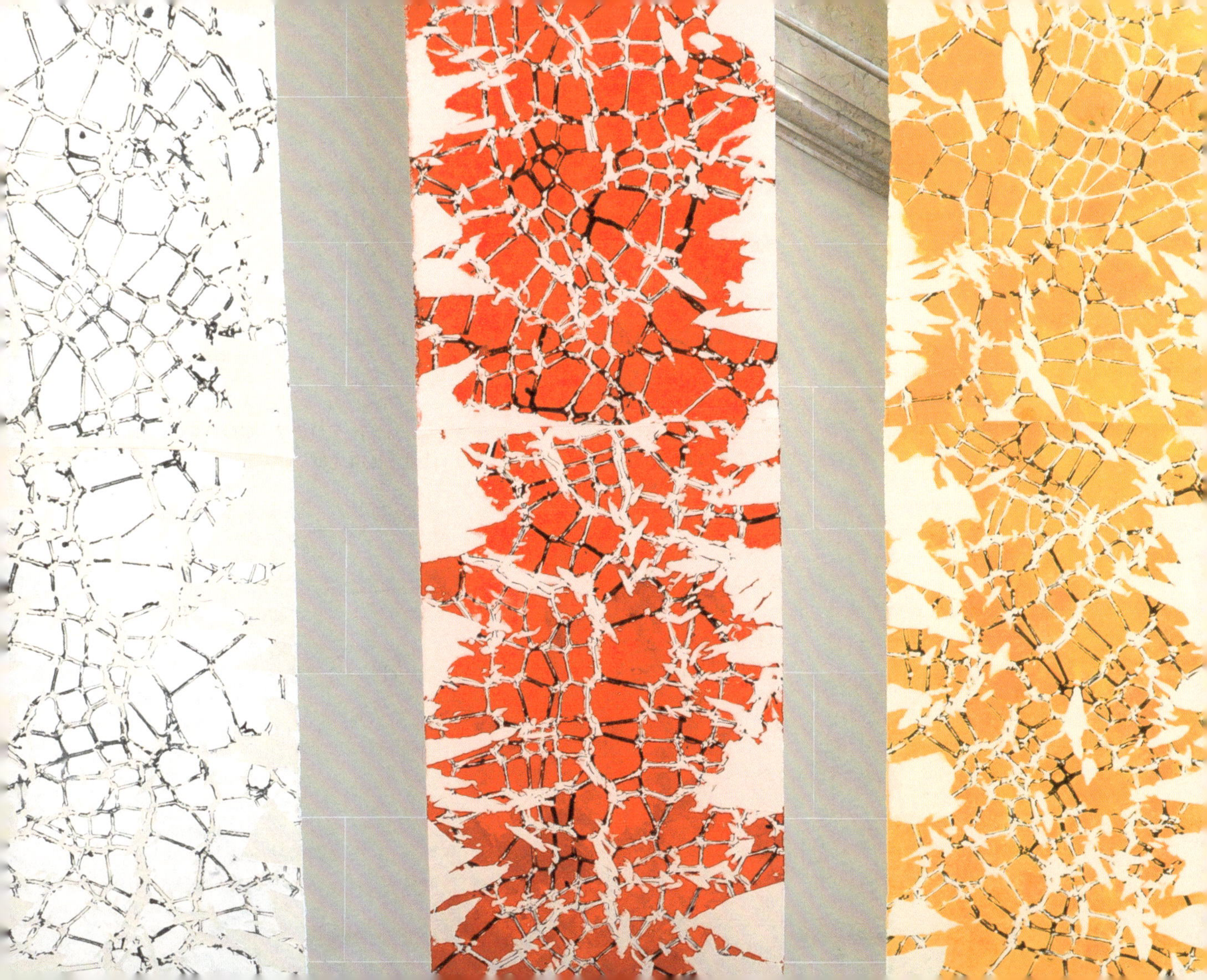

we are born soft creatures
our   cells
create a web

of latitudes and longitudes

they convene overla
a tight map of a tight city

streets

blocks

off thye map
off the skin   g r i d

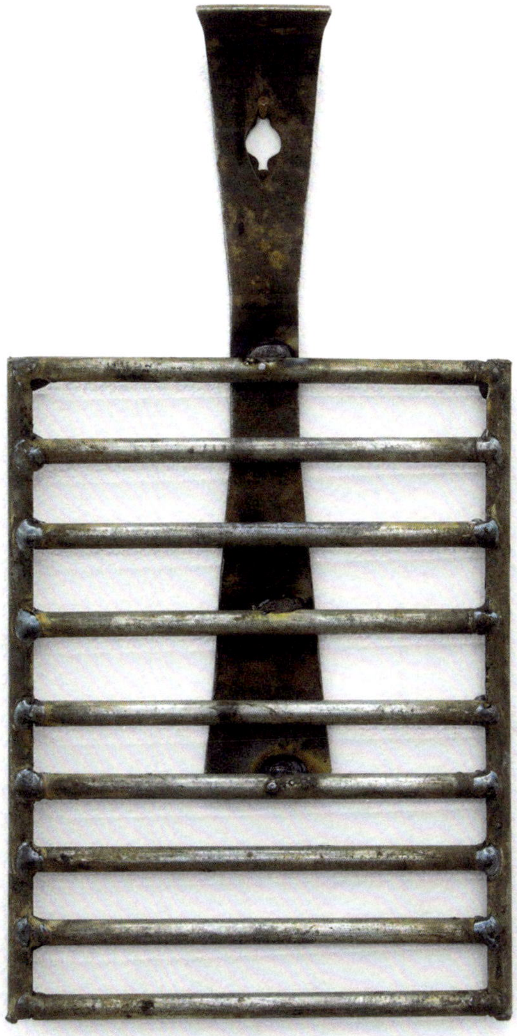

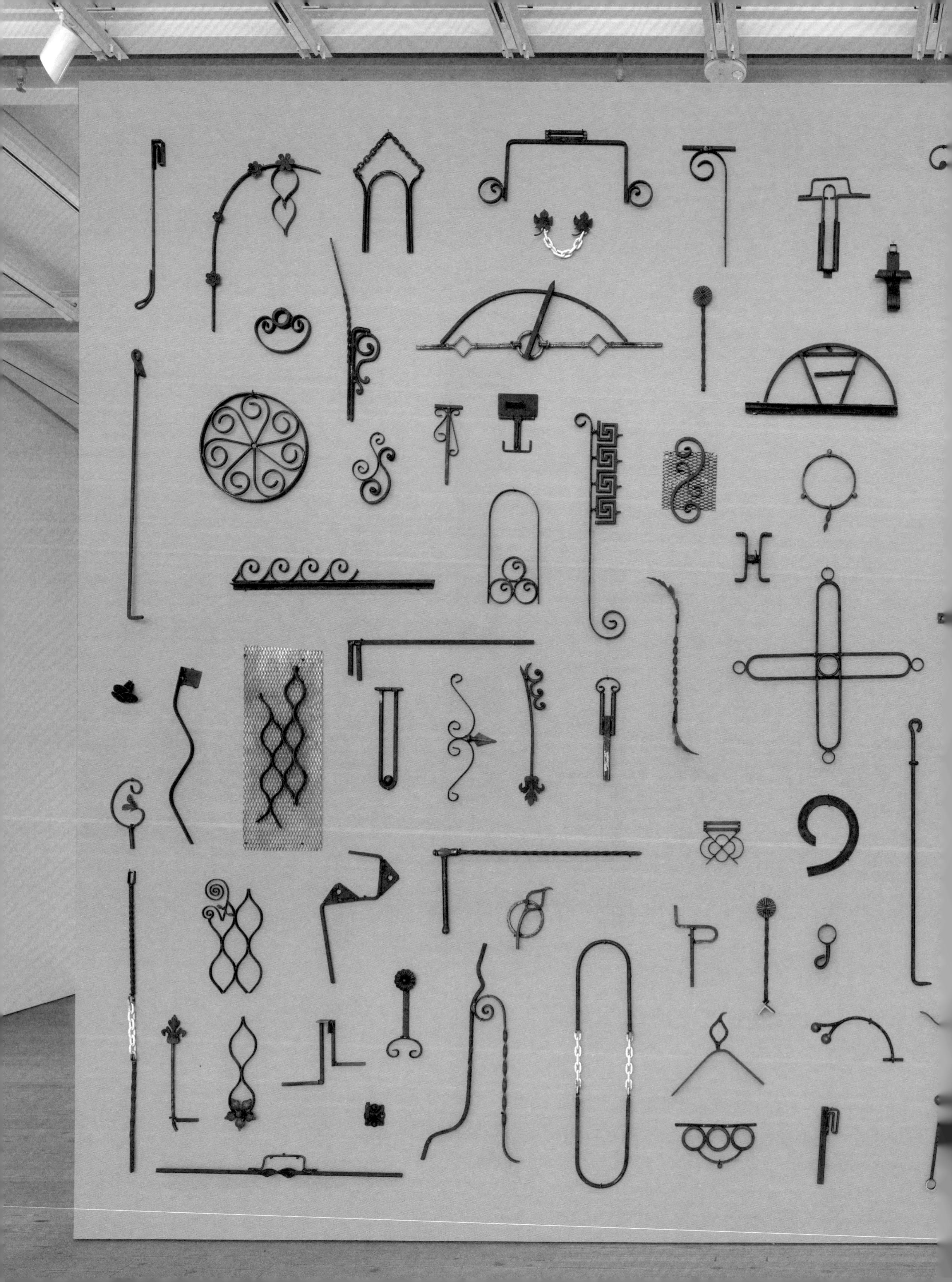

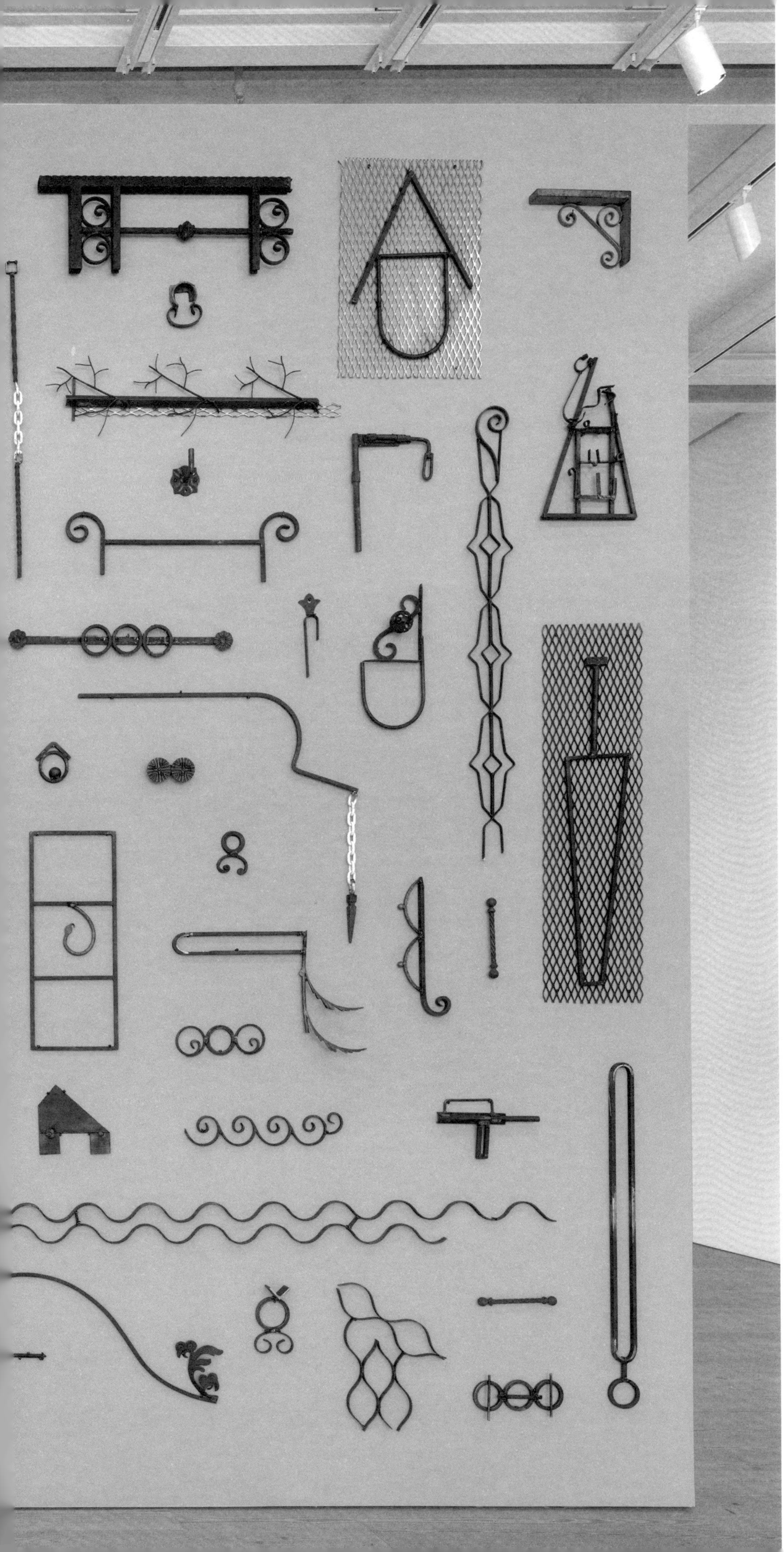

PAGES 134–135:

LABYRINTH, 2019
steel; 15 × 20 feet (4.6 × 6.1 m)
in the Whitney Biennial, 2019
curated by Jane Panetta and Rujeko Hockley
Whitney Museum of American Art, New York, NY
courtesy of the artist and Whitney Museum of American Art
photo: Ron Amstutz

OPPOSITE:

B.B.LATTICE 1-5, 2025
acrylic ink on canvas
57 × 59 inches (144.8 × 149.9 cm)
courtesy of the artist and Tina Kim Gallery
photo Hyunjung Rhee

PAGES 138–139:

THE LETTER [STILL], 2023
duration: 22:23; color, sound

PAGE 140:

BONDAGE BAGGAGE PROTOTYPE 1, 2018
tarp, tape, rope, cardboard, used bedding
45 × 27 × 23½ inches (114.3 × 68.6 × 59.7 cm)
courtesy of the artist and Jack Hanley Gallery

PAGE 142:

B.B.P. 1-3, 2024
acrylic ink and India ink on canvas
63½ × 58¼ inches (161 × 148 cm)
courtesy of the artist and François Ghebaly, Los Angeles and New York
photo: Paul Salveson

PAGE 143:

B.B.P. 1-2, 2024
acrylic ink and India ink on canvas
63¾ × 58¼ inches (162 × 148 cm)
courtesy of the artist and François Ghebaly, Los Angeles and New York
photo: Paul Salveson

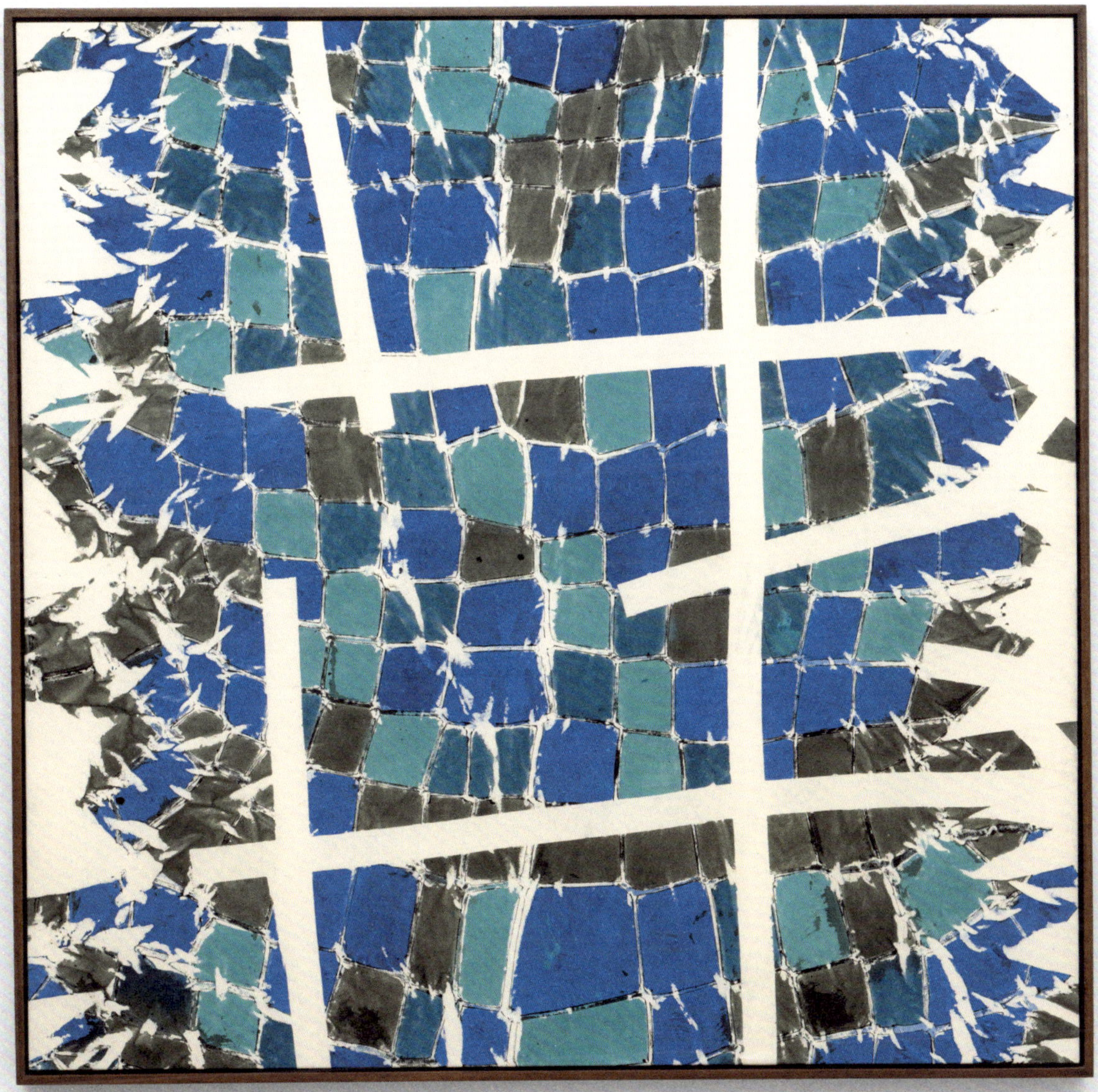

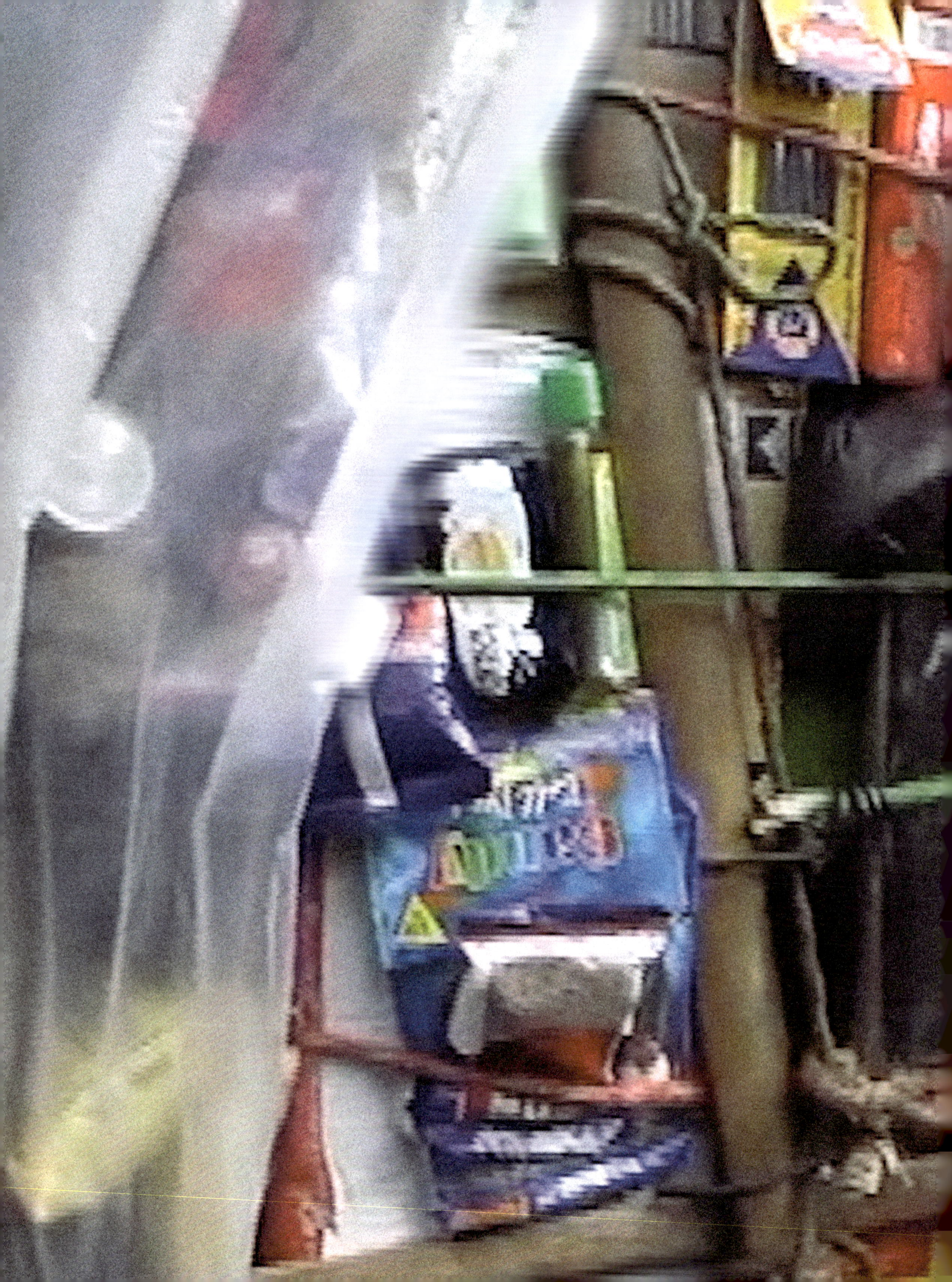

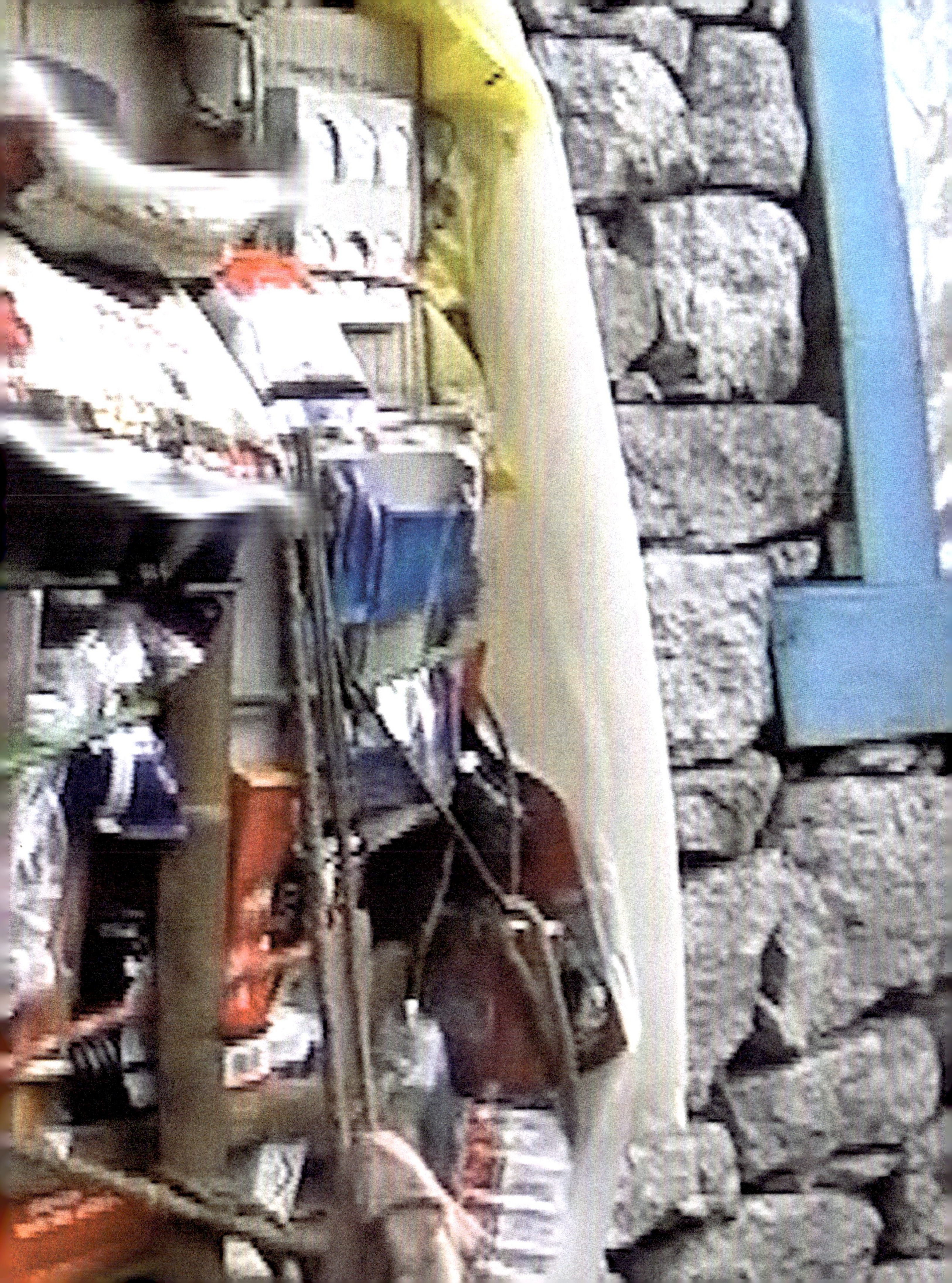

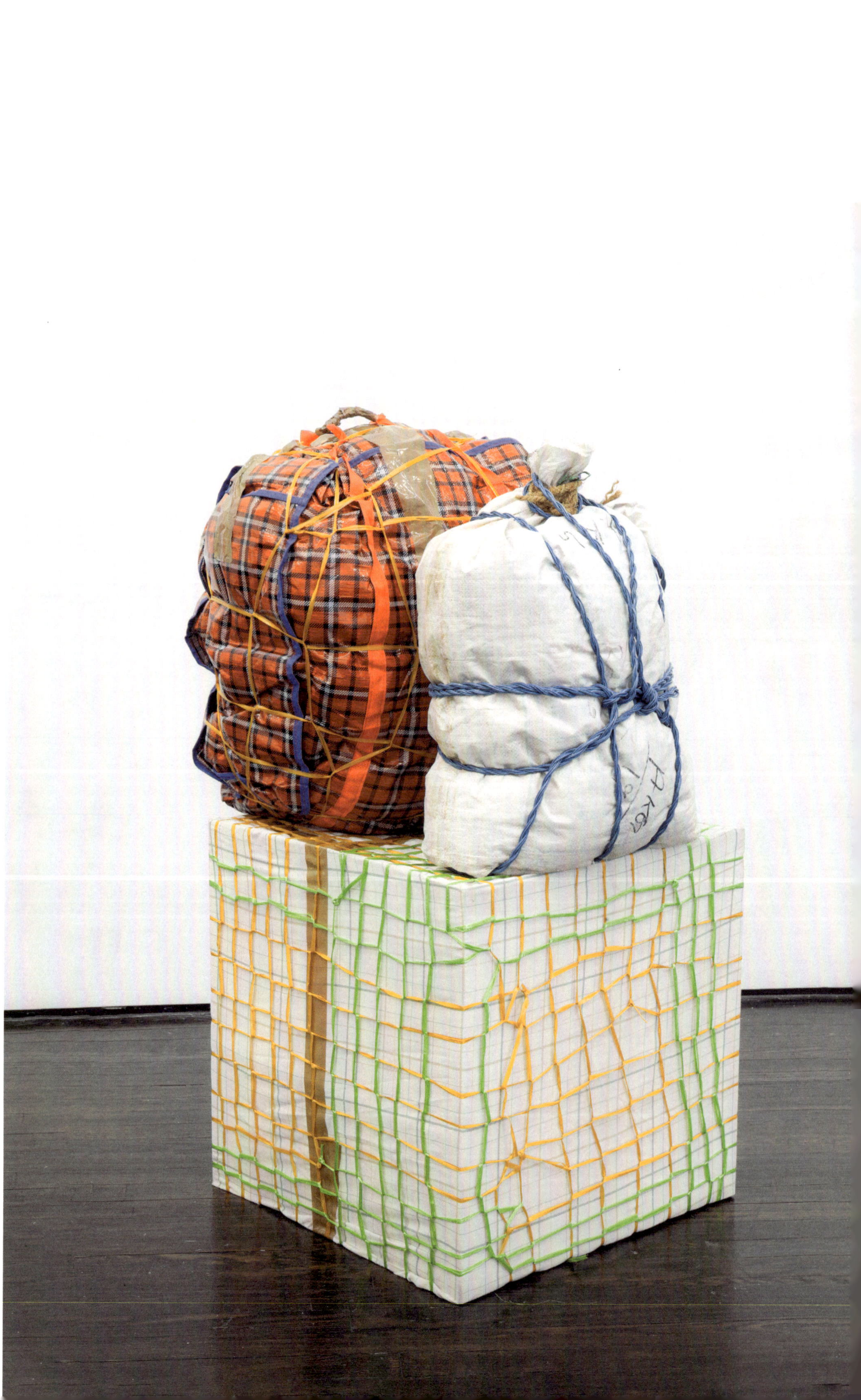

:s that held structures in place, and th
:tures, the more value it suggested. Val
their belongiggs.
ie surface on which the steel gpyhs are
ıindow, or a home.,
ıed together all my experiences. languag
ıts, therefore it was important to us. I
ıce in our lives, that language becam th
ıguage meant wihhout identity, and that
ı our childhood, my korean0ness was only
je. it meant that I needed to not only g
i was to go to bible studies in koream
week, and summers or winters in korea.
with everyday. I am neither fluent in e
communicating, but it is difficult for
even to myself. i was neither accepted b
:al nepali community, nor by my own peop
ıg, but what is it to understand what yo
peech and language are two very differen

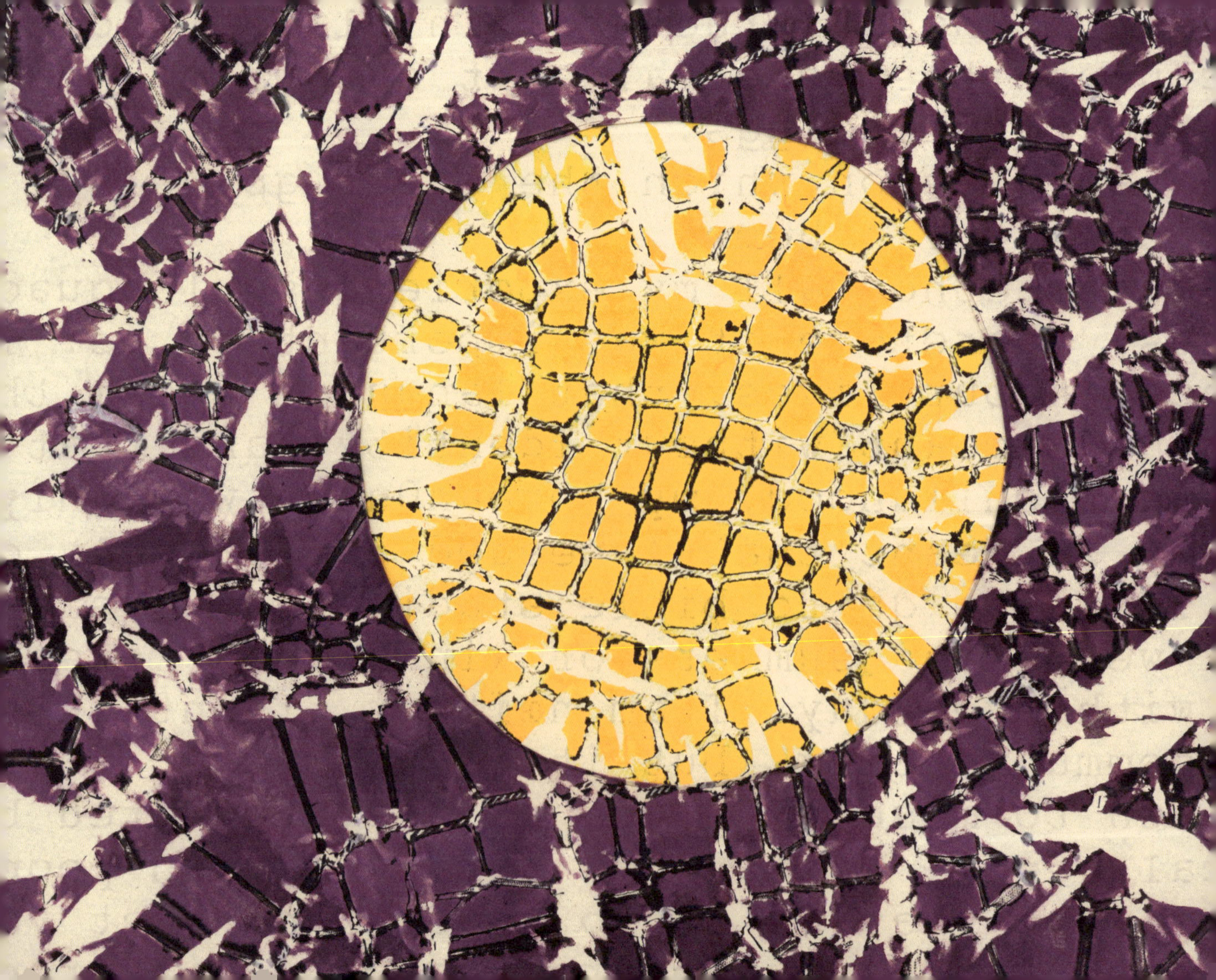

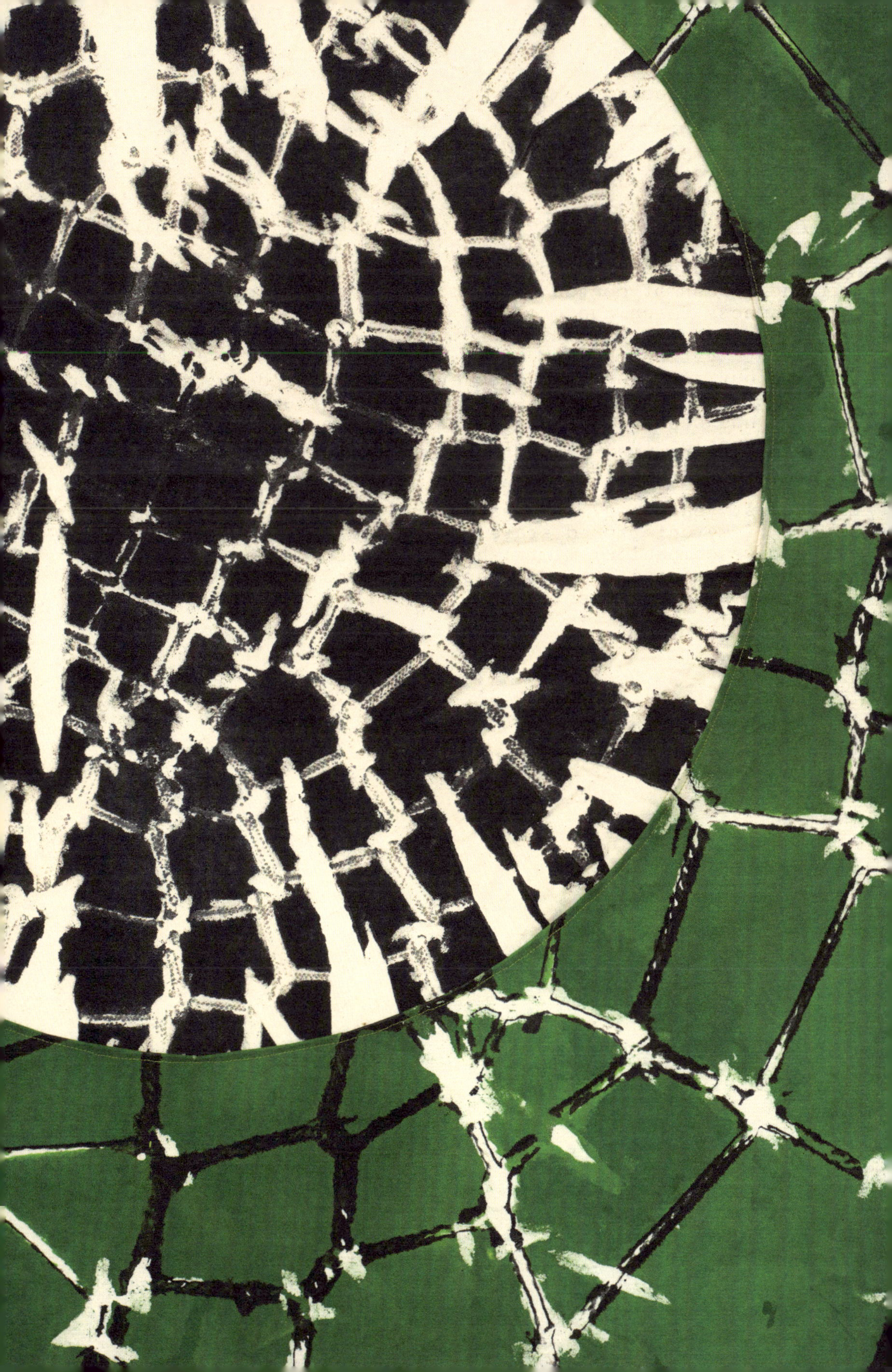

The symbol of Feeling

The other night as i smoked halfway through my joint, alone,
in my living room where it was dark and quiet - and as i moved
around my house in silence as not to wake up my child and husband
- i had a rush of contentment roll over me while i physically felt
the calmness reach the crown of my head. i was thinking deeply abo
-ut my art, and how it has accompanied me my whole life. and as i
enter into yet another chapter, into my forties, i looked back to
think about all the other chapters in which i'd abandoned my pract
-ice, the indefinite breaks buried in doubt and neglect. but my
art, it has been relentless, still present through my cowering and
despair, patiently waiting for the right moment to act,and in spit
--e of the many shifts and transformations i've forced it through,
it has been reliable, in attendance, and in constant tandem with
my deepest yearnings. as i sat there, joint in hand, i was in tota
-l awe of my unfettered state, i started to visualize my art as a
figurative companion, my friend who has followed me here, and
despite our on and offs, our ups and downs, i know that we can onl
-y be stronger together.

july 20, 2023
salida, colorado
maia ruth lee

‡ MRL GLYPHS FOUNDED IN 1983

Twenty-One GLYPHS of NYC 2016©

21 - 21 - 21 - 21 - 21

SALON 94 EDITION

RE DISCOVER YOUR PERSONAL SOURCE

GET ♥♥♥♥ 2KNOWU≈

THE MRL Chart

2016 = The Year of Decision-making

MAKE THE DECISION(21) YOURS OR SOMEONE ELSE WILL MAKE IT THEIRS.

Anxiety is the dizziness of freedom !

PRACTICE INTENTIONAL ACTS OF EVOLUTIONARY KINDNESS!

LET KINDNESS RULE !!

√ **K** INESTHETIC
√ **I** NTERDEPENDENT
√ **N** EUROLOGICAL
√ **D** EVELOPMENT
√ **N** ATURALLY
√ **E** VOLVING
√ **S** ENSITIVE
√ **S** OLUTIONS

** *Nine Universal Laws*

❶ 
KARMA

❸ 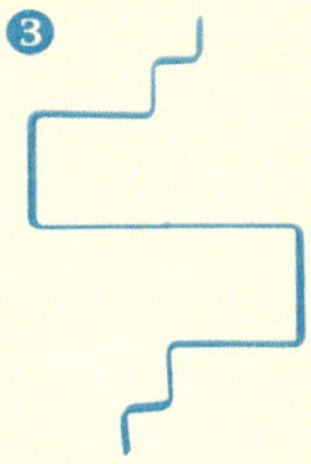
PERSPECTIVE

❺ 
HEALING

❼ 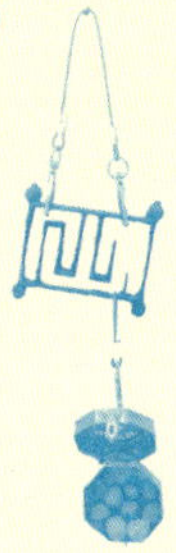
FERTILITY

ONLY TRUE SELF CRITICISM CAN SAVE THE HUMAN SPECIES

❷ 
CHARITY

❹ 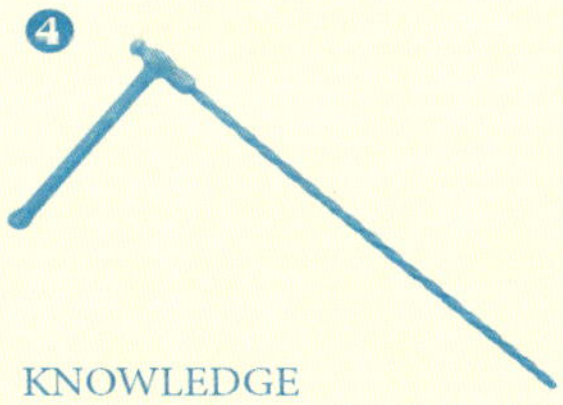
KNOWLEDGE

❻ 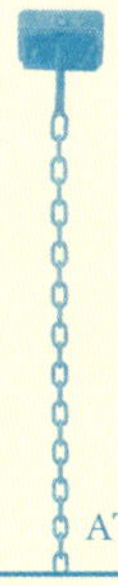
ATTRACTION

❽ 
HARMONY

❾ WISDOM
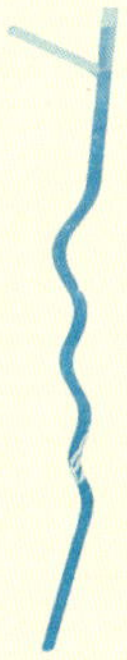

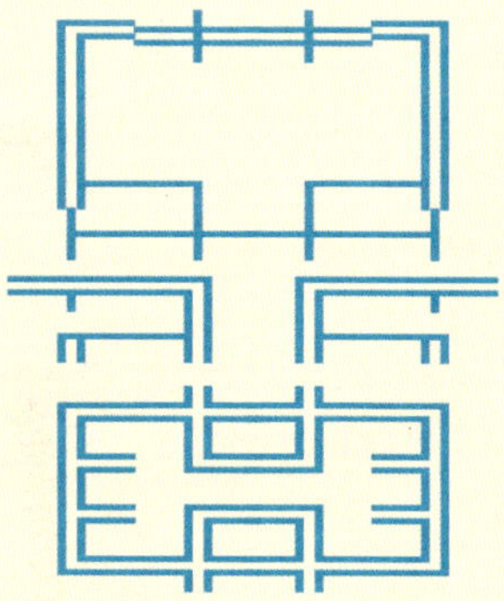

THE GLYPH-OSCOPE 2016

ENHANCE YOUR POTENTIAL

✖✖✖✕✕✕××✓✓👍👍👍

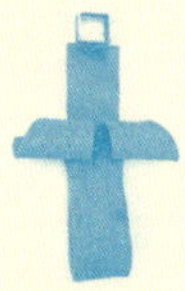

ARIES

Horizon
Exploration
Long-term

New opportunities to reinvent yourself. Stay away from dogma and rigid approaches. Avoid risky decisions.

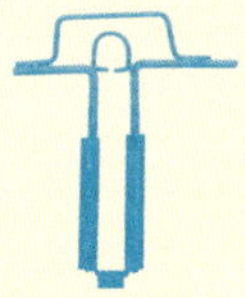

TAURUS

Mystery
Knowledge
Growth

Relationships can be tough this year, in your job or in love, but do not worry about the first half of 2016. There will be blossoming and renewal in the second half.

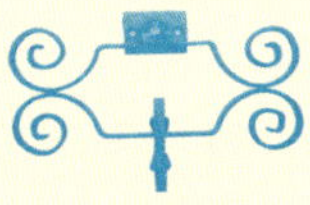

GEMINI

Future
Improve
Victory

The first 9 months can prove difficult in partnerships, but with patience you will improve and expand. Big year for learning.

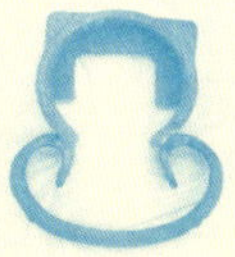

CANCER

Ideas
Renovate
Enlightenment

More complex responsibilities, and tensions may amass in August and October, but you will overcome your current situation in November.

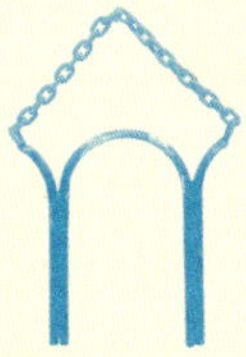

LEO

Strength
Influence
Evolution

Until fall '16 you should be leery of offers that promise easy, effortless opportunities. But you will win big by working hard.

VIRGO

Energy
Focus
Bold

You would like more action in terms of love life, but stay optimistic. Prioritize you and your needs. Your magnetism will be hard to turn down.

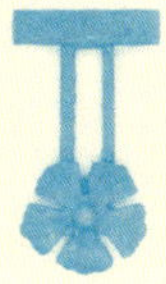

LIBRA

Security
Confidence
Logic

2016 is a mixed year, but it will bring the most significant events. Act on decisions that you've likely been postponing. Now not later.

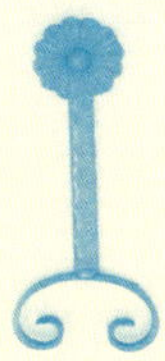

SCORPIO

Power
Passion
Charm

Power of persuasion, mental strength, talent for research are your strengths this year. But you must defend yourself from excessive self criticism and tendency to manipulate others.

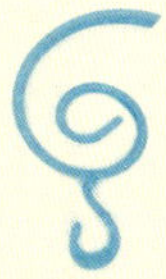

SAGITTARIUS

Freedom
Thought
Simple

A lot of frustration and restrictions this year as things happen slowly. Keep it simple but aim high. September is your lucky break. Being a good listener will help you.

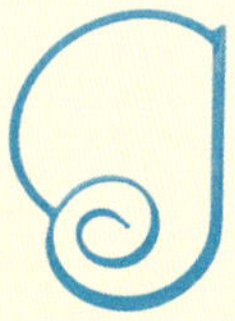

CAPRICORN

See
Unbounded
Liberate

Be on high alert, especially in August, and there will not be much turbulence this year. Your horizons widen through travel and spiritual study.

AQUARIUS

Collective
Understanding
Change

Much growth within a community this year, but try not to mix group activities with financial interests. Stimulated by competition, your career will reach a new step.

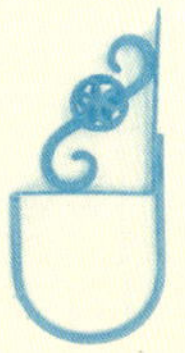

PISCES

All
Calibrate
Adapt

Professional ambitions are running high, but you have to act with diplomacy and tenacity to obtain a durable outcome. Especially with the ones closest to you.

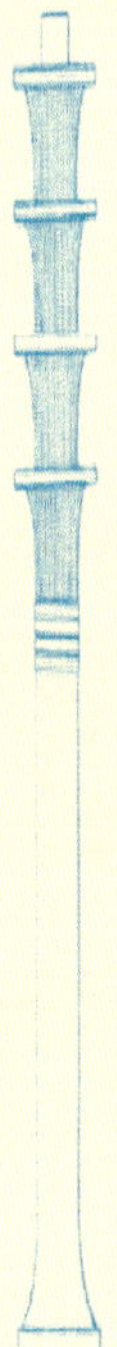

Together We're Better

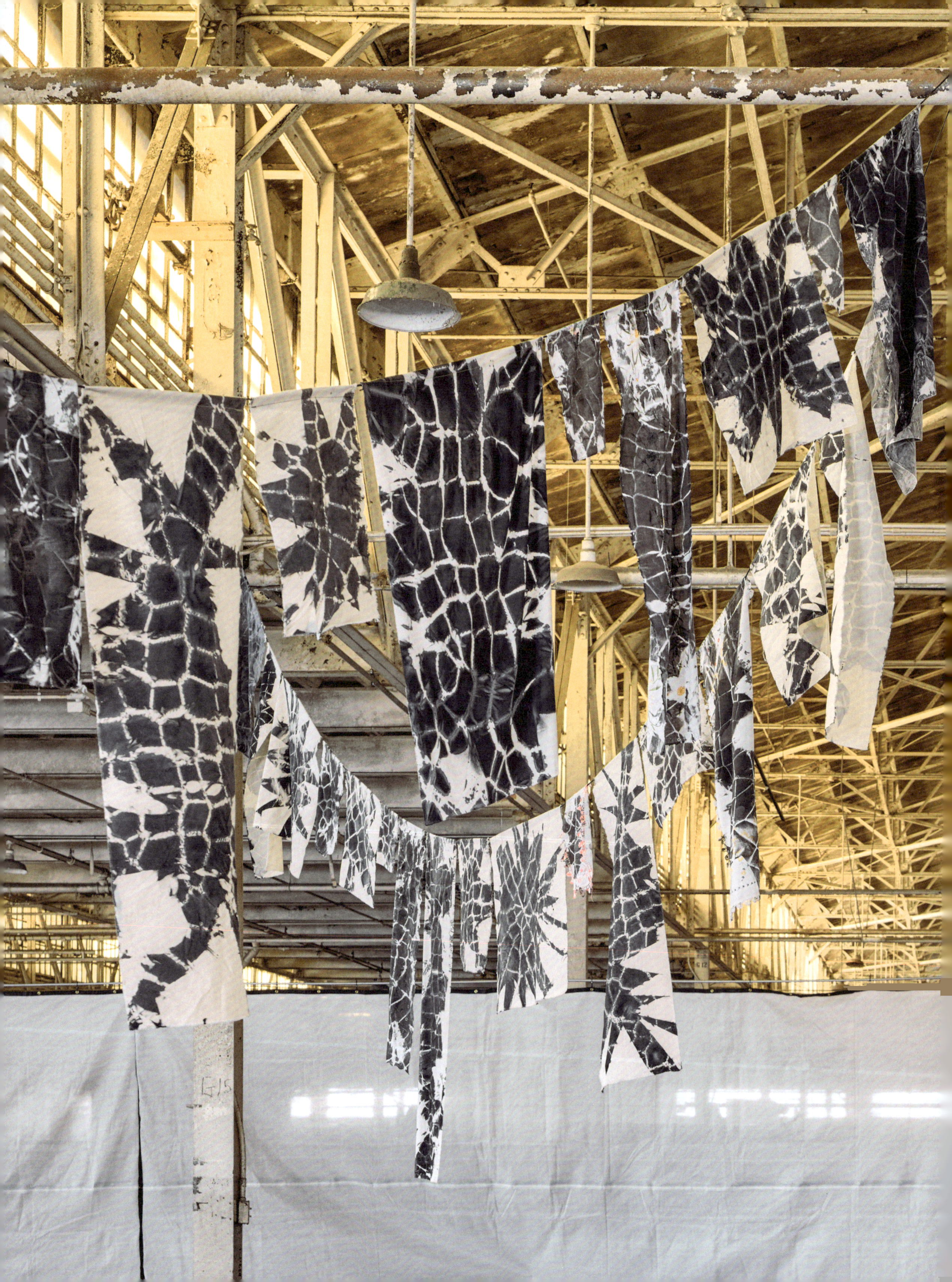

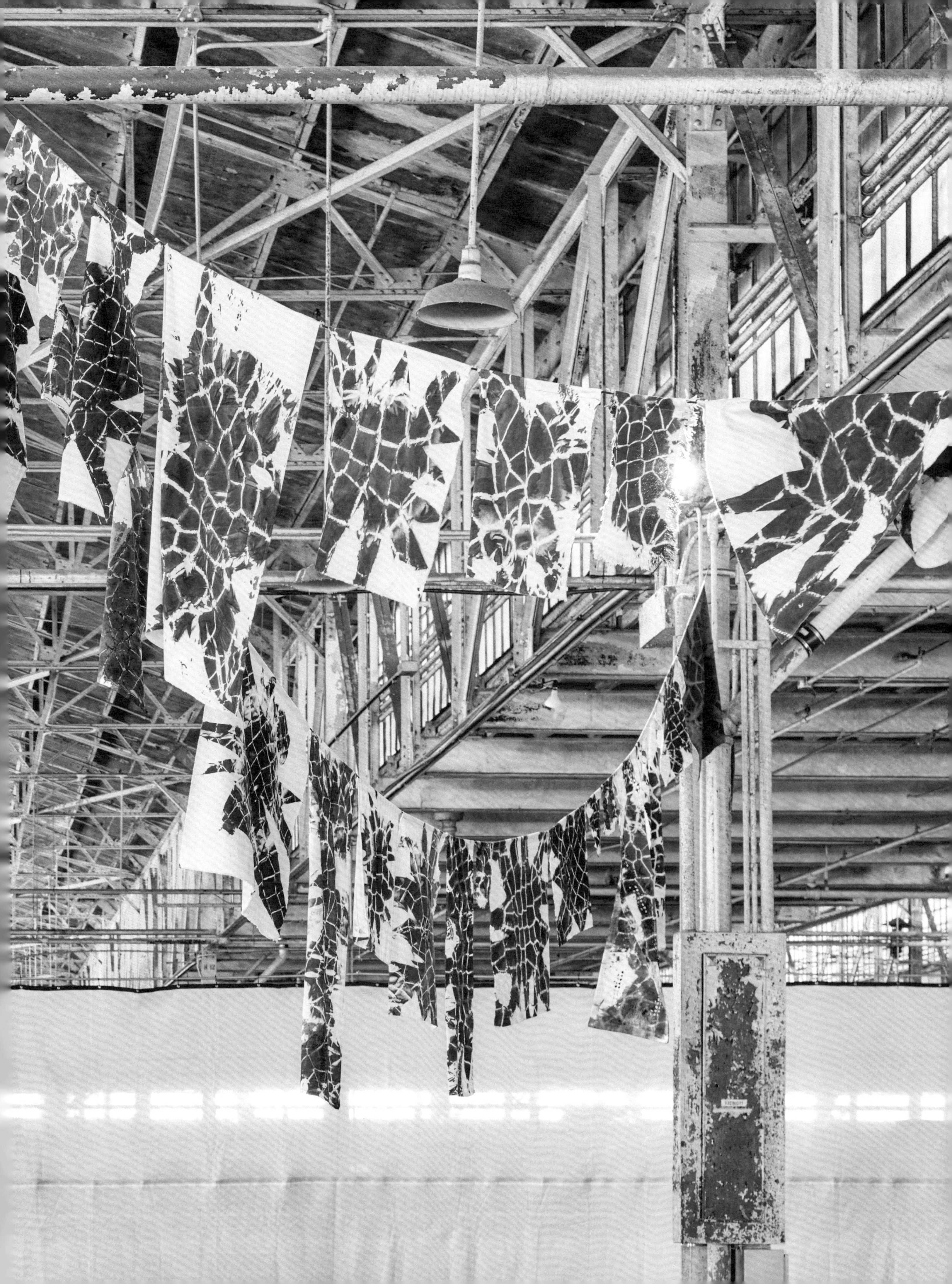

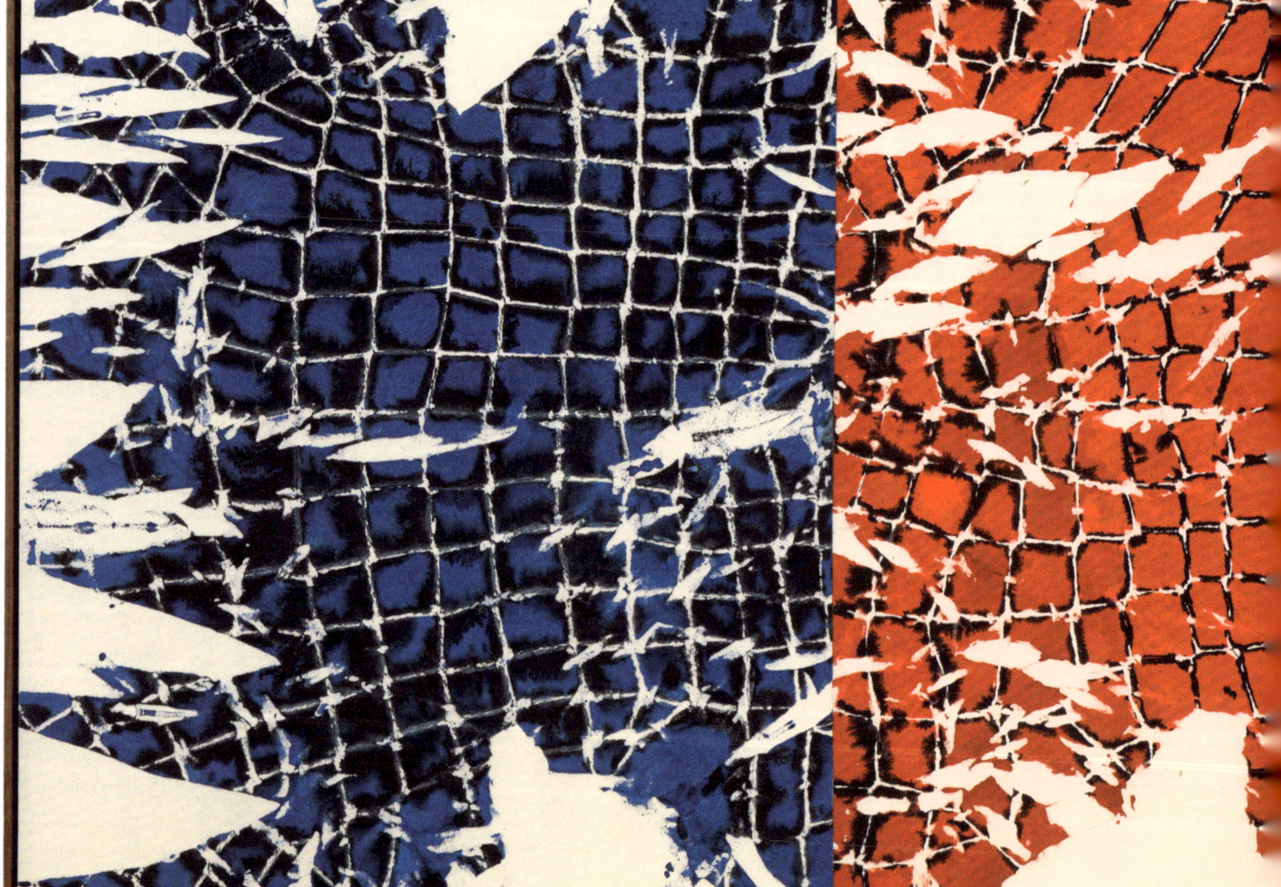

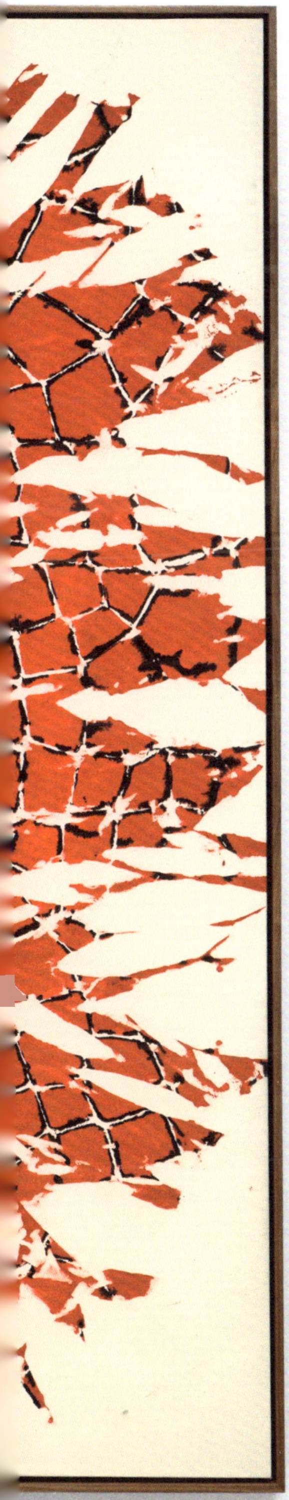

PAGE 145:

AUSPICIOUS GLYPH CHART, 2016

PAGES 146–147:

INSTALLATION VIEW OF **THE CONVEYOR**, 2024
in Prospect 6 Triennial, 2024
curated by Miranda Lash and Ebony G. Patterson
supported by Art Production Fund,
Ford Motor Plant, New Orleans, LA
courtesy of the artist and Prospect 6
photo: Alex Marks

OPPOSITE:

B.B.L. 2-1, 2024
acrylic ink and India ink on canvas
65 × 75 inches (165 × 190.5 cm)
courtesy of the artist and François Ghebaly, Los Angeles and New York
photo: Paul Salveson

PAGES 150–151:

THE LETTER [STILL], 2023
duration: 22:23; color, sound

PAGES 152, 153 [DETAIL]:

BONDAGE BAGGAGE HOLOGRAPH, 2025
ink on canvas
56¾ × 18½ inches (144 × 47.2 cm)
courtesy of the artist and UBP4

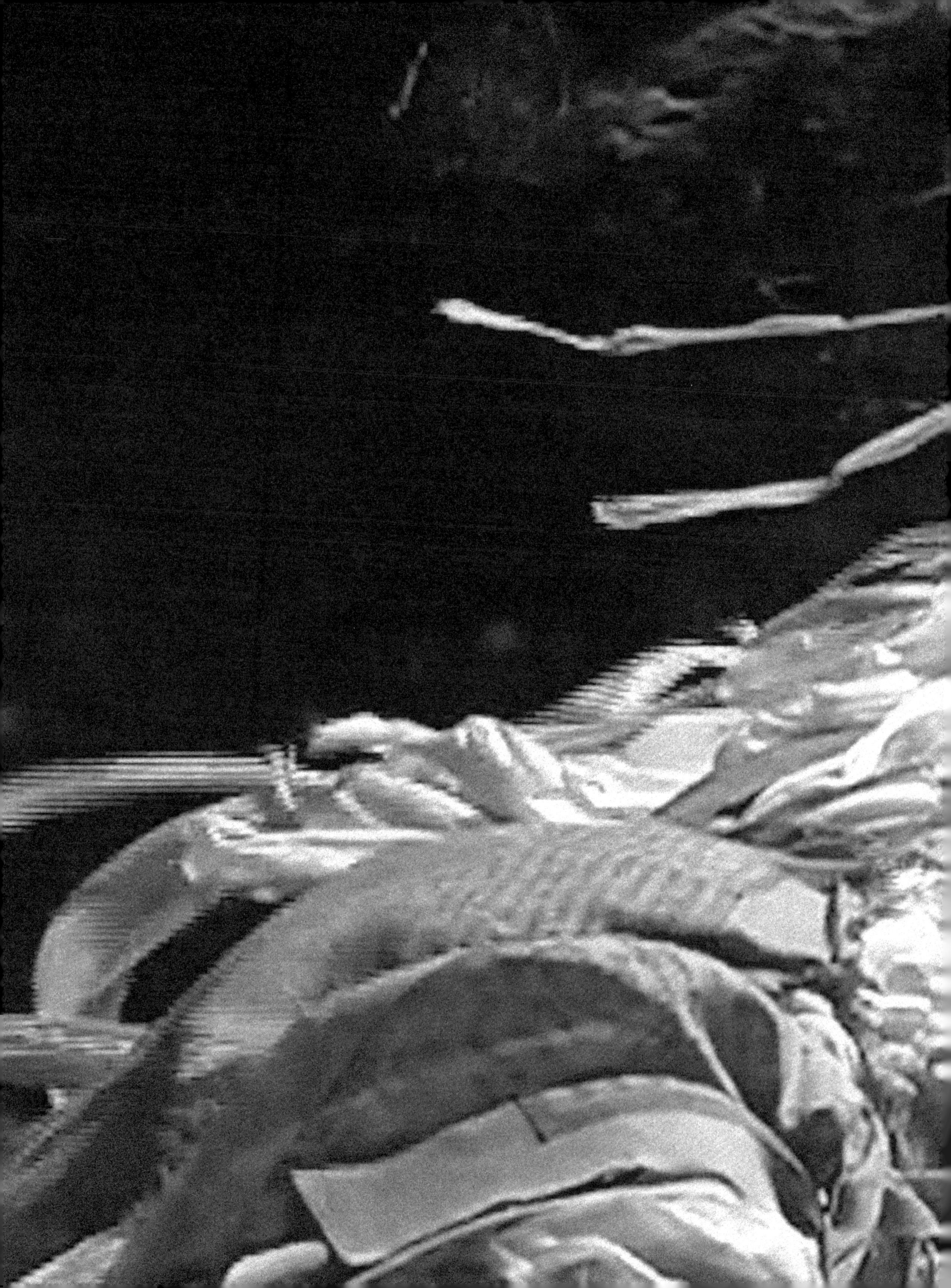

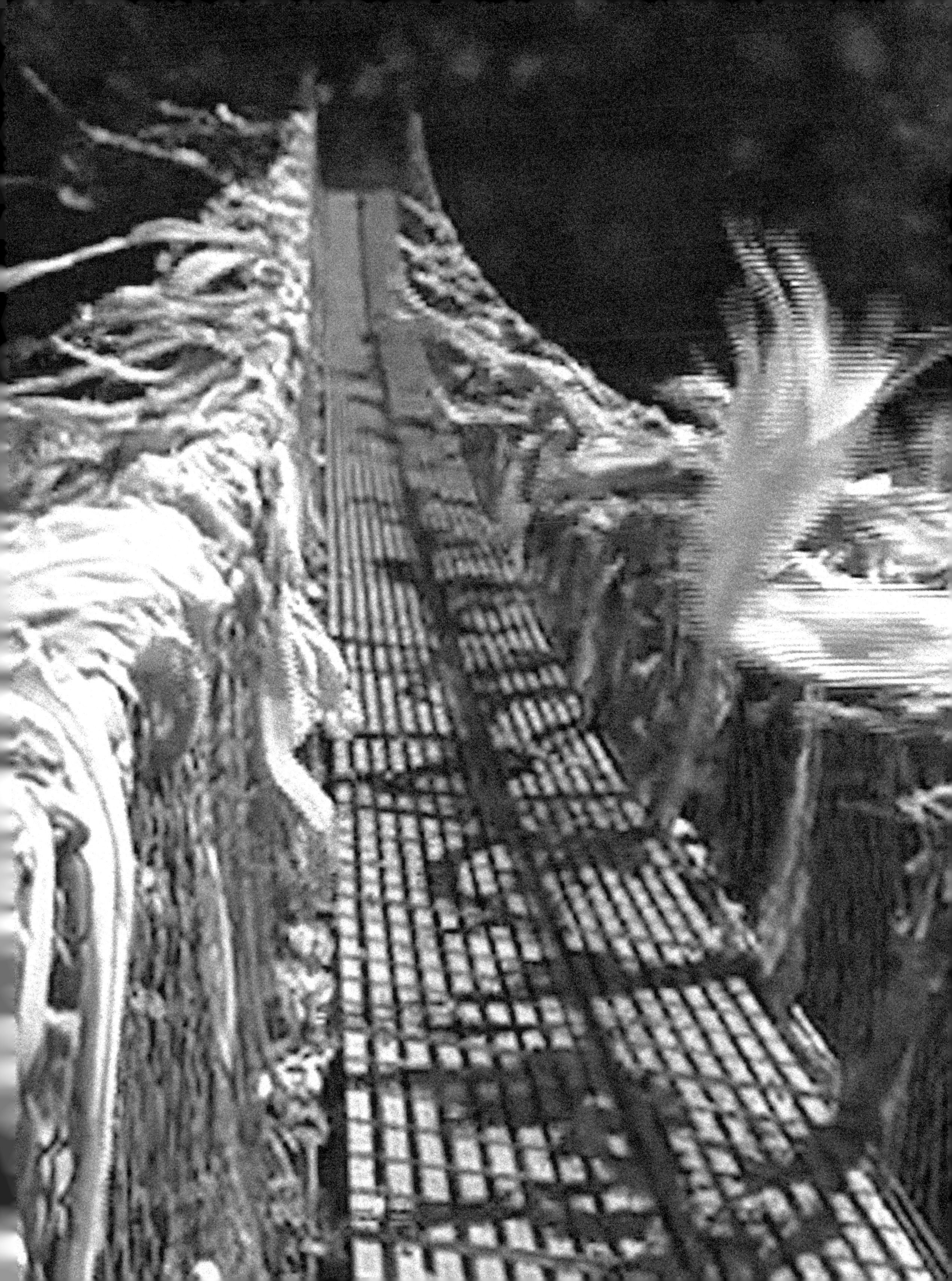

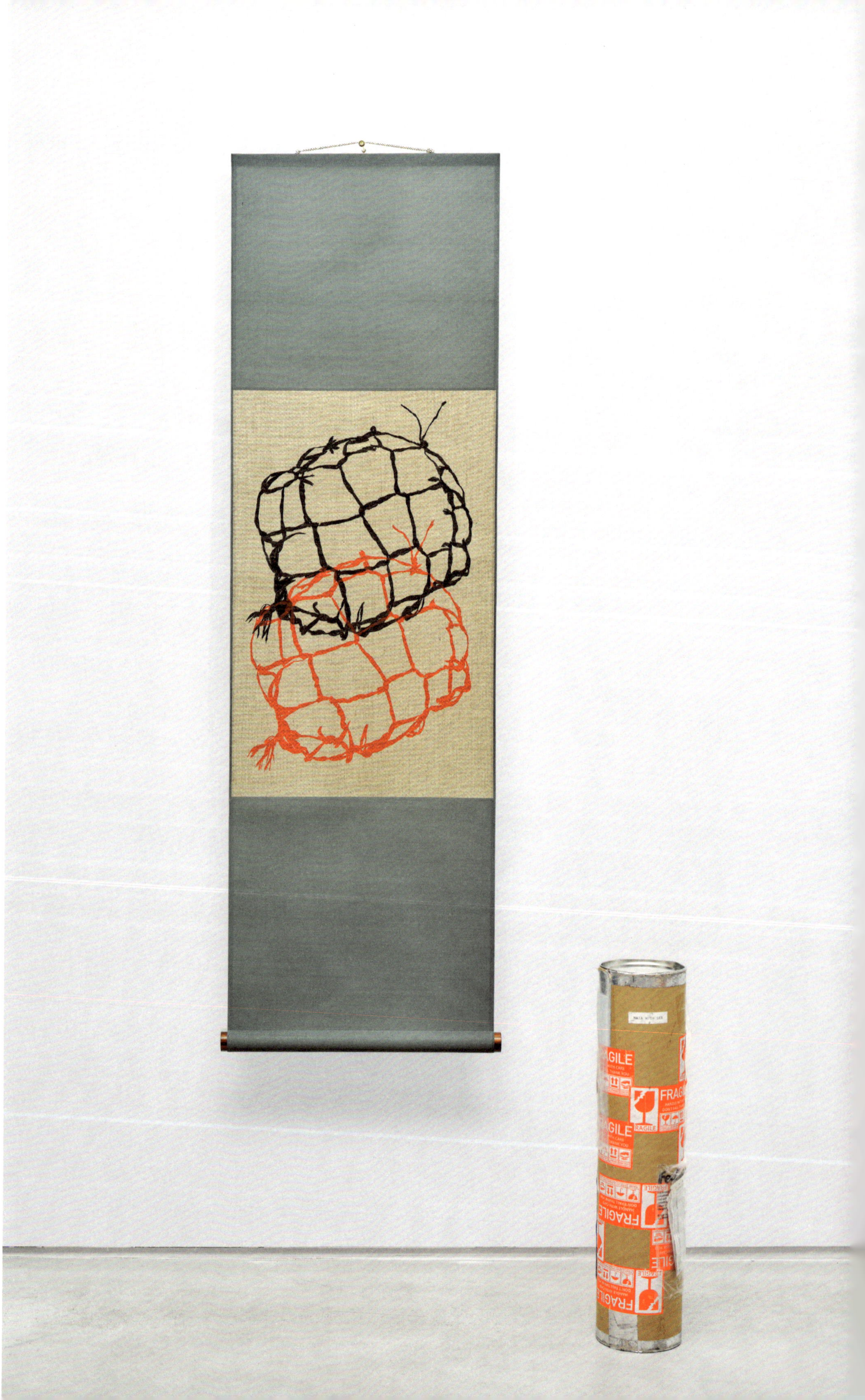
FRAGILE

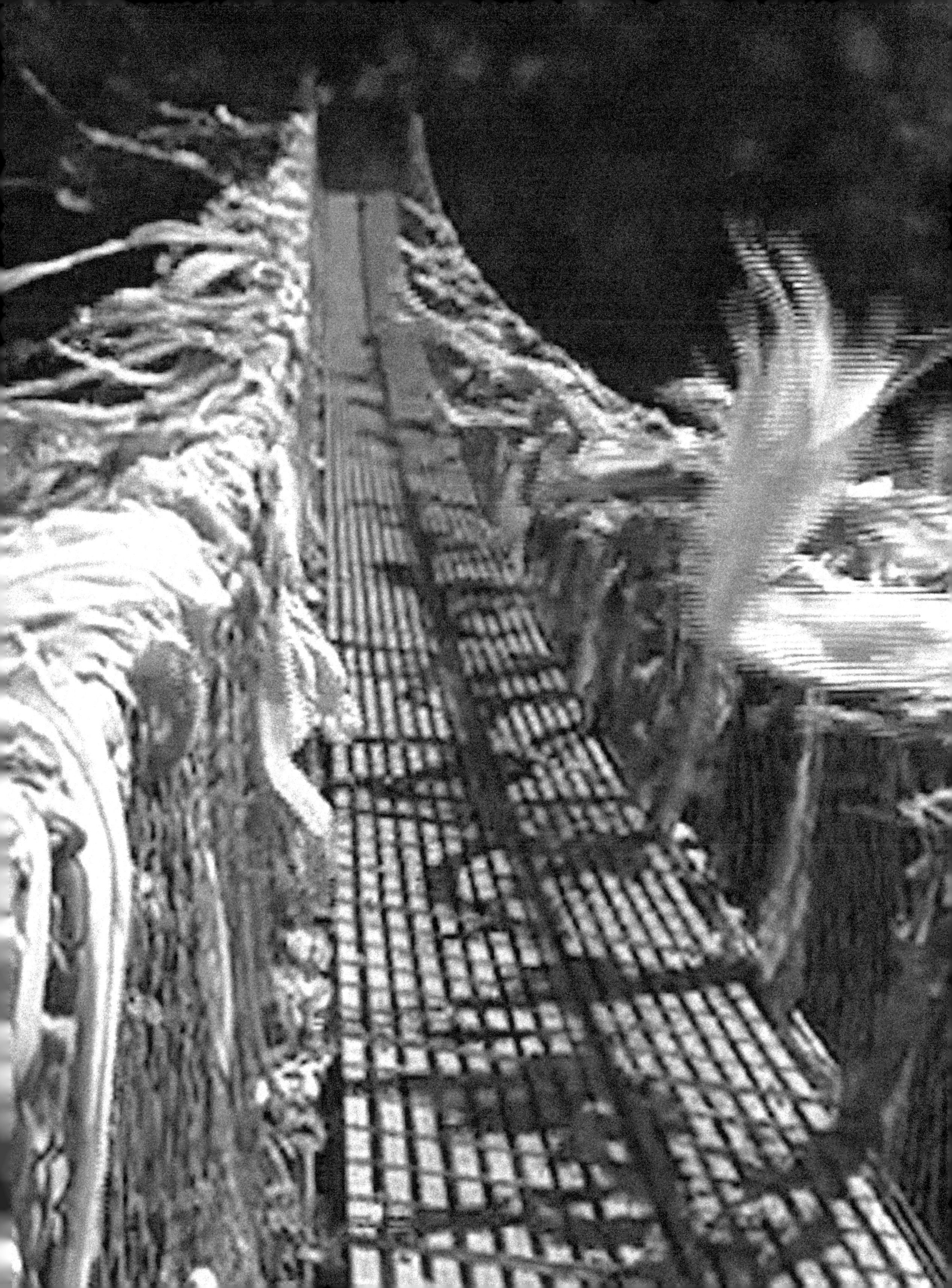

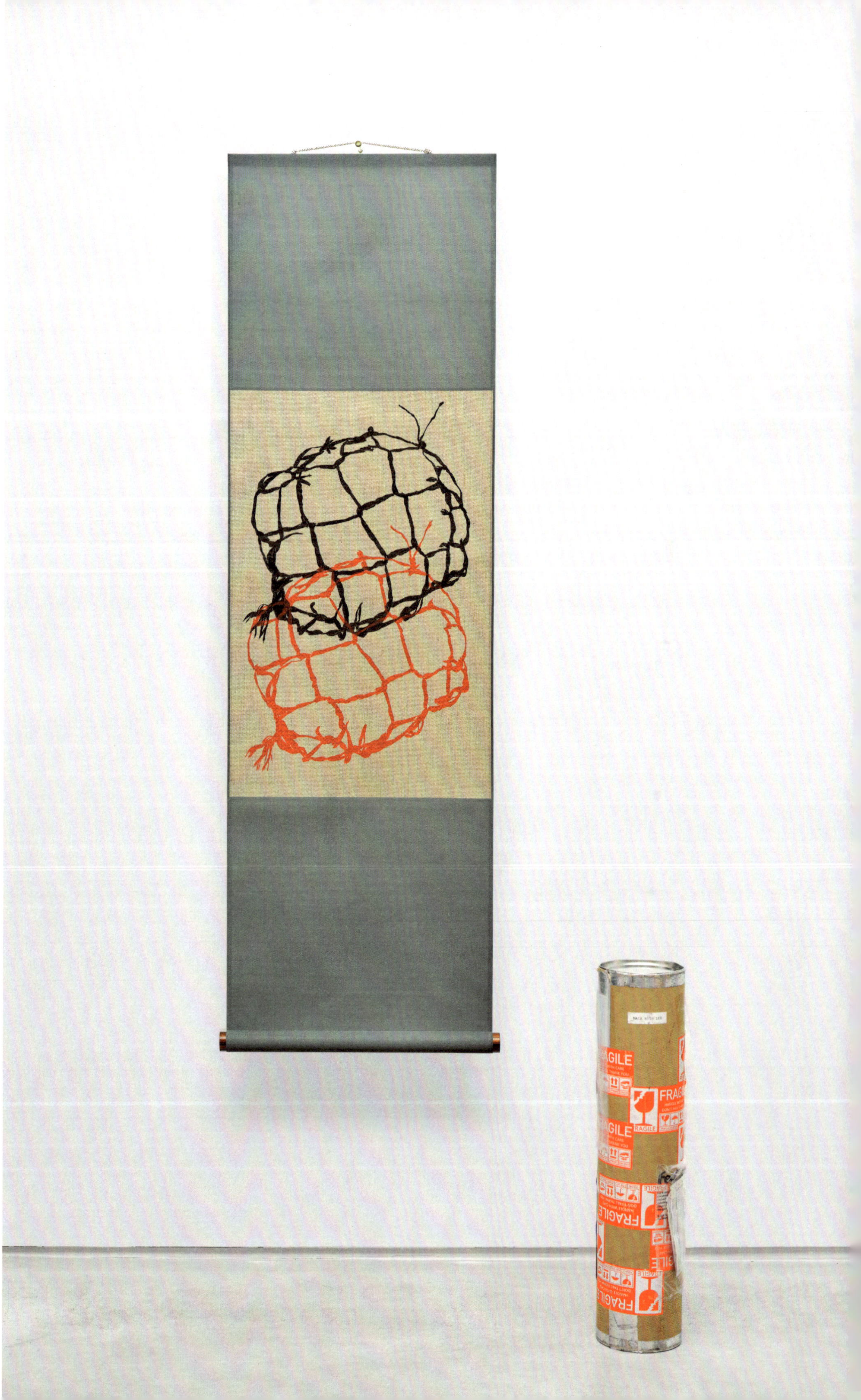
FRAGILE

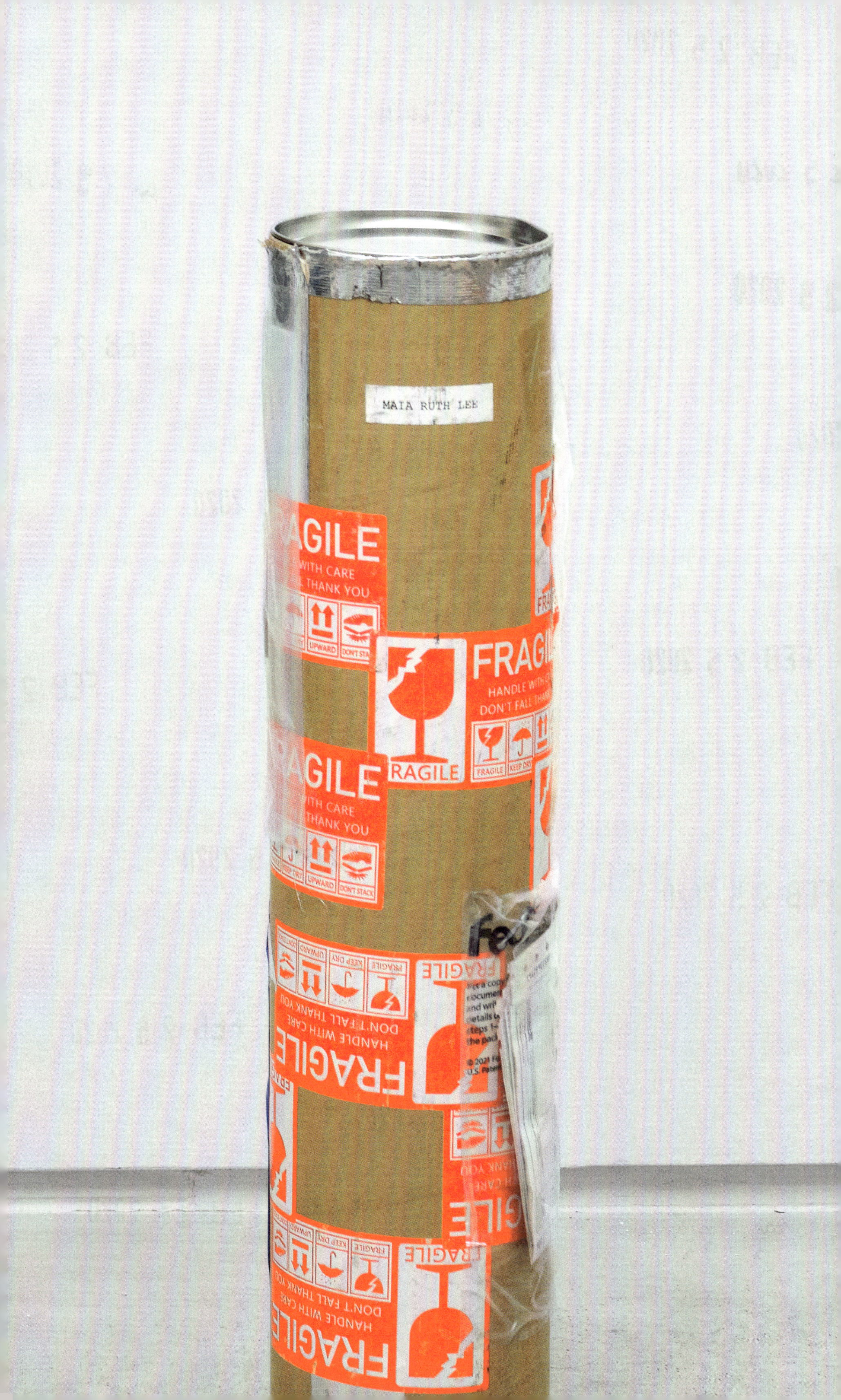
MAIA RUTH LEE
FRAGILE
HANDLE WITH CARE
DON'T FALL THANK YOU

FEB 25 2020
FEB 25 2020
FEB 25 2020
FEB 25 2020
FEB 25 2020
FEB 25 2020
FEB 25 2020
FEB 25 2020
FEB 25 2020
FEB 25 2020
FEB 25 2020

2024

"the year of tenderness"

- Tenderness will awaken the true meaning of care and community this year. Let this modetake over your central nervous system and feel the melting of a hardened heart. this year will break certain assumptions and judgements you carry. this is a good year to break the ahbig habit of jumping to conclusions.

-Take time to calibrate, the cogs of your mind + soul may feel misaligned. Spirituality is key this year. Your spiritual guide, whether in the form of a person, book ~~or~~ experience or place, will lead you to a new state of consciousness.

-unravel the tangled knots from within, one by one. the tangles are examples of a full life you have already lived. as you look at each tangle, admire its colors and energy. observe the tnderness it took ~~for you~~ to create its beautiful chaos. this year the chaos ~~may likely~~ continue, but you will find a brandnew perspective of it make sure you document each movement of your thoughts process, and you will find some v~~lau~~aluable clues.

-this is the year to lift the clouds. the air cleared, vision amplified. mind and body activated. place the tip of your fingers on your hearth chakra and feel the tenderness. this is the pl;ace where all your decisions should be made this year. the void you have been feeling should soon ~~b subside and~~ be filled withnew beginnings.

The fog will part + you can relax now. Concepts become clearer as you ~~start~~ to see that

- we are working for a revolution. you are at the precipice of collective change. small and large, you can make a huge difference if you yuse your voice. as socrates put it the secret of change is to focus all of your energy, not on fighting the old, but on building the new.

- don't wait for others to change first. that will only plant resentment in your heart. look deeply at what you want in others and exemplify with your own actions. true change comes when you can be moved by it. they will notice and t follow your h lead.

If you have felt you have become less reliable, that is probably because you have taken on too much.

- Doubts can kill more dreams than failure ever will. Doubts are b boomerangs with a vengeance. but remember you can always choose t not to throw them in the first place. this is the year to start shedding self doubts, and with less blockage you will see that your dreams are closer to reality than you think.

-Truth is like the sun; you can close your eyes but you cannot turn it off altogether. Actively seek the truth this year and keep facing towards the sun. Elevate your leadership by leaning into this truth; you- it will build you up and everyone around you.

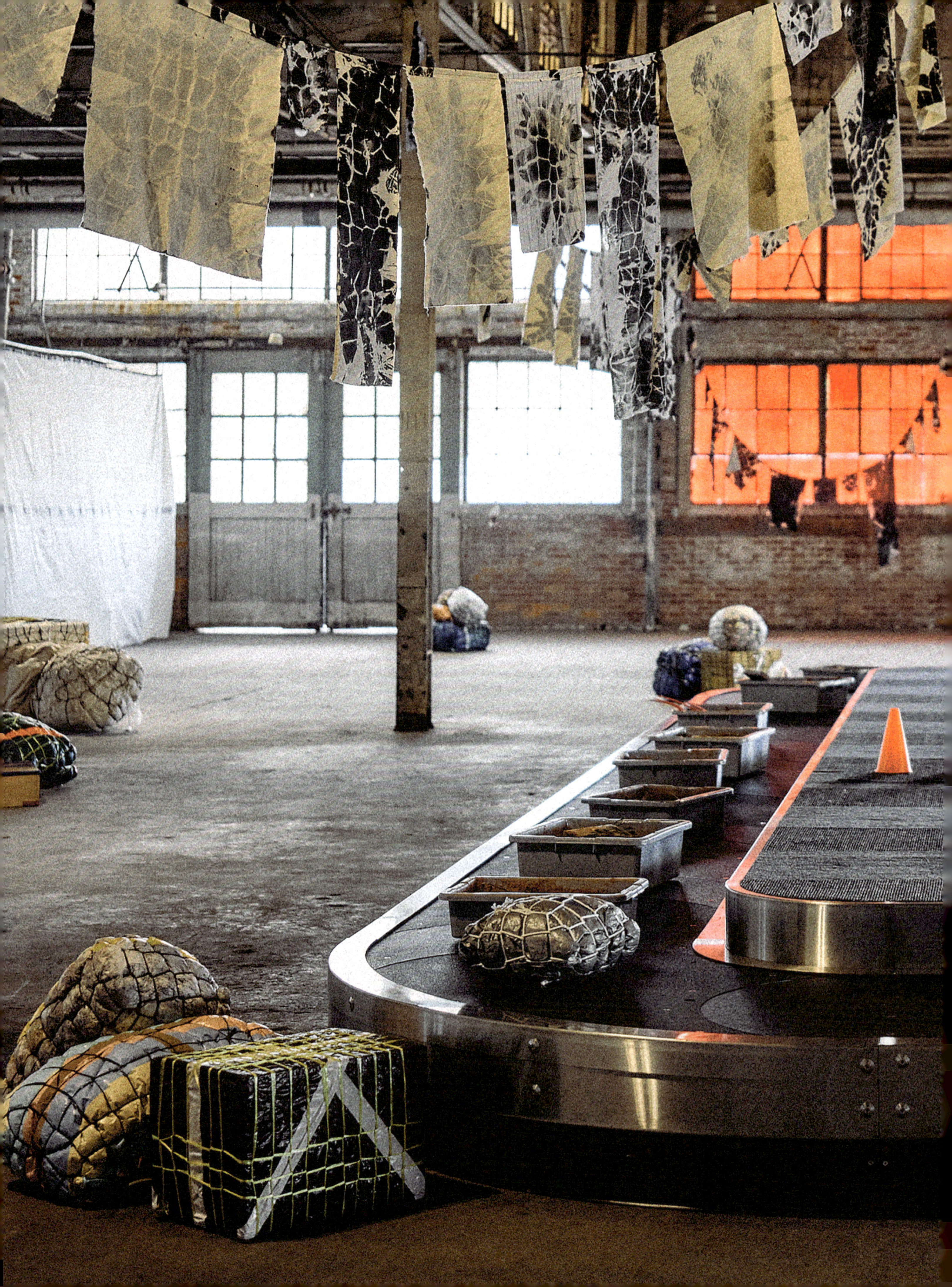

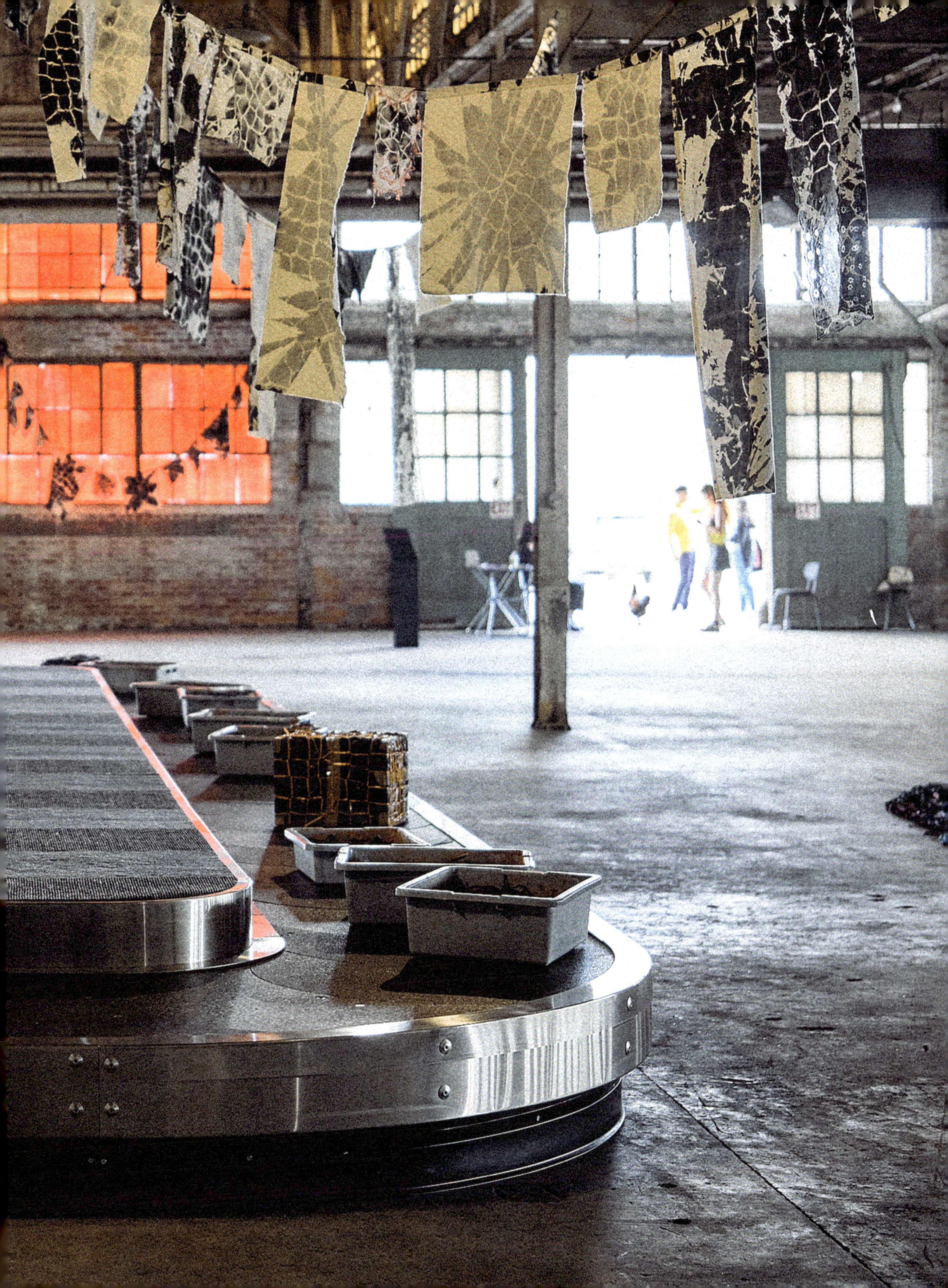

PAGES 160–161:

INSTALLATION VIEW OF **THE CONVEYOR**, 2024
in Prospect 6 Triennial, 2024
curated by Miranda Lash and Ebony G. Patterson
supported by Art Production Fund,
Ford Motor Plant, New Orleans, LA
courtesy of the artist and Prospect 6
photo: Alex Marks

OPPOSITE, PAGES 164–165 [DETAIL]:

INSTALLATION VIEW OF **HUMAN LIFE IN MOTION**
curated by Jade Foster, Primary, Nottingham, UK, 2025
courtesy of the artist and Primary, Nottingham, UK
photo: Reece Straw

PAGE 166:

INSTALLATION VIEW OF **B.B. PRAYER FLAGS,** 2025
India ink on textiles
courtesy of the artist and Mai 36 Galerie, Zürich, CH

PAGE 172:

B.B.M. 2-22 [DETAIL], 2024
acrylic ink on canvas
59¾ × 59¾ × 2 inches (151.8 × 151.8 × 5.1 cm)
courtesy of the artist and Tina Kim Gallery
photo: Hyunjung Rhee

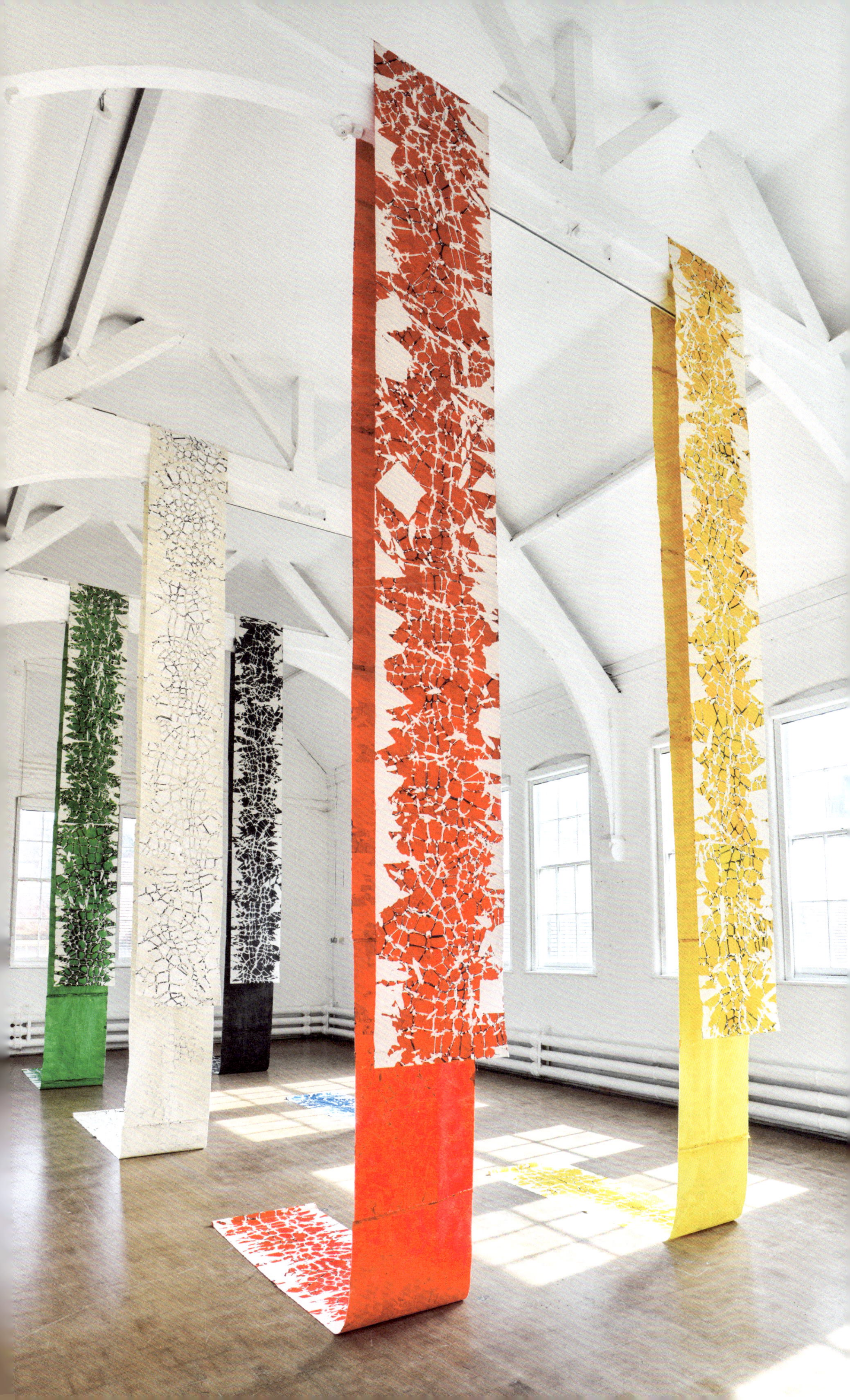

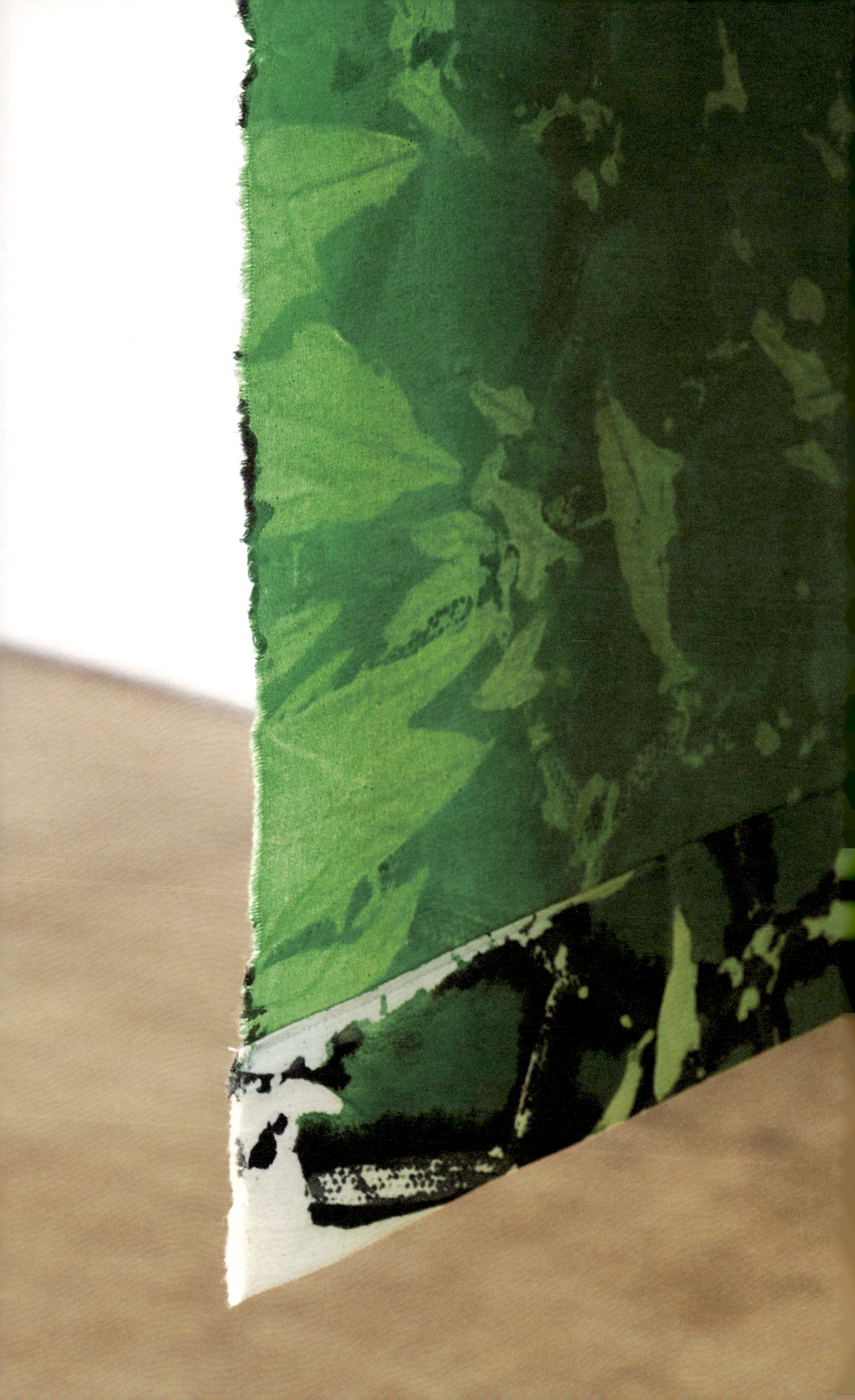

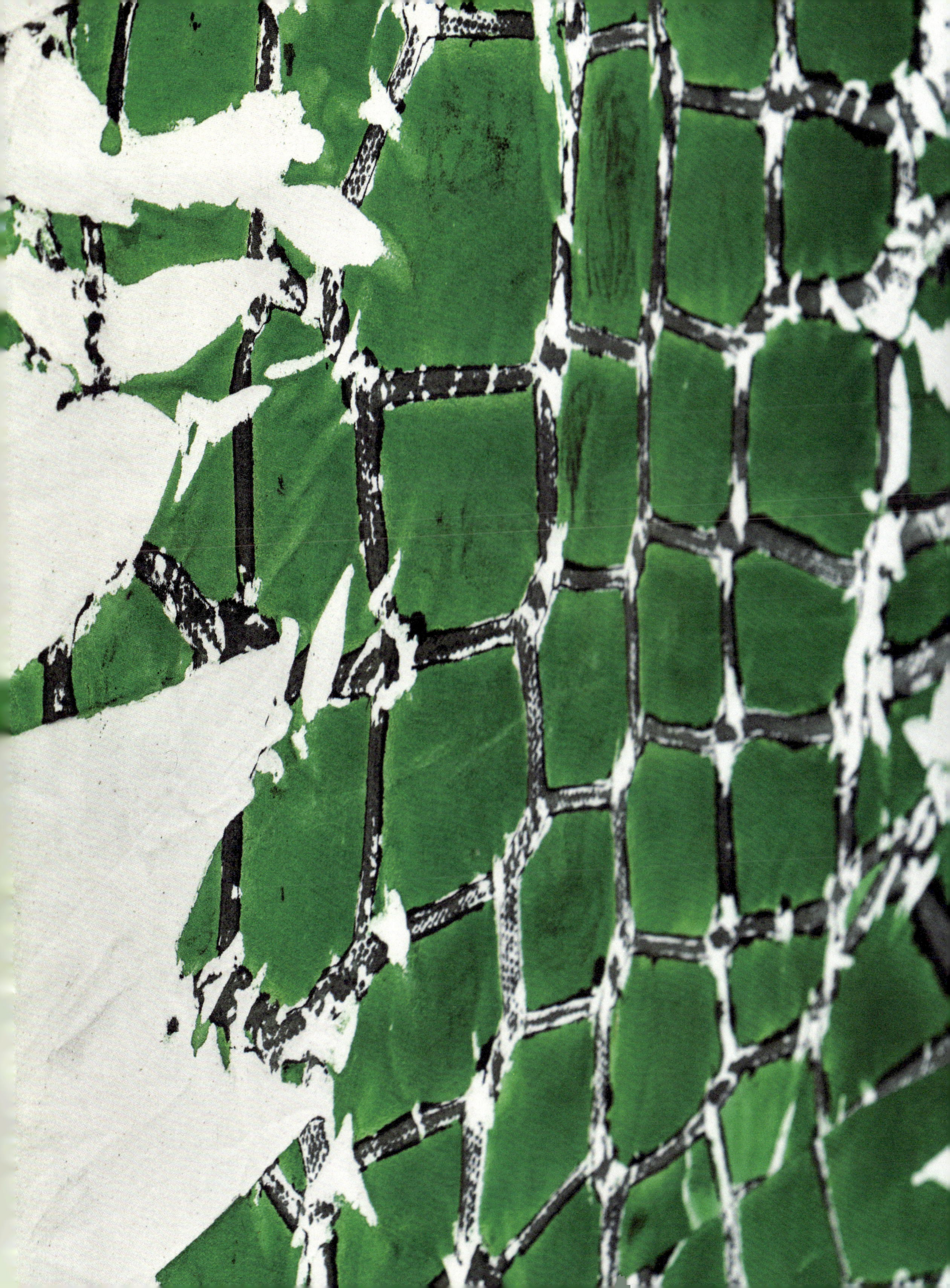

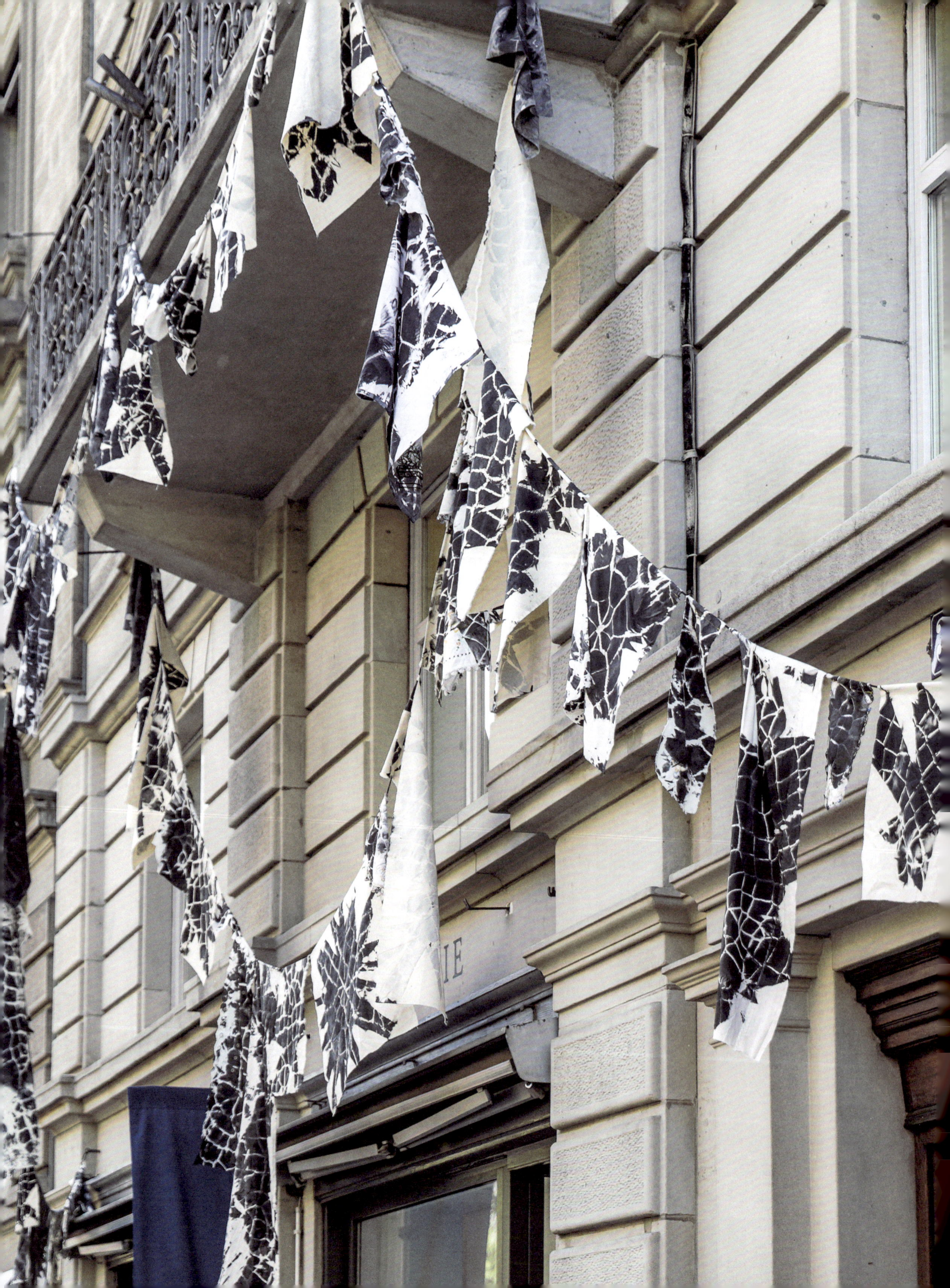

[]   ▌] [ ]]   [ ] [ ][ ][ ][ ][ ]][ ][ ][ ][ ]
guess the ten letter word

s t o r a g e b o x
h e a v y d u t y

]
askoqipogjp;bhp;j--   p;mnlkgnosbkjs pjlnkadnskjbadkj ca'la'klja
(nima)

i woke up today

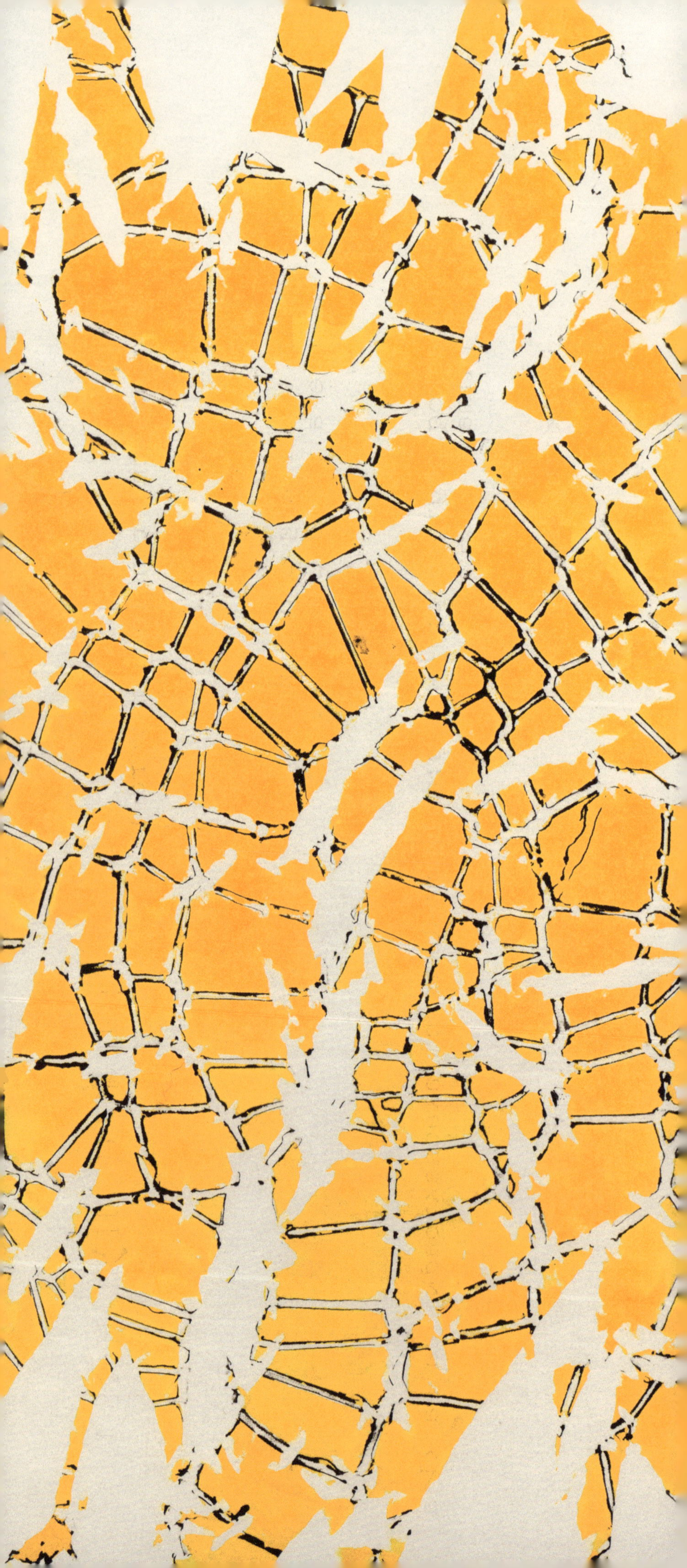

colonial knowledge systems are rapacious

(X) — stress apathy — guilt

october 22, 2024

i am dayt 2 on meds. first time inmy bl8fe i've been diagnosed with high adhd, with possibility of bipolar disorder.
i feel finally seend, been told that there are chemical reasons and not just crazy thinking. for as long as i can remember my life has been foggy and unclear. like light veil has always covered my view to the world, lifted only at unexpected times if i'm lucky. this veil has largely kept my own experience out of reach, almost as if i have to strain and lift myself out of my own body to get a better view, which results in great fragmentation from my own truth - my life has felt like someone else's . i've worked hard to clmain it as my own, take control and articulate it. everytime i c -lose my eyes i see faces, visions of the past that dash past me t -oo qu8ckly that i lose it again right away. i want toretrive all of those things, names, places, experiences but i simply cannot. i'm not sure if the meds will reboot my senses, but 41 years of my li8fe may be lost in the broken hard drive of my memeories. this year has been up and sdown in a way it has never been. almost daily i struggled to keep up with myself - my moods and my anxiety, i kept searching for some answers, but the moment i turn my head it would be lost in the fogginess. sometimes i'll see or read something like it is my first tije, only to - halfway through - realize i had already seen or read it before. this wi8ping of my mind, it happens so often so that it is aomost impossible for m -e to retain any information, let alone even things i have said. or promised. i want to be better. i want to wake up alive and not as if the ceiling is crubling over me. i want to look out into the world without dread and anxiety. i want to face nima and look him in the eye with confidence that everything will in fact be okay. but those confident moments come and go like the fluttering of butterlfly wings. by the time i turn to grasp it has completely disappeared. i am judgemental purely on the way i feelabout them. there is nologic to the way i judge, if the energy doesn't match mine i am keen to look away. it is not even worth my time. this arrogance i know will haunt my sleep, sometimes the things i disregard show up at night. as if to say - heay! that's not fair give me another chance and let me p]rove myself. i will still scof my work is making more sense to me as i uncover more of my mental states. yhe constant concealment and revealing is not just a coincidence, the act of cover and uncover, is beyond just an act, but a n obvsession i can't quite figure out why. i have built for myself a tall fort. i can look out but people cannot look in. i feel safe but utterly alone. i think it is safe to say that i n need to change something before i am forever changed.

(A woman of our group says: My village is the bundle on my back — Mahmoud Darwish)

Mu	무	巫

(two people dancing side by side) 人+人+工

= connects the two worlds (— of not singular but multiple)

무신간 → "god pillar" = apparatus to receive spirit / community

ie. vertically erect tree, a long stick, or mountain

→ a transporting device

OPPOSITE, PAGES 176–177 [DETAIL]:

B.B.M. 3-1, 2024
acrylic ink on canvas
63¼ × 57½ inches (161 × 146 cm)
courtesy of the artist and François Ghebaly, Los Angeles and New York
photo: Paul Salveson

PAGES 178–179:

INSTALLATION VIEW OF **THE CONVEYOR**, 2024
in Prospect 6 Triennial, 2024
curated by Miranda Lash and Ebony G. Patterson
supported by Art Production Fund,
Ford Motor Plant, New Orleans, LA
courtesy of the artist and Prospect 6
photo: Alex Marks

PAGES 180, 193:

INSTALLATION VIEW OF **THE STRANGER**, 2018
duration: 23:45, color, sound; in *Mountain/Time*,
curated by Chrisse Iles, Simone Krug, and Anisa Jackson
Aspen Art Museum, Aspen, CO, 2022

PAGES 181–192:

THE LETTER [STILLS], 2023
duration: 22:23; color, sound

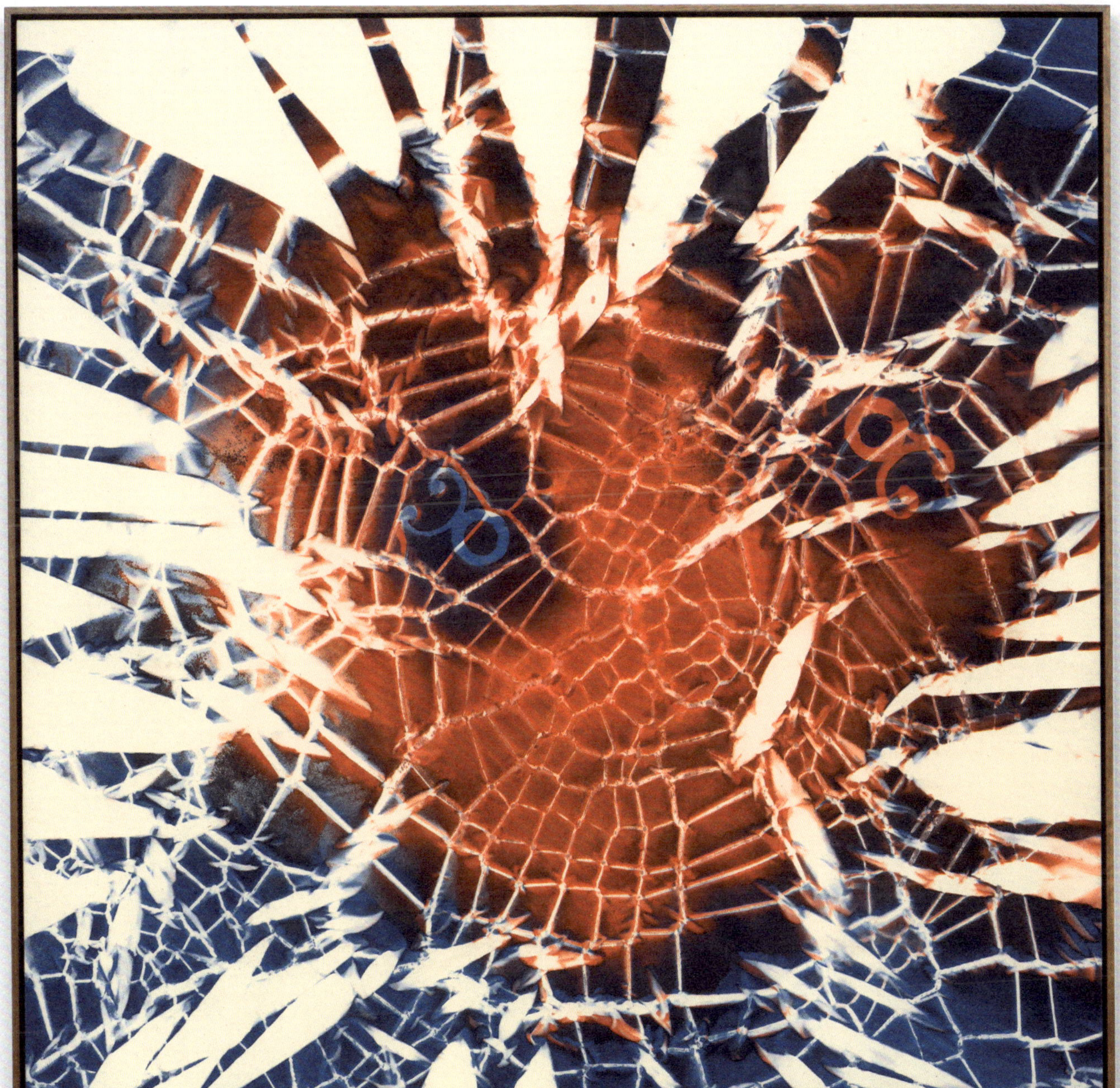

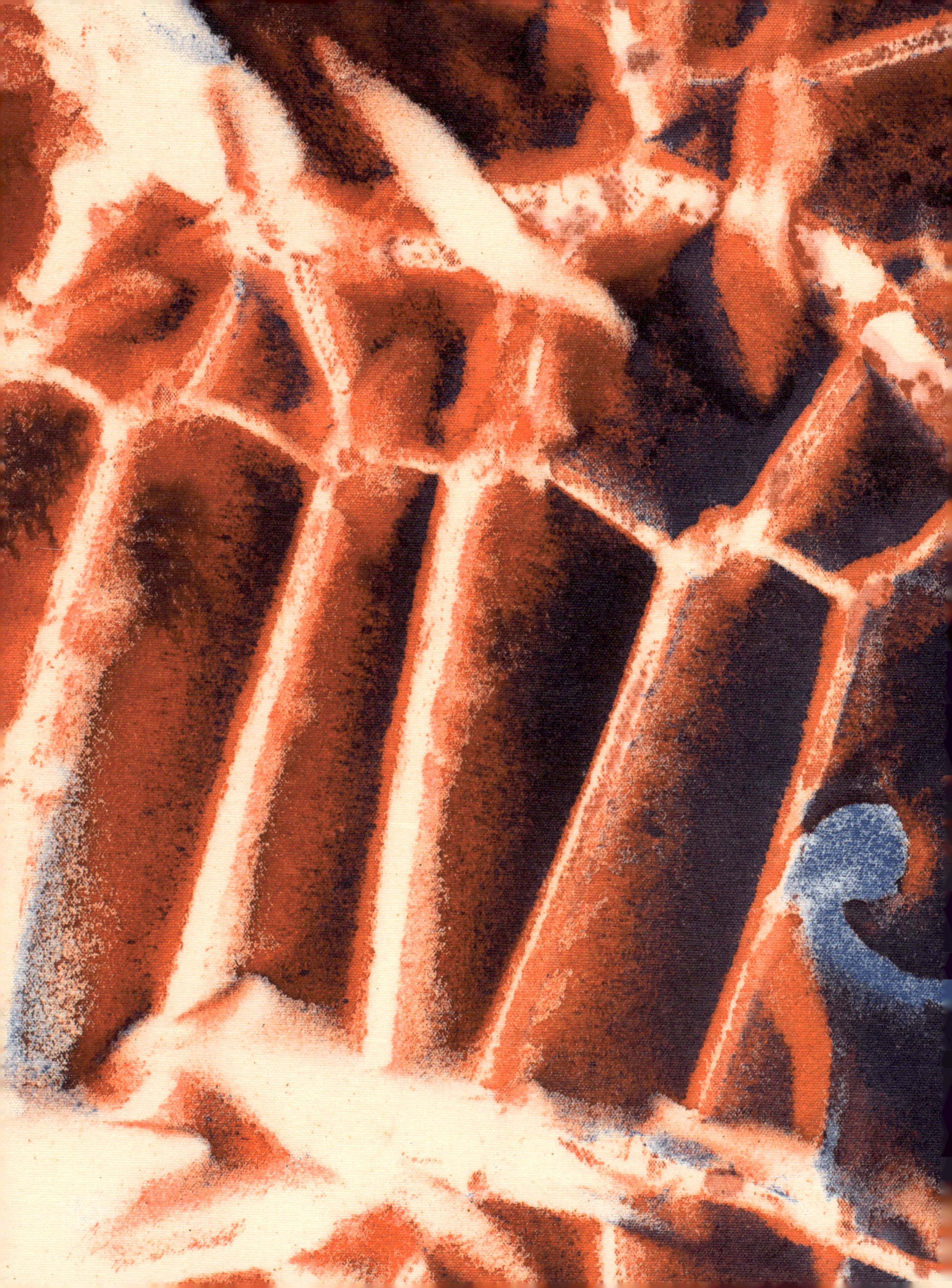

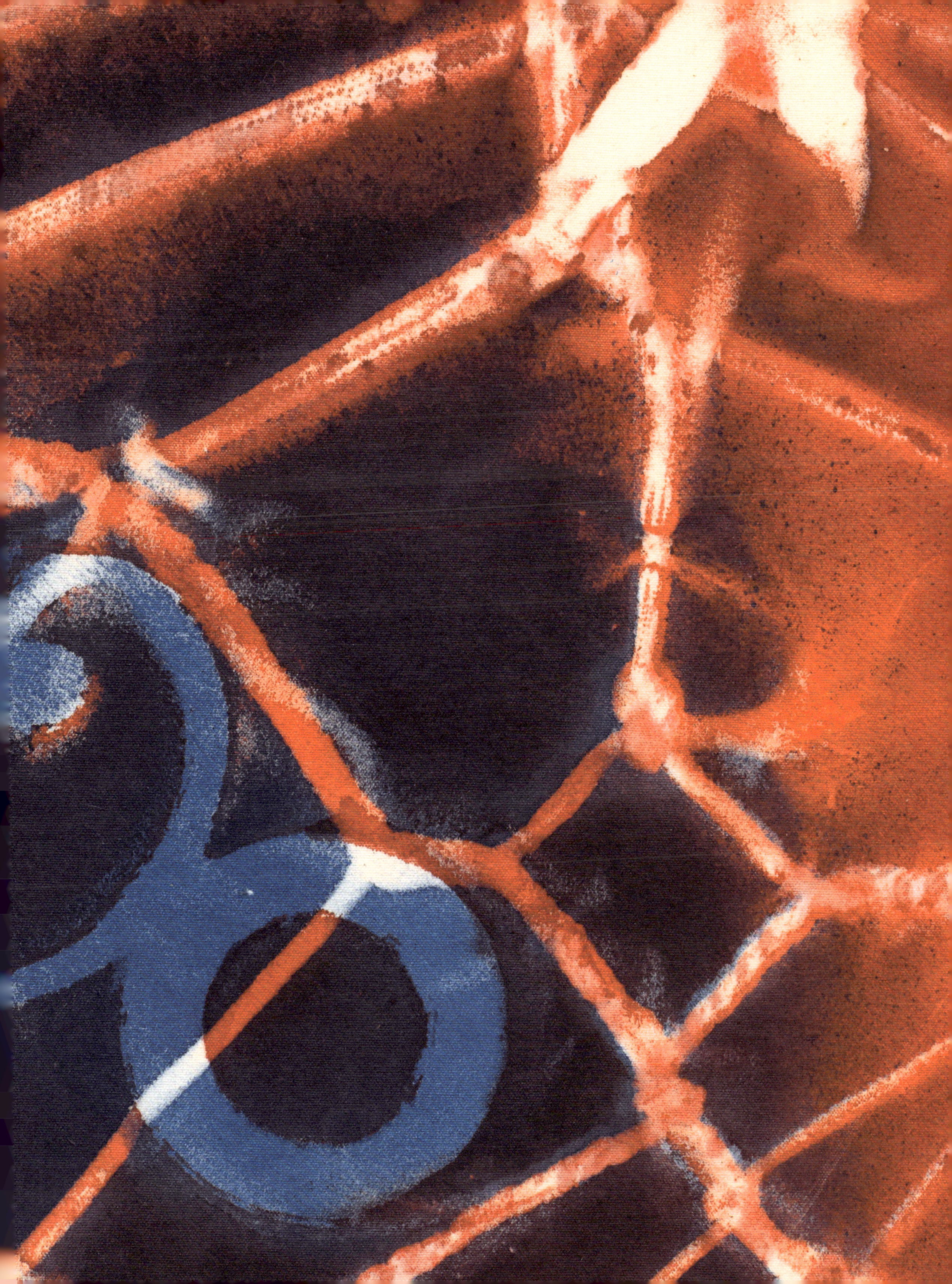

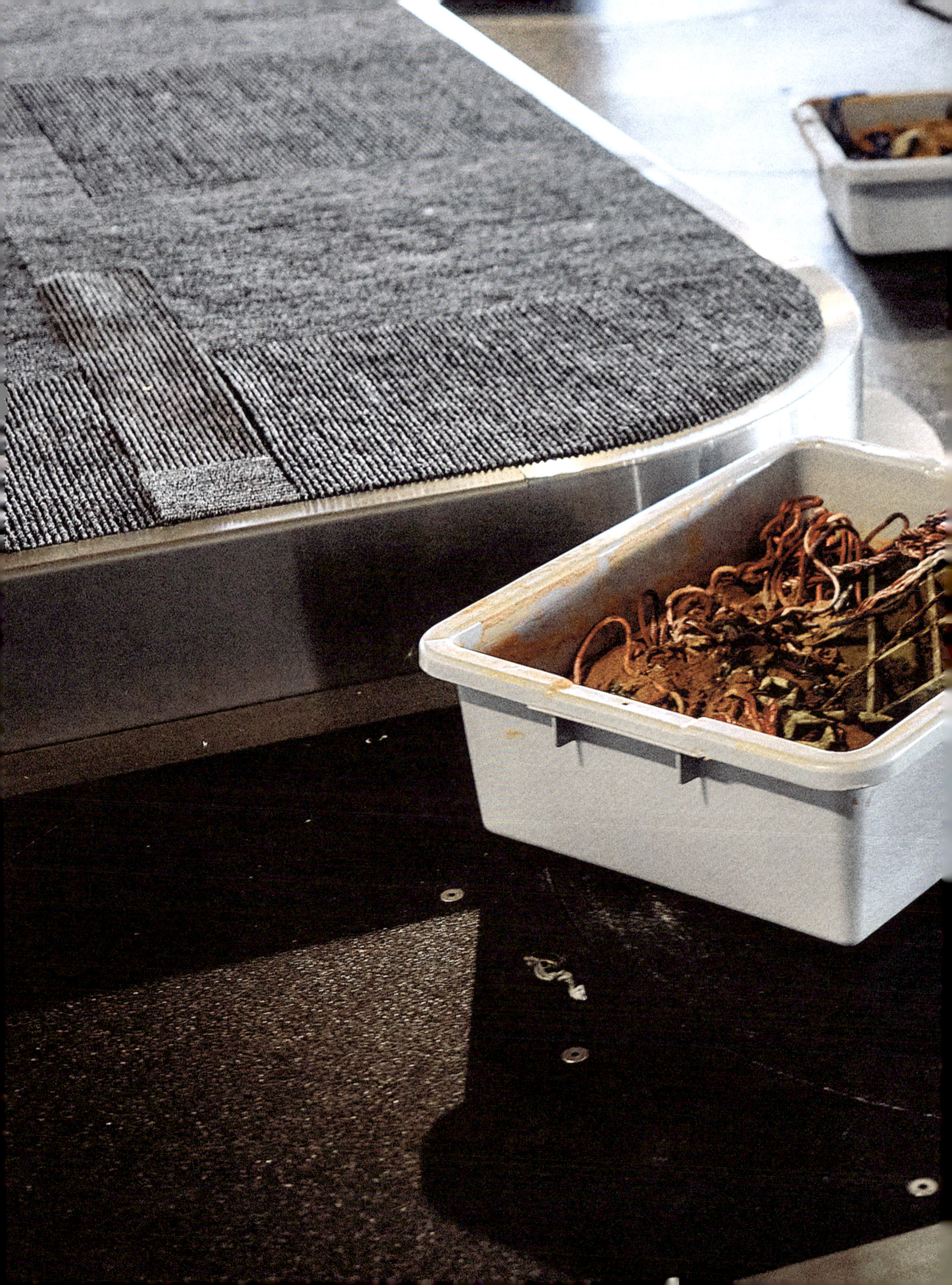

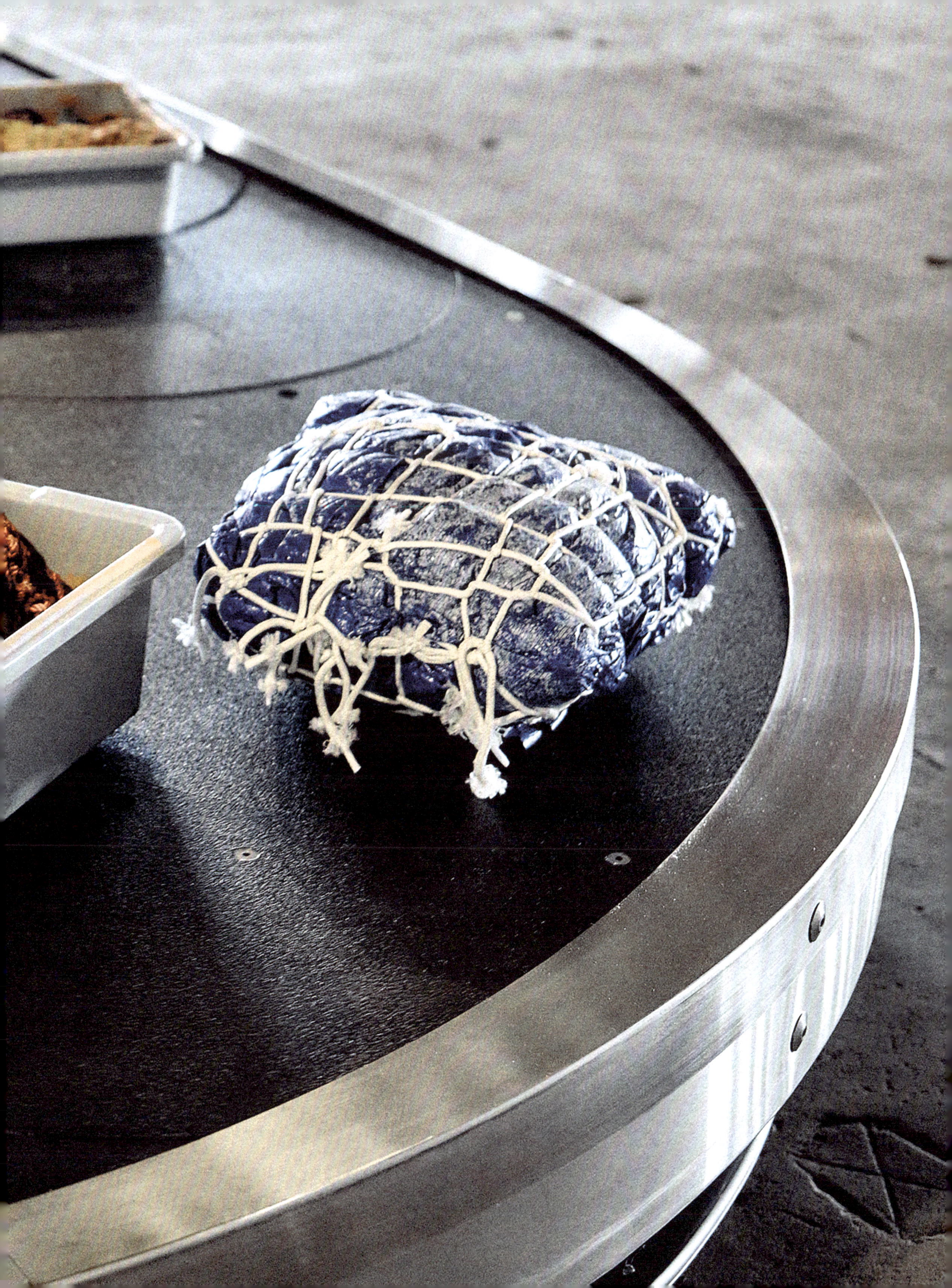

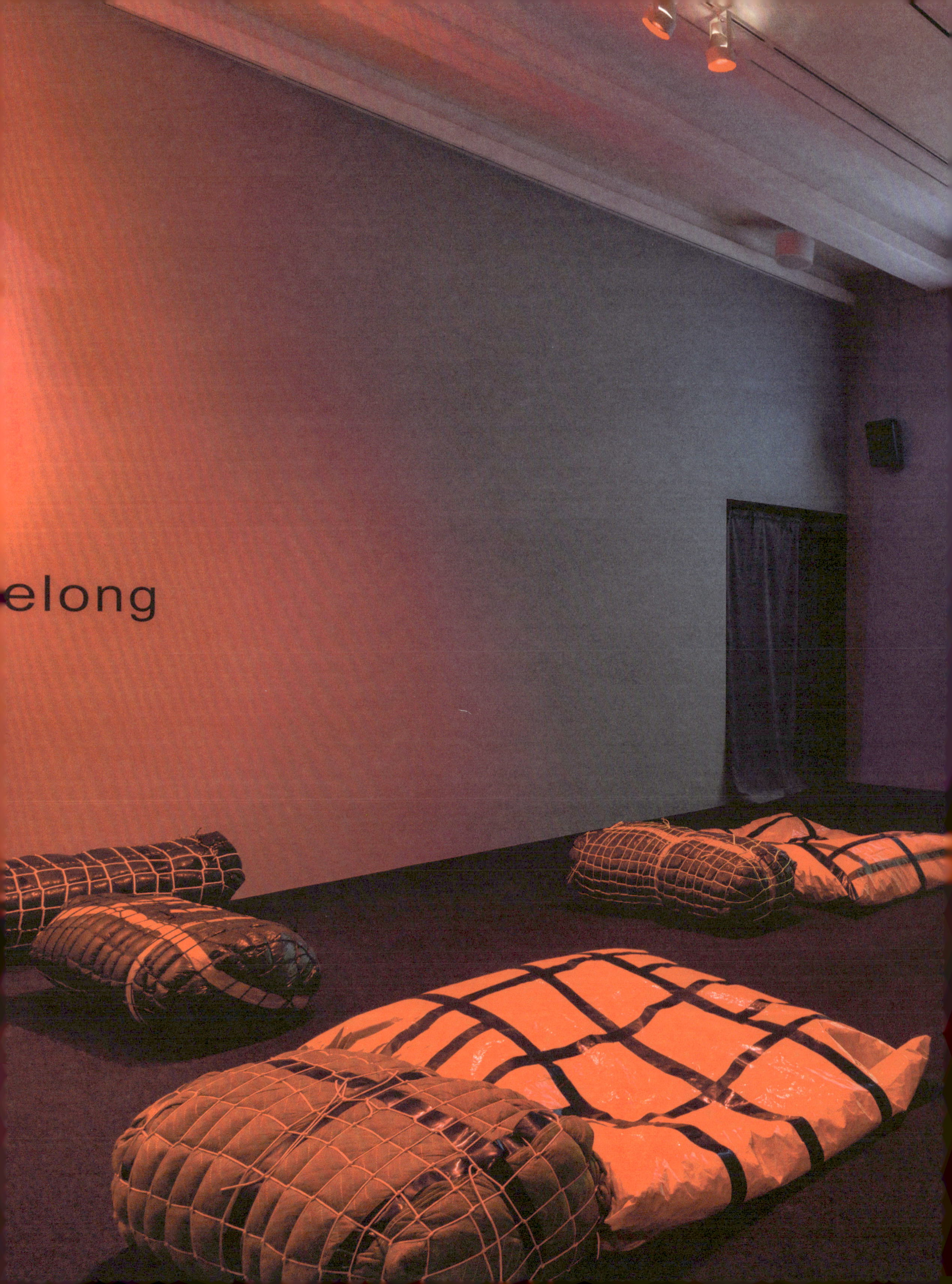
elong

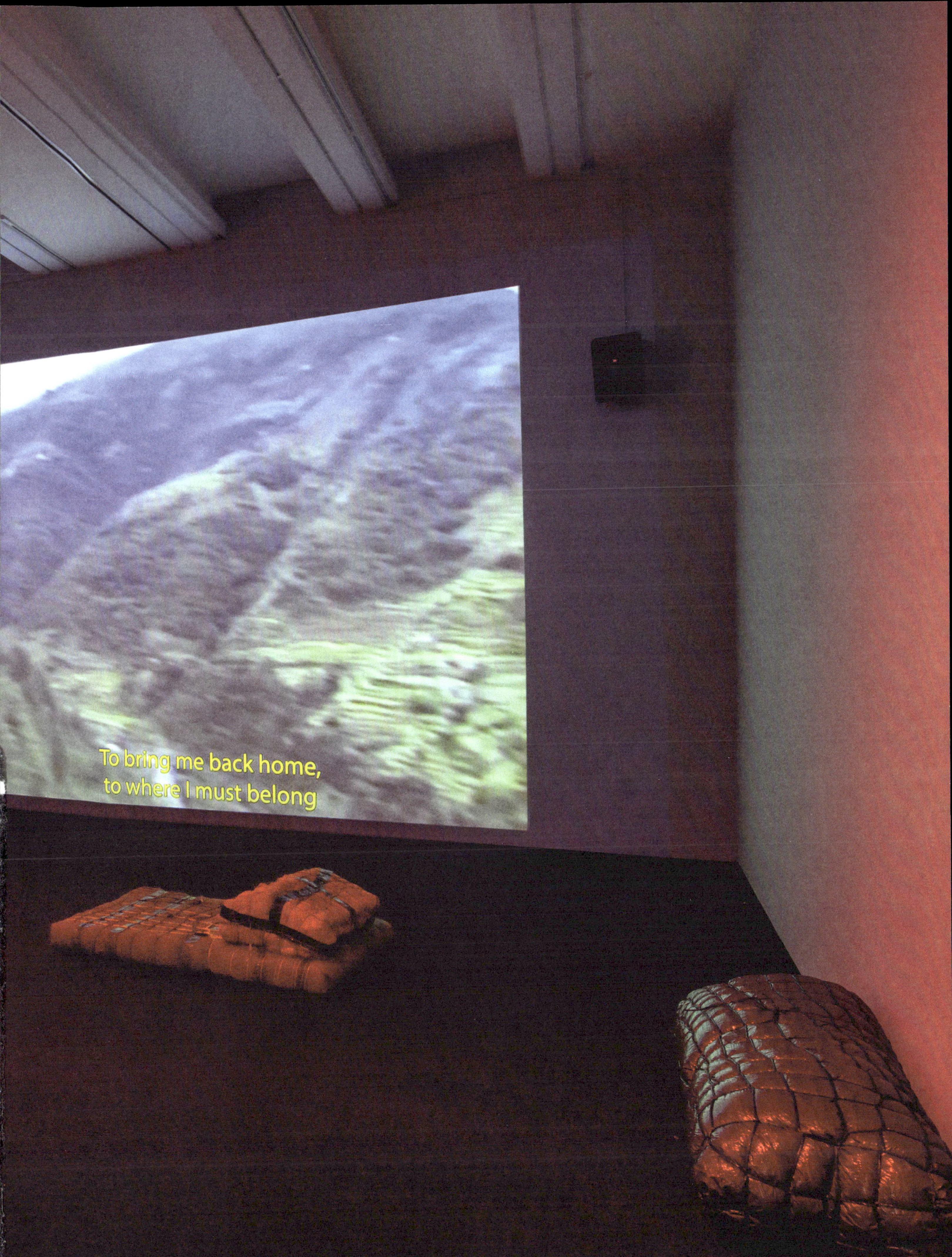
To bring me back home,
to where I must belong

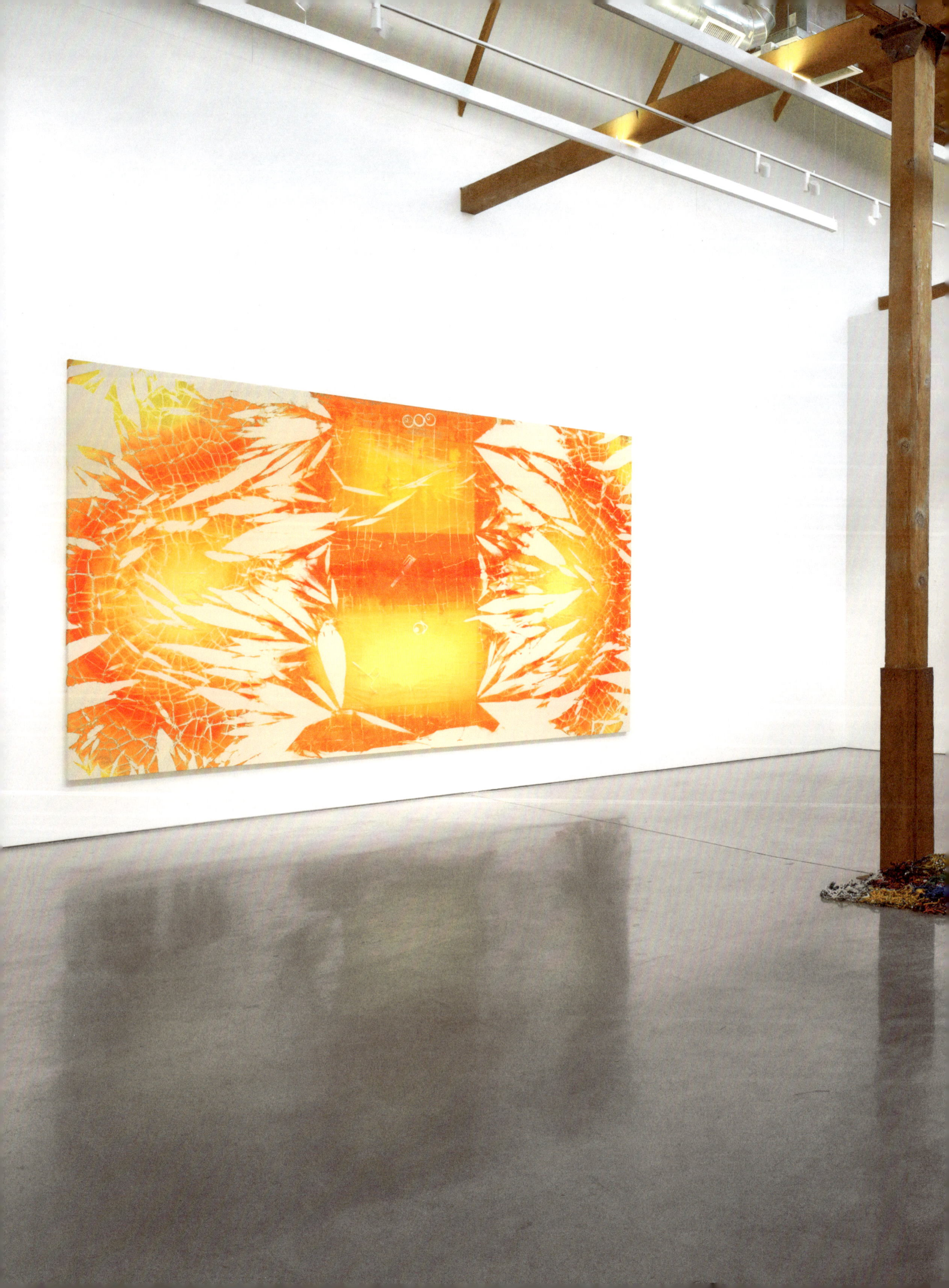

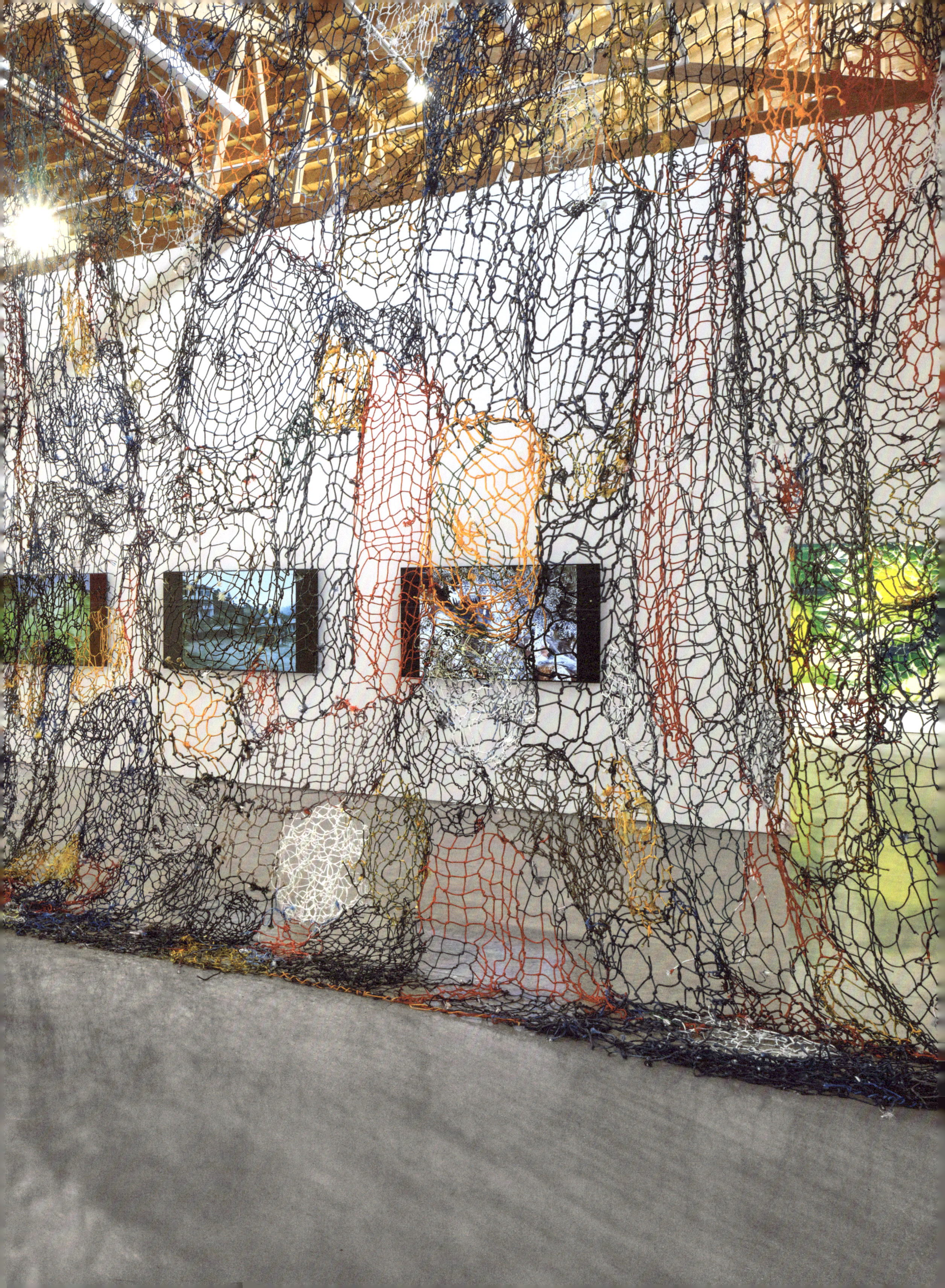

in early september the tepperature dropped from 90s to 30s in a matter of days, freezing the landscape and even morese with a blizzard snow storm. the trees creaked in pain and anguish, dropping sideways with unbearable weight, no one, not even the birds knew what was to come, and to their horror most freezed overnight, some found huddled together on the freezing ground. more upsetting to me than the idea of climate change, was the feeling of inevitable doom that was now so visible before me. a pile of dead birds, there is nothing more upsetting than this. nothing more symbolic, nothing more metaphoric. no one to warn us of any danger. we are alone in our own mess. birds are the symbols of freedom, life, rebirth, intelligence, peace hope, love and so much more. they have the ability to roam the earth and fly in the skies. but spiritually, they are considered messengers from the spiritual realms. but a dead bird, a dead bird symbolizes deaparted souls, soetimes immprtality. more specifically, it symbolizes the end of something and the start of something else. if this is true, than what are we parting with and what are we about to embark on? perhaps their death is the message, the message that change can only be the answer.

PAGES 194–195:

INSTALLATION VIEW OF **MAIA RUTH LEE: HOLD SHIMMER WIND**
François Ghebaly, Los Angeles, CA, 2024
courtesy of the artist and François Ghebaly, Los Angeles and New York
photo: Paul Salveson

PAGES 200–201, 202–203 [DETAIL]:

B.B.WEBS, 2024
acrylic ink on canvas
121 × 184 inches (307.3 × 467.4 cm)
courtesy of the artist and Jeffrey Deitch, Los Angeles
photo: Charles White/JW Pictures

PAGE 204:

BONDAGE BAGGAGE VERTICAL, 2023
rope, India ink, glue
187 × 41 × 39 inches (475 × 104.1 × 99.1 cm)
in *Revolt of the Body*, curated by Simon Wu
Tina Kim Gallery, New York, NY, 2024
courtesy of the artist and Tina Kim Gallery
photo: Susan Behrends Valenzuela

MRL,

It is one thing to have a vision, but it is another to materialize it. It is one thing to imagine a destination, but it is another to take the journey to be there.

What makes us leap?
What makes us do what we do, and how do we do it?
What do we value, what makes us more whole, who we are?
What do we choose to hold on to?

How do we move through this world, unrooted and/or fractured, and still remain connected to ourselves and one another? Especially those who are forced into movement, violently thrust into worlds of borders and limitations imposed by the fear and lovelessness of others?

How did we get from "heres" to "theres" when we cannot yet see the way?

How can we begin to grasp and gather others' multitudes until we have woven our own ropes into a web strong enough to bind us together with ourselves, with the misty world that we move through, that we move all kinds of our things through?

We stay moving, gathering, bonding, breaking, and binding together, spread it out, and repeat it again, ad infinitum.

Baggage in all its forms—some have so much to carry and others carry almost nothing at all, by choice or privilege or fate. Sometimes luck, sometimes willingness, sometimes misfortune, sometimes it's just sometimes—it is always just the way that it is.

What do we choose to continue to carry with us and why?
How do we choose what we need to carry now for a future we haven't met yet?

Do we choose for utility, for love, for safety in a world and time where most things feel precarious? How is who we are just as much what we carry as things themselves?

I would like to think that we choose to carry each other in love, that our relationships are the frameworks that give form to our nebulous selves. We tie our ropes together into infinite shapes, amorphous containers that accommodate the unique quality of existing amongst infinite universes of other beings.

I wonder what I would want you to know if I wasn't here to tell you anymore. I think it would be to remind you that you are a force of energy, an embodiment of dreams once carried, now manifest. How you are what it means to build yourself and your world with the pieces you find and gather from all around the self. A life well lived with intention, care, awareness, love, compassion, patience, beauty. Impressive not in your productivity but in your expansive talents for connection with other beings, with being present in love and curiosity in a world designed to foreclose possibility. You are so precious and rare. Twin soul, friend of a long time, likely lifetimes. Different paths and places, yet so much we find is the same. What a joy to see myself in your brilliant mirror, to tie my rope to yours. I'll always love you.

Yours,
AAA

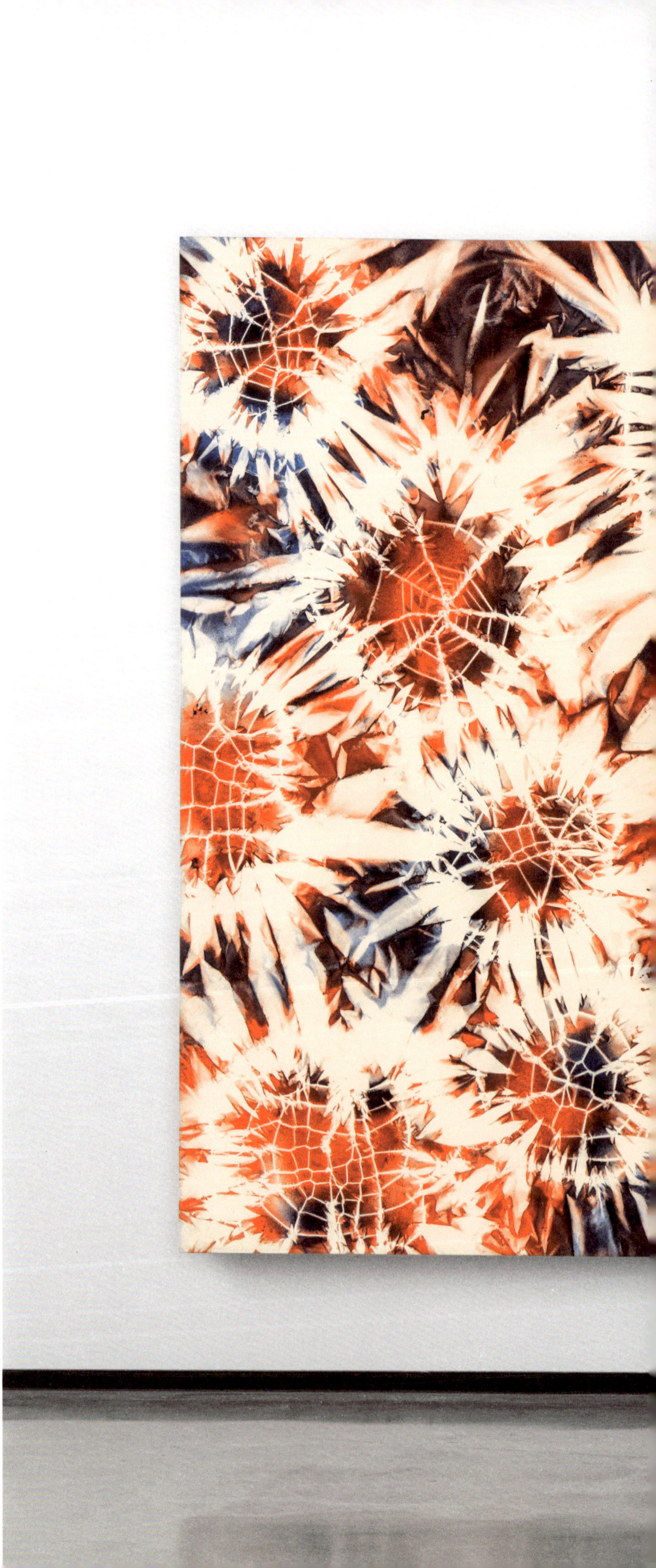

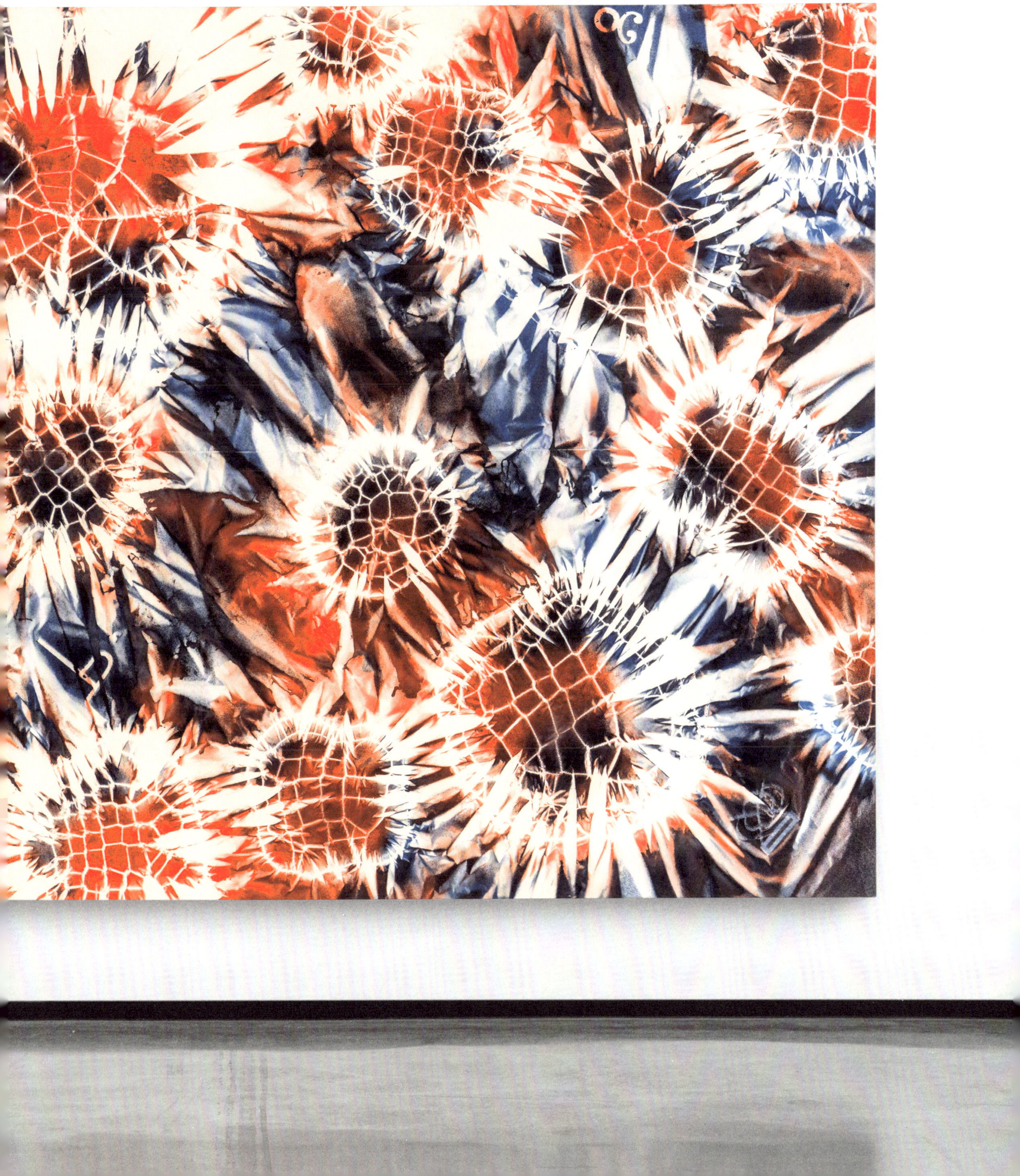

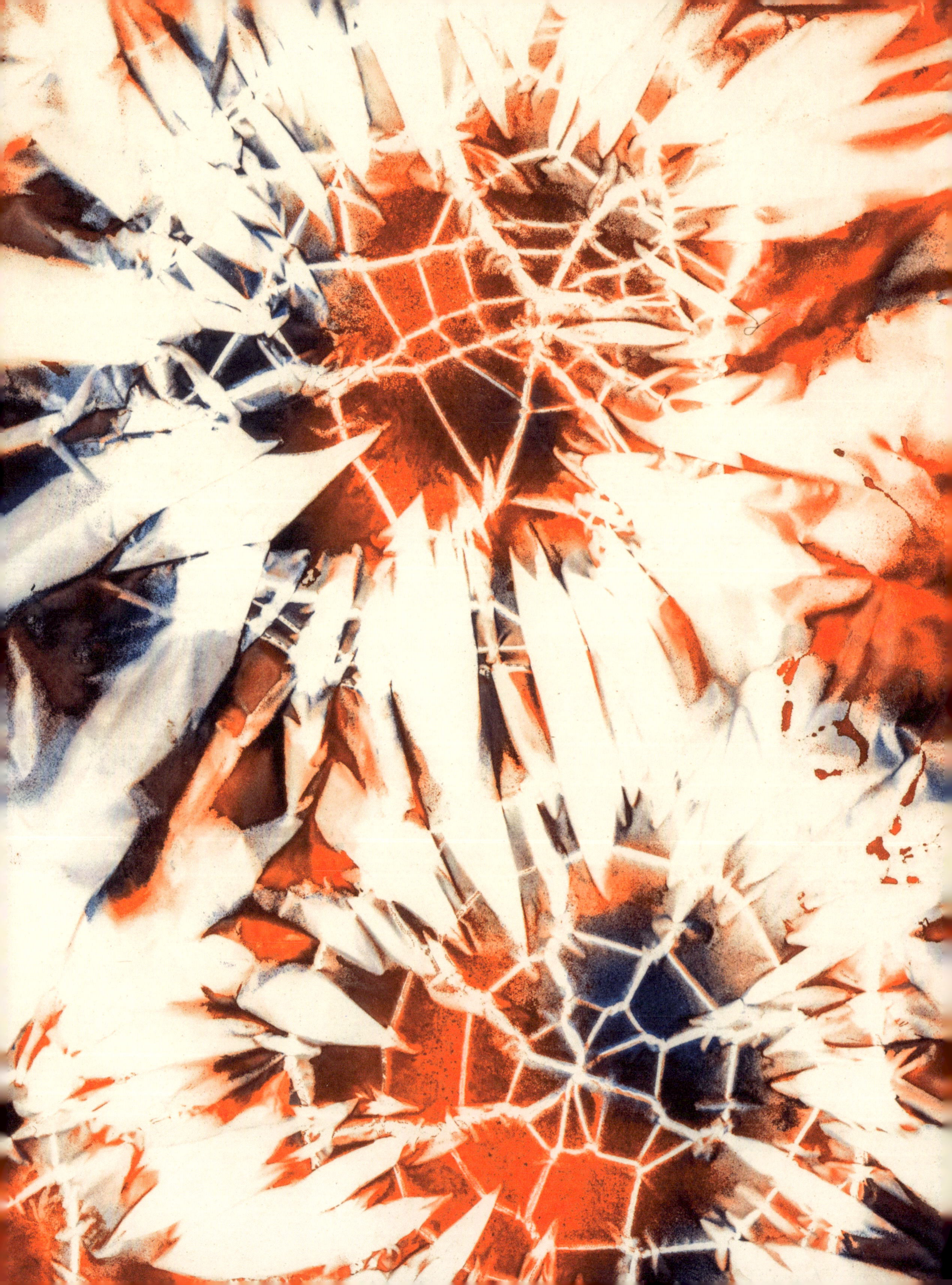

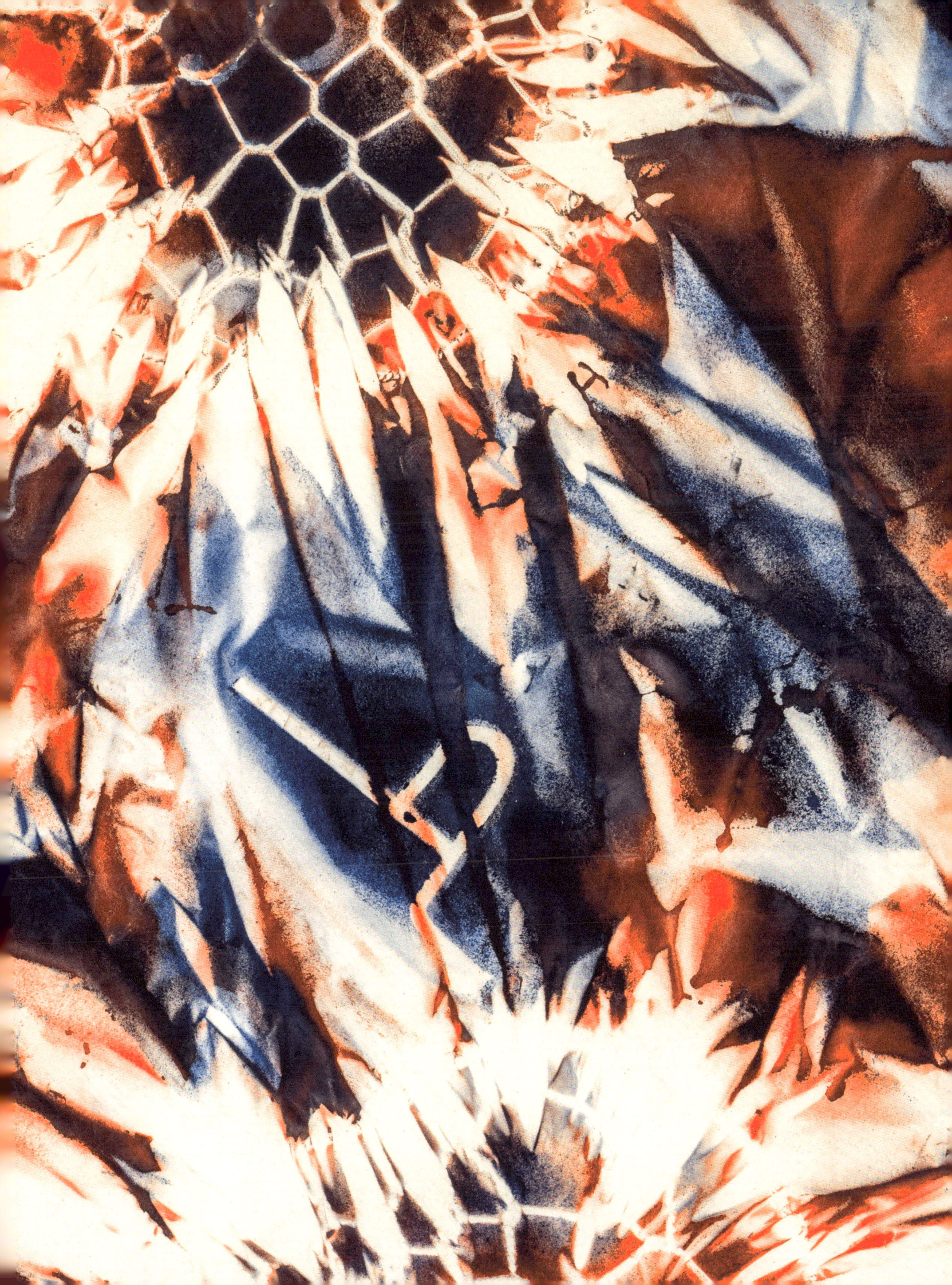

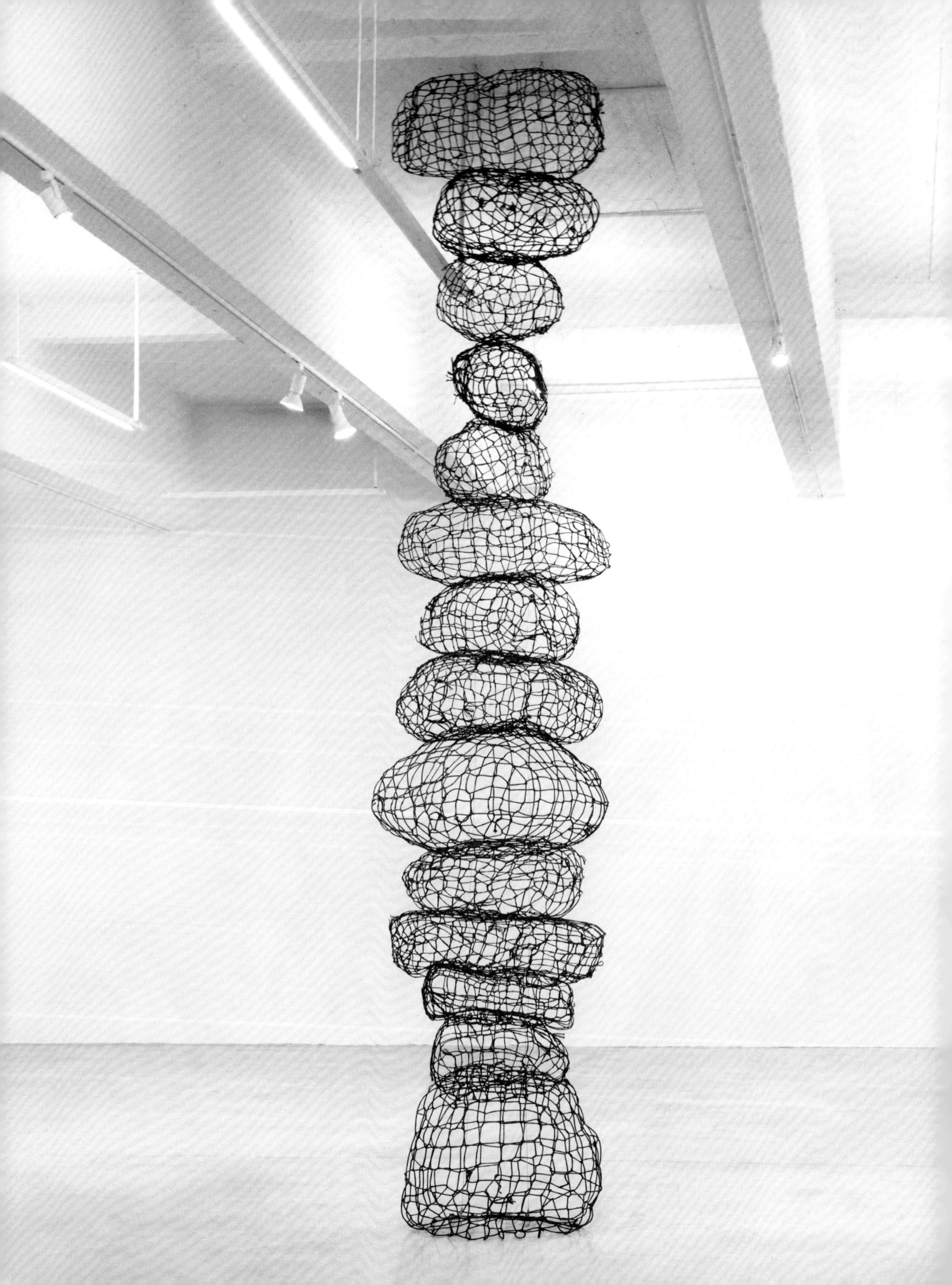

ACKNOWLEDGMENTS

The works in this book carry traces of many people, places, and moments—none of which exist in isolation. I'm thankful to everyone who supported, challenged, and tolerated me, and especially to Amanda Minami + Radius Books for extending the life of this work through this beautiful book. This book speaks to a kind of suspended arrival—a gentle trajectory toward something sensed but not yet reached. It is both an endpoint and a beginning.

[in no particular order]

David Chickey, Nick Larsen, Inga Hendrickson, Tina Kim, François Ghebaly, Shawn Larsen, Olivia Oyamada, Jane Panetta, Jade Foster, Yoma Ru Smith, Nora Abrams, Casey Fremont, NayanTara Gurung Kakshapati, Jimin Seo, Miranda Lash, Chrissie Iles, Candace Squire, Cole Lu, Elizabeth Jaeger, Miyoung Lee, Christine Sun Kim, Jordan Nassar, Valerie Rose, Violet Dennison, Rujeko Hockley, Jenny Le, Aine Vonnegut, Gan Uyeda, Amanny Ahmad, Megan + Dan Lombardo, Sandeep Salter, Ebony G. Patterson, Ellie Hunter, Sonya Sombreuil, Fern Clark, Farah Al Qasimi, Morgan Connellee, Brook Hsu, Martine Syms, Eliza Ryan, Henri Gisler, Victor Gisler, Francesca Wade, Kelly Huang, Stella Bottai, Kathleen Lynch, Sara Gates, Alexann Susholtz, Mariel Williams, Lyndsy Welgos, Frances Perkins, Lele Saveri, Jiminie Ha, Tauba Auerbach, Hyunjung Rhee, Zadie Xa, Gabrielle Rucker, Julia Trotta, Blaize Lehane, Priscilla Jeong, Eli Ping, Jim Mangan, Pia Sofyanti, Stephanie LaCava, Emma Allen, Ingrid Song, Cynthia Leung, Ana Kraš, Jaye Kim, Daniel Piwowarczyk, Kenny from ship'n'things, Shaniqwa Jarvis, Raj Debah, Maria de Victoria, Cathy Park Hong, Nick Stillman, Hannah Sage Murphy, Lily Foster, Minsun Jeon, Diamond Stingily, Lotus L. Kang, Aayushi Khowala, Jane Kim, Jack Hanley, Felix Harlan, Junni Chen, Amanda Marsalis, Alia Dahl, Nina Veazey, Ruiqi Wang, Malaika Newsome, Clarice Lee, Fiona Yu, Catherine Quan Damman, Diana Seo Hyung Lee, Andrew Sutherland, Kristina Klochok, Agathe Pinard, Danielle Lindenbaum, Valeria Napoleone, Simon Wu, Gala Porras Kim, Darren Tuozzoli, Carolina Ebeid, Jim + Jan Weston, 엄마, 아빠, 오빠, and Peter + Nima, thank you for it all.

Letter writing has long been a way that Maia Ruth Lee has maintained contact and reached out across distance to her community all over the country and around the world. That practice took on new significance during the COVID-19 pandemic and Lee's subsequent move, with her family, to a small mountain town in rural Colorado. In addition to letters she wrote—some reproduced in full, others in fragments—Lee also asked several close friends and fellow artists about including letters they had written to her in this volume as well. Engaging with many of the themes she had been considering in both her artwork and her writing—independence/interdependence, language/legibility, motherhood, place, and belonging—the correspondence reveals a world of shared questions and concerns, all woven with a sense of humor and understanding that comes through close connection. The letter contributors are Amanny Ahmad, Brook Hsu, Christine Sun Kim, Jimin Seo, and Martine Syms.

This book is the fourth in a series made possible by a generous multi-year grant from Amanda Minami. When RADIUS BOOKS was founded in 2007, our primary goal was to get as many thoughtfully crafted art books into underserved libraries, community centers, and arts organizations as possible. To achieve this goal, each title is a discrete entity that is wholly funded before we go to press. Through the sale of limited editions, collaborations with foundations, donations from collectors, and co-publications with museums and galleries, we have always created books along this financial model, on a project-by-project basis.

As we looked to the future and considered a more forward-thinking, proactive model, we worked to widen the scope of our support network with a special emphasis on funding series of books over several consecutive years. Ideally, these projects fulfill a particular need both in terms of amplifying the work of an artist and offering curricular potential of their subject matter.

The Minami Grant was seeded with these goals in mind. The initiative, which focuses on art and scholarship at the intersection of Asian American and Pacific Islander history and culture, aims to provide access to and a deeper understanding of these themes through school curricula centered on these titles. *Maia Ruth Lee: Bondage Baggage* not only provides the reader with a significant selection of this artist's work, but we hope that it will also provide a gateway to educational outreach and inspiration.

Operating on the belief that the arts—all arts—are vital to our culture, RADIUS BOOKS is a 501(c)(3) non-profit organization with a focus on photography and fine art book publishing.

In addition to publishing, RADIUS BOOKS encourages aspiring artists through educational workshops and community events and distributes books of artistic and educational value for a wide audience.

RADIUS BOOKS donates copies of every title we publish into a nationwide network of libraries and schools, with the hope and expectation that these books will reach and inspire new audiences.

RADIUS BOOKS
227 E. Palace Avenue, Suite W, Santa Fe, NM 87501
t: (505) 983-4068 | radiusbooks.org

Available through

CONSORTIUM BOOK SALES & DISTRIBUTION
34 Thirteenth Avenue NE, Suite 101, Minneapolis, MN 55413
t: (800) 283-3572 | www.cbsd.com

ISBN 979-8-89018-122-0

Library of Congress Cataloging-in-Publication
Data available from the publisher upon request.

DESIGN: David Chickey, Inga Hendrickson, and Nick Larsen
EDITORIAL: Nick Larsen

Printed by EBS SRL, Verona, Italy

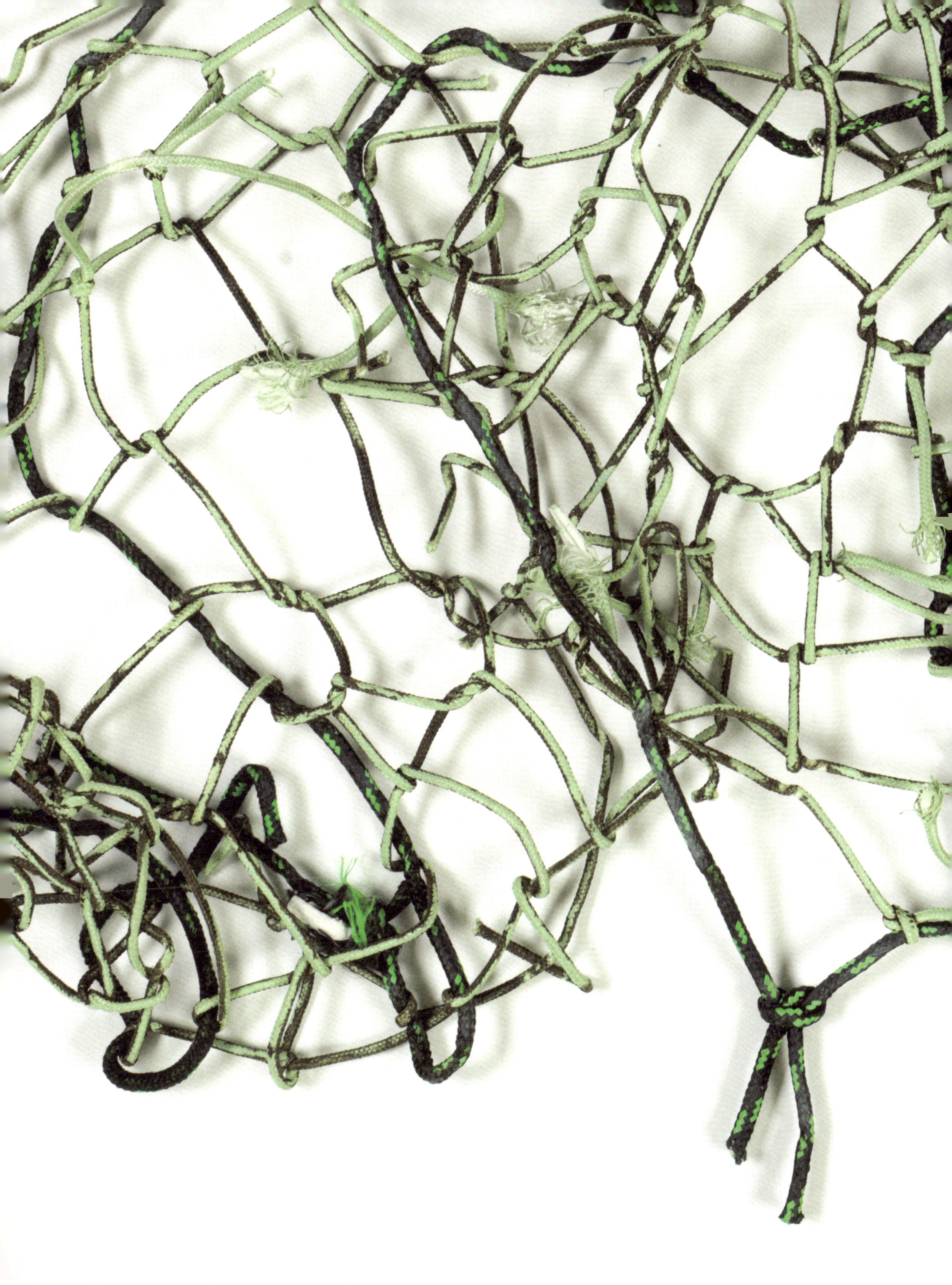